BEAT

THE
SPORTS BOOKS

BEAT
THE
SPORTS BOOKS

An Insider's Guide to Betting the NFL

Dan Gordon

Cardoza Publishing

Cardoza Publishing is the foremost gaming publisher in the world, with a library of over 175 up-to-date and easy-to-read books and strategies. These authoritative works are written by the top experts in their fields and with more than 8,500,000 books in print, represent the best-selling and most popular gaming books anywhere.

FIRST EDITION

Copyright © 2005 by Dan Gordon
- All Rights Reserved -

Library of Congress Catalog Card No: 2005920562
ISBN: 1-58042-174-1

Visit our web site —www.cardozapub.com)—or write for a full list of books and computer strategies.

CARDOZA PUBLISHING
P.O. Box 1500, Cooper Station, New York, NY 10276
Phone (800) 577-WINS
email: cardozapub@aol.com
www.cardozapub.com

About the Author

Dan Gordon is widely regarded as one of the three best handicappers in the sports world and has a winning record as a professional sports bettor for over two decades. His sports betting columns have appeared in the *New York Daily News*, *San Francisco Examiner*, *Boston Herald*, *Los Angeles Herald Examiner*, *College and Pro Football Weekly*, and other magazines and newspapers. From 1984 to 1991 he served as handicapping consultant to Pete Axthelm of NBC, ESPN, and *Inside Sports* magazine, and is currently a consultant to some of the most successful sports bettors in the world. He also is an oddsmaking consultant for the top sports books worldwide. For information on Dan's NFL and NBA picks service, contact him at: danlgordon@aol.com.

Dedication

I dedicate this edition of *Beat the Sports Books* to my late father, Murray A. Gordon. An idea that he shared with me over a dinner in early 1980 helped give birth to this book. I hope that I am as good, honest, and competent in my fields of handicapping and betting sports and writing as my father was in his field as an attorney.

TABLE OF CONTENTS

CONTENTS

Acknowledgments

I want to thank Avery Cardoza of Cardoza Publishing for his understanding of and respect for both authors and professional gamblers. I also want to thank Megan Jones of Cardoza Publishing who did a good job editing this book, and Sara Cardoza, for her excellent layout of *Beat The Sports Books* which makes the book much easier to read. Finally, I want to thank Radar O'Reilly for editing both the first and second editions of this book and helping it to be published.

Foreword

Every once in a while, a book comes along that you realize instantly is a seminal work, a treatise so sweeping in its scope that it is destined to become an instant classic in the field. *Beat the Sports Books: An Insider's Guide to Betting the NFL*, by Dan Gordon is such a book.

My fascination with gambling of all kinds, and with sports betting, in particular, goes back well over 30 years. There's little I haven't read on the subject, and although I never had much success actually handicapping on my own, it wasn't for lack of trying! But, I recognized quite early that the amount of preparation, commitment to detailed record-keeping, and studying required to be truly successful in this endeavor was more than I was willing to devote to the venture. And then I met Dan Gordon.

It's difficult to put into words how unique an individual Dan is. I've certainly never met anyone like him, and I've spent a fair amount of hours in casinos and sports books all over the world. Dan is the genuine article: a handicapper of professional football and basketball so skilled at what he does that he has picked about 57%

winners in the two sports for the past twenty years, with a 60% NFL win rate in 1999 and 59% in 2000! For the last four of those years, I have personally received every one of his NFL selections, by e-mail, before the games were played, so that I might serve as an impartial monitor of his picks.

I first met Dan about six years ago, interestingly enough, to discuss a separate matter that had nothing to do with his sports wagering. But, it didn't take lone before the topic of conversation turned to Dan's particular field of expertise, and he began to regale me with stories of his days as a journalist for some of the country's top newspapers, where he wrote handicapping columns and made weekly selections for readers. Indeed, his "Smart Money," which appeared in both the *Los Angeles Herald Examiner and the San Francisco Examiner*, in the '80's and his "Between the Lines," which he penned for *College and Pro Football Newsweekly*, were the epitome of the kind of low-key, responsible, yet searingly accurate brand of prognostication that was to become the hallmark of this consummate professional.

The years passed, and Dan continued to do well wagering on a very specific sector of the overall sports-betting market "sides" in the NFL and the NBA. That he has had such great success is all the more remarkable when we note that many experts consider professional football to be the hardest of all sports to beat on a consistent basis.

Beat the Sports Books is Dan Gordon's magnum opus, his life's work on the fine art of how to pick NFL spread winners, so complete in its approach, so meticulous in its detail, so mesmerizing in its mastery of the intricacies of the game, that you won't be able to put it down. It's as if we've been permitted the luxury of crawling inside Gordon's head, from the day he turns his attention to the upcoming NFL season, to the moment the gun goes off, signaling the end of the Super Bowl. Along the way, we're invited to examine every handicapping tool, every angle, every piece of information that Dan deems pertinent for picking winners. Indeed, in the last part of the book, as he craftily weaves theory and practice together, Gordon treats us to the week-by-week rationale behind every one of his selections for an entire NFL season. And, we marvel at his insight.

Is this the first book ever written on handicapping the NFL? Hardly. Is it, by far, the very best? Without a shadow of a doubt. Looking for easy money? Move on! Looking for shortcuts or "touts" to do all the work for you? Wrong book! Looking for a total "game plan" for a complex subject, so far reaching in its scope, yet so unpretentious and honest in its exposition that you will greatly appreciate the candor? Then *Beat the Sports Books* is what you've been waiting for all your life.

Go get the money! Dan Gordon is about to tell you how to do it. And good luck.

-Don Schlesinger, Notable Author and Gaming Authority

1

Introduction

The first edition of *Beat the Sports Books* was widely read among smart football bettors—perhaps too widely read! Many of the readers used my winning NFL betting models in their own betting, which has increased early-week movement in the NFL betting lines. This makes it more difficult for bettors without early access to NFL betting lines to find the numbers they need to place a good bet.

I also suspect that some linesmakers—especially those in the offshore sports books—used the information in my book to toughen up their opening NFL betting lines.

In this new edition, I have added a number of strong betting models that have withstood the test of time and for the first time, I show exactly how many points my betting models change the power ratings on a game. These precise adjustments have made my power ratings more accurate than they had been. Also, I now use value in selecting games during the first four games of the season, while in the first edition, value was used only from the fifth game on.

Year after year, NFL bettors go into the season filled with confidence—and end up losing. How can this happen? This is the question I answer in the book you are about to read. I will tell you how you can become a winning pro football bettor. My approach is more detailed than any written before. Someone using it will forever be a favorite to overcome the 11 to 10 odds in betting pro football, as I have done in the twenty-plus years I've wagered on the NFL.

2

My Sports Betting Journey

This book has been over twenty years in the making. Early in 1980, I ended a disastrous 1979 season betting the NFL, marking the first of exactly two times in my career when I went virtually broke betting. (The second time was to come in the 1980 NBA regular season.) My failure was especially shocking to me since I had done well betting the NFL in late 1977 and 1978, the first seasons I had ever tried NFL wagering.

Over dinner one night, my father suggested a way to alleviate my recent discouragement. Why not write a book about the pitfalls of betting on the NFL, he suggested. I could call it *Hey, Sucker!* I told my dad I would think about it. Though I didn't really know it then, I still had much to learn.

For the immediate future, I was determined to do better. I'd keep more careful records, chart trends better than anyone, and try to spot psychological weaknesses in the teams that no one else could see. I worked odd jobs and saved some money. Thus staked to a few thousand dollars, I was ready to wager on the 1980 season.

Full of confidence, I even hosted my own cable television show in New York City, called *Dan Gordon's Football Picks*, in the 1980 and 1981 seasons. Fortunately, I ended up with winning records both seasons, happy to have some public proof of my success. Quoting stats and trends and their seeming use in helping me beat the point spread was nice—in fact, for me it was even better than the actual money I won betting the games. Through the show, I also met other NFL bettors and even received phone calls from a sports service or two.

In my actual betting those years, I was much more conservative than I had been in my first seasons. There is nothing like going broke to learn the value of money. In addition to being conservative, I also started using several bookmakers to shop around for the best prices on games and came to pride myself on my shopping.

But when it came to evaluating lines for when to wager, I still relied on mainly feel or instinct, with no power ratings or line of my own as anchors. In retrospect, I see I was lucky to have won in 1980 and 1981.

I decided not to renew my cable show for 1982, which was fortunate since it turned out to be another losing season for me. Because of an eight-week players' strike, that season lasted just nine weeks, with the first two weeks played before the strike and the last seven played after. The season was a losing one for me largely because I made most of my bets based on emotional edges that I felt one team would have over another, which had been a successful tactic for me in 1980 and 1981. That year, however, I didn't realize that the short season would negate many of the trends I depended on. Teams played according to form in almost every game because the emotional fatigue that normally sets in over the course of a 16-week season simply didn't occur in this much-shortened one.

Though I lost money, the season wasn't anywhere near the financial disaster I'd experienced in 1979. My conservatism in betting came in handy during the frustrating weeks of 1982. Instead of losing nearly my entire bankroll, as in 1979, I lost less than 10 percent of it.

On a happier note, I met Pete Axthelm during the strike, who at that time predicted games against the point spread on NBC and wrote a betting-oriented column for the magazine *Inside Sports*. Pete liked my attention to spread statistics and other insights. After the strike—and for the next eight seasons—he called me every week for my views, and by 1984 was paying me as a consultant. Until his death in early 1991, Pete was the most consistent winner against the point spread of anyone who selected games on television.

Another person I met during the players' strike was John Walsh, who at the time was the editor of *Inside Sports*. John suggested that Pete do an article about the research I was doing for betting NFL games. Unfortunately, *Inside Sports* folded when the article was just about to come out.

Before I had time to get depressed, John decided to edit a book about college and pro football called *Inside Football 1983*. John wanted part of the book to deal with NFL wagering, and he recruited me to write it.

John also thought highly enough of my work to encourage me to start writing a football-betting column in 1983 and help me get it into *College and Pro Football Newsweekly* and the *Village Voice*. By this time, I was developing a number of statistical models to help me in my handicapping and, by 1984, I was winning consistently enough that the illegal bookmakers in New York started telling me to take my action someplace else.

That was when I discovered that bookmakers do their own shopping. If a bettor is considered smart at all, a number of bookmakers will throw him out. To their way of thinking, why have "wise-guy" bettors when there are hundreds or thousands of suckers willing to bet on every phone call?

As I'll talk more about later, shopping for the best price is critical in betting the NFL (or any sport). So is selectivity. When you are giving 11 to 10 odds (putting up $11 for every $10 you want to win) you can't afford to give up even a fraction of your edge.

In any case, by the middle of the 1984 season, I had just three places left to bet. And in two of them, I was giving my bets to "movers," or people who actually placed the bets for me. That is, I was until I caught one of them "scalping" me by quoting prices slightly worse than the ones that were really around. It seemed that my only option was to spend the 1985 NFL season in Las Vegas. There, I would not be hassled if I shopped around for the best prices on games. And since I would be making all my bets myself, no one would be scalping me.

Unfortunately, my 1985 season in Las Vegas was a rough one. Favorites had a very good year, covering nearly 55 percent of the games. This hurt me (and most other professional bettors) since the smart bets are almost always on underdogs. And, in a devastating personal blow, my father died of cancer during the season.

On the brighter side, my media audience continued to grow larger that year. Through John Walsh, I landed jobs at the *New York Daily News* and the *San Francisco Examiner* writing NFL handicapping columns.

But the biggest plus about 1985—though it didn't pay off in that year—was that I started to use power ratings in my handicapping. No longer was I determining the value of a line mainly by feel.

MY SPORTS BETTING JOURNEY

The 1986 season was a better one for me. I again spent the season in Las Vegas, picking up the *Los Angeles Herald Examiner* and Washington's *Home Team Sports* as clients. And though Pete Axthelm was no longer with NBC and not yet with ESPN, he continued to purchase my stats and insights.

More important for my bankroll, my use of power ratings had started to pay off as I won in 1986 at the betting window as well as in my column.

In 1987, anticipating another NFL players' strike, the second in six years, I decided not to go to Las Vegas. Though the strike lasted only four weeks, starting after the second week of the season, my decision not to go to Las Vegas put me on the sidelines in terms of betting for the entire season.

My two years in Las Vegas had shown me exactly how much the worst of it bettors outside Nevada had it for line shopping. In New York at that time, I was totally shut out of the early-week NFL betting action—a time when pros in Las Vegas take advantage of poor opening numbers. And late in the week, the lines in Las Vegas sports books tended to move more than those in New York. The average bettor in New York was taking between a half point to a point the worst of it on every bet he made. Plus, of course, in New York, winning bettors were still often getting chased from offices. Since I hated getting the worst of it and didn't relish getting chased, I decided to sit the season out.

Despite not betting, I stayed busy. I still had handicapping columns to write and had another strong season in the media, winning for the second year of three in print and the sixth year of seven in all media. And, partly due to my stats and insights, Pete Axthelm made his first season at ESPN a winning one. In addition, I picked up some private clients who paid me for my selections.

Still, I was frustrated not to be betting the NFL myself. So by 1988, I found some money movers in Las Vegas who would place my NFL bets for me. Through these movers I would have access to early Las Vegas numbers as well as out-of-line late numbers.

On the negative side, I lost the *San Francisco Examiner* as a client when Charles Cooper, my editor, left the paper in early 1988. From the beginning of my time in the big print media, I thought Cooper had a unique understanding among editors of what I was trying to do and what handicapping should be. He often likened my work to someone giving advice on how to buy and sell stocks, and praised my professionalism. He even noted that I sometimes came up with trends about the 49ers (the home team of the *Examiner*) that had been missed by the beat writers.

The loss of Cooper was particularly important to me because I was beginning to feel discouraged about my experience with other newspapers. By 1988, I was down to two papers, the *Los Angeles Herald Examiner* and *Boston Herald*, and I was unable to pick up any others. Cooper had praised my writing and many pro bettors had told me my competency in handicapping was unmatched in the media. Yet writers like Benjamin Lee Eckstein, who lost consistently in all sports, and Gerald Strine, who "saved" several lost seasons by plunge bets on the Super Bowl, were getting in more and more papers as I was getting shut out.

A number of people advised me that it was not a smart move to have just a couple of selections a week—that editors wanted handicapping writers who gave a lot of selections. I explained that picking against just one number, which newspaper writers do, forces a handicapper to be selective (Remember, shopping is key to betting success). However, I was told that if I wanted to write for more papers, I would need to pick more games. For 1988, I reluctantly decided to do this. I often had five or six games as selections even if I myself bet just two or three.

Predictably, the results were bad. I endured my second losing season in the media. Meanwhile, I had a winning season in my own betting using my Las Vegas money movers. The difference between my media and personal betting results came down to the lines I could get by shopping in Vegas and those extra picks I wouldn't have put my own money on.

Ironically, despite my losing season in print, I picked up two more newspaper clients: the *Tacoma News-Tribune* and the *Citizen's Voice* of Wilkes-Barre, Pennsylvania. Nevertheless, I decided to go back to my old way of limiting my selections to only the games I myself would bet at a given price. I also decided to make 1989 my last season in the media. I had come to see that competence in handicapping had nothing to do with getting published and I wanted to go out with a winning season for my readers.

As for the readers who wanted to continue following my selections, I decided to start a 900-number service instead.

In the meantime, I was continuing to refine my power ratings. I had also started to make my own oddsmaking line to compare to the lines the sports books put out. I was able to discover true value in this way, and in 1989 I had a very strong season.

Strangely, this very success began to hurt both my newspaper column selections and Pete Axthelm in his ESPN Sunday spots. I was still using money movers, and on my early-week bets against the weakness of the early Las Vegas numbers, my movers—who bet a lot more than I did—had begun to follow me. In addition, other people followed them. By Thursday, when I made my newspaper selections, the line had more often than not moved by at least half a point. This meant fewer selections for my newspaper readers than I was getting. Pete Axthelm, who followed my selections closely that year, didn't get to give his ESPN selections until *Sunday!* Despite this, I am happy to report, he had another winning season.

The third week of the 1989 season was a classic example of what happened that year.

On Sunday night and Monday morning I made four bets for the coming week: Falcons plus 8 over the Colts; Packers plus 10 1/2 over the Rams; Bucs plus 3 1/2 over the Saints; and Jets plus 5 over the Dolphins. I knew I needed at least eight points on the Falcons, ten on the Packers, three on the Bucs, and 4 1/2 on the Jets. By Thursday, the lines had changed to the Colts by seven, the Rams by ten, the Saints by 2 1/2, and the Dolphins by four. Only one of the four games (Packers plus ten over the Rams) was still bettable. All four games won, but in the media, I was just 1-0.

Of course, my movers didn't much care about my newspaper readers or how Pete Axthelm might be hurt. They were just happy to jump on a winning train.

Despite these problems, I had another winning season in the media. It was my third in five in the large print media, my fifth in seven going back to 1983, and my seventh in nine going back to my cable television show.

I was also running my 900 line at this time, which was active through two basketball seasons and one football season. But I discovered that most people who called were looking for someone who claimed to pick 75 or 80 percent winners. The people who advertised claims like that tended to be the ones with the most successful 900 numbers. I closed the 900 number in late March of 1991.

Pete Axthelm remained a client until he passed away in early 1991, at which time ESPN hired Norm Hitzges to fill its on-air NFL handicapping job. Hitzges lost badly in 1991, as he did in 1992 and 1993. In all three years at ESPN he finished below the .524 win percentage that is needed to beat the 11 to 10 odds. His stats were often inaccurate as well. I couldn't understand why ESPN suddenly cared so little for accuracy.

Week Four of 1992 provides just one of many examples. That week Hitzges incorrectly picked the Patriots, a 15 1/2 point underdog, to cover against the Bills. A stat that Hitzges used to support his selection was that teams that had scored seven or fewer points in their last two games, as the Patriots had, were 45-18 against the spread the following week. But in reality, the seven-and-under stat had gone 31-29-2 the last sixty-two games (a losing record giving 11 to 10 odds). The Bills routed the Pats, 41-7.

I was actually upset enough to call John Walsh, now an executive editor at ESPN, about the matter. It's hard enough for the average bettor without having TV commentators giving them inaccurate statistics.

Though I still followed the game, I decided to take a break for a while from handicapping football and spent the next two years in other pursuits. But in 1995, I decided to come back to betting. One of my old reliable movers was willing to help me find the best numbers around. I reopened my consulting business. That year, I ended up behind by about five bets in my NFL wagering. But in 1996, I bounced back in a big way in the NFL, ending up with a win rate of 62 percent. My lifetime average win rate in the NFL, including my early years, is roughly 57 percent. During 2003 and 2004 combined it was 61 percent.

I now always base my handicapping and betting decisions on betting models and power ratings rather than feel or instinct. I make my own line on every game *before* seeing the sports books' lines.

It is my hope that the information and handicapping models in this book for betting the NFL will help make you a winner as well.

3

Overview

As Labor Day approaches each year, one of the biggest businesses in the world prepares to restart. It's a business that generates well into eleven figures over a five-month period and involves the participation of millions of Americans and citizens from other countries—and those numbers grow every year. This business is wagering on National Football League (NFL) games.

Pro football is the biggest betting sport in the United States, with total wagers on it now running more than $1 billion a week. According to *USA Today*, over half of the American adult population had a financial stake of some sort in the outcome of 2004's Super Bowl. That meant over $5 billion wagered on that game alone.

A few hundred thousand people wager on NFL games legally in Nevada in scores of sports books. They put their bets up front on just about any NFL game of their choosing. The yearly Nevada sports book handle in NFL wagering has grown to $1 billion in recent years.

Millions of people wager on the NFL illegally. They deal with local bookmakers who usually extend them credit. Their NFL bet is just a phone call away, and both bookmaker and bettor trust each other to make their losses good. The possibility of being busted by the police is but a small obstacle for these bookmakers, especially the larger ones. Most large bookies who get busted are back in operation in two or three days with a new phone number. The amount wagered on the NFL illegally is about $35 billion a year, according to Bob Daluga, formerly of Las Vegas Sports Consultants.

OFFSHORE AND INTERNET BETTING

In recent years very large numbers of bettors have been betting with offshore and Internet sports books. For the most part, money must be put up front with these sports books. While a few of these offshore and Internet books have stiffed bettors for money, most pay reliably. These sports books have been taking money away from the illegal bookies in the United States. For bettors, a wager with these books is but a phone call or computer hookup away.

PARLAY CARDS

Millions of people also wager on what are known as **sheets** or **parlay cards**. On sheets, a bettor must pick the point spread winner of at least three games to win, with a loss on any pick meaning the whole bet is lost. The lure of the sheets is that the bettor can put up a little money to win a substantial amount, especially if he correctly selects a large number of winners, like nine or ten games. The huge house edge on these wagers (see Part Two of this book: "Obstacles in the Bettor's Path") provides a serious amount of profit for both illegal sheet operators and Nevada sports books.

A number of factors make pro football the most popular betting proposition.

MEDIA COVERAGE

The NFL receives thorough coverage on television. The average fan can now view, if he chooses, five of the fifteen games played each week, and those viewers with satellite dishes can now watch them all. Highlights of the games that are not broadcast are covered on halftime shows and post-game wrap-ups on networks like ESPN and CNN. With nearly every big play shown in replay during the game and many times thereafter, a viewer can't help but see who made the big runs, catches, or blocks. Feeling like an expert, he remembers these key plays as he tries to beat the bookmakers' spread on next week's games.

During the week following the games, many cable stations continue to report on the NFL, giving prominent mention to key injuries, roster pick-ups and drops, and angles on upcoming games. But that's not all. The print media also cover the NFL very closely. Box scores and colorful stories by sportswriters can give fans a strong impression of what took place in a game. National newspapers like *USA Today* not only publish box scores of every game, but also list every scoring drive. Both national and local papers devote daily sections to the NFL to report on injuries and other important team information. On Fridays, newspapers preview the upcoming games.

And every day more and more people access computers and the Internet where they can read NFL news from sports Web sites and newspapers all over the country. This increases the feeling of expertise among bettors.

In addition, though betting on the NFL is illegal in nearly every state, the point spread on games receives extensive coverage in both the print and televised media. Late in the week, many newspapers use handicapping writers or staff members to make selections against the point spread. Many radio shows in NFL cities have staff members who not only make predictions against the point spread, but also explain the reasons behind their selections. And ESPN's Chris Berman and Hank Goldberg make weekly selections against the point spread as well.

All of this coverage makes the point spread enticing for many viewers. The information encourages them to form their own opinions. Some bettors follow the advice of favorite writers or commentators. Others go out of their way to try to prove that they know more than the experts.

EASY TO FOLLOW

Yet another factor that makes the NFL the most popular betting sport is that each team plays just one game a week. This makes the sport much easier to follow than basketball, hockey, or baseball, where games are played virtually every day.

SPORTS SERVICES, TOUTS, AND BOOKIES

And for any fans who still find keeping track of the NFL too time consuming, hordes of sports services or touts offer to fill the gap. Most of them promise fabulous returns. For a comparatively small fee, they do the work of handicapping and selecting games for their clients. Most sports services promise 70 or even 80 percent winners, as if the people who book NFL games were the biggest suckers in the world.

Nothing could be further from the truth. Bookies love the NFL season. It provides them with their greatest profits in sports. Many local bookies operate *only* during the NFL season because the profit from these few months enables them to live well the rest of the year. Bookmakers represent the vast majority of people who make a profit from wagering on the NFL.

THE BETTORS

The average bettor, on the other hand, despite all the touts and information, loses season after season. In a routine NFL season fewer than one bettor in twelve turns a profit. Over the course of a large number of seasons, the percentage of bettors who turn a profit is minuscule. Bob Martin, former head linesmaker for the NFL, once told me that the number of bettors who win betting pro football is so small that "it is virtually the same as if no one won." In addition, extremely few sports services win. Usually, the bigger the promises, the more likely the service is to lose.

It should be noted that Las Vegas Sports Consultants has much less of an effect on the early numbers than they did in the late 1990s, and this change is addressed in the book as well. Offshore books like CRIS and especially Olympic (which puts out NFL betting numbers before anyone else) are more important in the early posting and betting of NFL games.

4

How Pro Football Is Bet

THE POINT SPREAD
BETTING THE ODDS

Before you can win betting pro football you have to know how the line is set.

Many years ago all sports, including football, were bet according to odds. If someone liked a favorite in a game, he could give, say, 2 to 1 odds on the game, meaning he would have to risk $2.00 for every $1.00 he hoped to win. On the same game, a bettor could take 8 to 5 odds if he liked the underdog (risking $5.00 for every $8.00 he hoped to win), thus making the "true" odds—or how the betting public perceived the game—9 to 5 for the favorite.

The odds of 9 to 5 are the midway point between 8 to 5 and 2 to 1, which could also be expressed as 10 to 5. The difference between the give on the favorite (2 to 1) and the true odds (9 to 5) was the edge for the bookie on the favorite; the difference between the take on the underdog (8 to 5) and the true odds (9 to 5) was the bookmaker's edge on the underdog.

A problem with this type of betting on football came in mismatches, where a bettor might be asked to give 5 to 1 or 6 to 1—or more—on the favorite. Few bettors wanted to lay such high odds because they had to risk so much to win so little. Nor would many bettors bet the underdog when it was perceived as having such a small chance of winning. Getting high odds was no consolation if your team seemed certain to lose. Thus, mismatches drew very little betting action and very little "juice"—or profit—for bookmakers. This was a situation oddsmakers could never feel happy about.

BETTING THE POINT SPREAD

This problem was solved with the advent of the point spread (also called the "spread"). As far back as the 1920s, point spreads were used on a limited basis. By the late 1940s, the point spread had become the accepted way to bet.

The **point spread** is a handicap given to the favorite in terms of points. In the last regular season game of 1996, for example, the New England Patriots closed as 9 1/2-point favorites over the New York Giants. In this game, the oddsmakers believed that the Patriots—in the eyes of the betting public—were 9 1/2 points better than the Giants. This meant that the Patriots had to win the game by more than 9 1/2 points—ten points or more—for a Patriots bettor to collect. An outright Patriot loss or a Patriot win of less than 9 1/2 points meant a loss for a Patriots point spread bettor.

If you bet the underdog Giants, on the other hand, you *received* 9 1/2 points on the Giants on your bet. If the Giants won the game outright or lost by less than 9 1/2 points—nine points or less—you won your bet. If the game landed exactly on the point spread, which obviously couldn't happen with a line of 9 1/2, the game was considered a **push,** or tie, and neither the bettor nor the bookmaker would win.

Thus, when you bet a favorite, you are giving (or laying) points; when you bet an underdog, you are taking the points. In the above example, a way of writing up a Patriots bet would be "Patriots -9 1/2." For someone betting the Giants, the bet would be "Giants +9 1/2."

The reason the point spread is considered better than odds is that, in theory, a handicap makes a game an equal proposition in the eyes of the betting public, with bettors just as likely to take one team as the other no matter how great the mismatch might be. In Week 4 of the 2002 NFL season, the first year expansion Houston Texans went to Philadelphia to play the powerful Eagles. The early line, or the very first line posted, had the Eagles favored by 21, but as bettors took 21, 20, 19 1/2, and 19 points on the Texans, they pushed the line down to as little as 18 1/2. Then Eagles bettors drove the line back up to 19, where it finally settled.

MOVING THE LINE

The point is that, because of the point spread, there was some action both ways on this game, whereas if the bookmakers had tried to post a money line on this mismatch there would have been little action. Virtually no one would have wanted to give over 15 to 1 odds on the Eagles (I would guess that bettors would have had to give about 17 to 1 on them) or take 12 or 13 to 1 on the Texans since they were perceived as having very little chance of defeating the powerful Eagles. The Eagles, by the way, won the game easily by a score of 35-17, but failed to cover the spread, making the Texans bettors winners.

The point spread method also makes it easy for sports books to adjust the **price,** or handicap, on a game as money comes in on one side or the other. Let's return to the 1996 Patriots-Giants game discussed above.

The people who work at Las Vegas Sports Consultants in Las Vegas, Nevada, the largest oddsmaking office in the world and the one with the most clients (sports books that use their numbers), felt that making the Patriots an 8 1/2 point favorite would make the game an equal proposition to the nation's bettors. However, as the week went on, more money came in on the Patriots than on the Giants. Sports books in Nevada and bookmakers around the country were quick to raise the price on the Patriots, moving their handicap (the **number** or **line**) to -9 and then -9 1/2. When wagers continued to come in on the Patriots despite the higher price, some books were even forced to move the number to -10. Finally, Giants money came in and most bookmakers closed the game at -9 1/2.

As you can see, betting on pro football is truly a free-market activity. Most bettors who wagered on this game considered the Patriots a bargain at -8 1/2 and -9. Their betting pushed the price on the Patriots up. When the line reached -10, bettors at last considered the Giants a good bet and their wagers pushed the line back down. The closing number on the Patriots, -9 1/2, was the result of pure supply and demand.

BETTING AGAINST THE POINT SPREAD

When you bet against the point spread, you are not only giving or taking points, however. You are also almost always giving 11 to 10 odds to a bookmaker or sports book, meaning that if you want to win $50 on a game, you must risk $55. When a bettor is giving 11 to 10 odds, he is bucking a 4.55 percent edge against him. To make this clearer, take two bettors who choose the opposite sides of the same game. If each one wants to win $100, each must actually risk $110, the extra $10 being a fee or commission for the sports book, called the **vigorish** or **vig**. After the game, one bettor will lose the $110 he risked while the other will get it back plus his $100 win. Thus, of a total of $220 risked, $10 goes to the bookie. Ten dollars of $220 is 1/22, or 4.55 percent.

In return for giving 11 to 10 odds, a bettor is compensated in the following ways:

1) He can bet the games of his choice and pass on the others.

2) He can shop for the best price on the games he wants to bet. In our Patriots-Giants game, for example, a bettor could have given 8 1/2 points on the Patriots or taken 10 on the Giants, at least in theory. In reality, the lines available to him depend on his access to the sports books. Such shopping goes a long way towards overcoming those 11 to 10 odds.

3) A bettor can choose the timing of his bets. Again using the Patriots-Giants game as an example, a bettor could have wagered early in the week on the Patriots, feeling that the line on the favorite would rise as the week went on, or late in the week on the Giants, when the points they got peaked and they had their maximum spread value.

5

Other NFL Wagers

OVER-UNDER BETS

In this type of bet, also known as **totals**, the bettor wagers against a number that represents the total number of points scored in the game, betting on whether more or fewer total points will be scored. For example, if a bookmaker's total on a game is 41, a bettor will win on an **under** wager if fewer than 41 points are scored in the game. If a bettor chooses the over, he will win if more than 41 points are scored. If the number of points scored is exactly 41, all bets are considered ties and no money changes hands.

A bettor must typically give 11 to 10 odds on this type of bet, but you must watch out for bookies who charge 6 to 5, which represents an 8.3 percent edge, on over-unders. You must also watch out for bookies with whom you lose on ties. I would suggest that over-under bettors stay away from bookies who have either of these rules.

PARLAYS

In this type of wager a player chooses two or more teams against the point spread and all must win for the bettor to collect. Thus going 1-1, with one win and one loss, on a two-team parlay produces the same result as going 0-2. In either case, the bettor loses.

A two-team parlay usually pays 13 to 5 odds. If someone bets $50 on a two-team parlay and wins, he profits $130. If he loses the parlay, he loses just the original $50 investment.

On a three-team parlay, a bettor who goes three for three, with three wins and no losses, is usually paid at 6 to 1 odds. Going two for three or one for three is the same as going zero for three: a losing ticket. A winning $50 bet on a three-team parlay gives the bettor a $300 profit.

A tie on any of the games reduces the parlay to the next lower number of games. For example, a tie and two wins on a three-team parlay make the bet a two-team parlay (at 13 to 5 odds).

In Part Two, "Obstacles in the Bettor's Path," I explain why most parlay bets are sucker bets, despite their seemingly great payouts. I also mention how some parlay bets can be winning plays—though this is the exception to the rule.

PARLAY CARDS

The lure of parlay cards is similar to parlay bets in that a bettor has to risk only a small fraction of what can be won. These cards can be put out by anyone with access to a printing press and a bankroll. Many Las Vegas sports books offer them. A person betting these cards must pick a minimum of three games, with the usual payoff for going three for three at 5 to 1. Though the mathematical odds of winning get worse after that, the payoffs continue to get juicier. Some cards offer payouts as high as 1,000 to 1 for going 15 for 15.

In most places, a parlay-card player loses the whole card if any of the games ends in a tie. Some Las Vegas sports books are an exception to this. This makes wagering on parlay cards worse than parlay bets. Another difference is that a parlay-card bettor almost always puts his money up front, before the games are played. He must trust the operator to pay if he wins.

In Part Two of this book, I explain why, like parlays, parlay cards are almost always sucker bets. I also point out the few instances where parlay cards can actually be used to get value.

REVERSES

These are almost always bet with illegal bookies. The most common reverse is the two-team reverse. What seems juicy about this bet to the novice is that a bettor is paid at 4 to 1 odds if both teams cover the spread. However, the same bettor is penalized if he goes 1 and 1 on the bets.

Using a $100 reverse as an example, here is what can happen:

A) If both picks win, the bettor wins $400.
B) If one pick wins and the other loses, the bettor loses $120 (a win of $100 on the first game minus a loss of $220 on the second.)
C) If both games lose, the bettor loses $220.

In Part Two, I explain more about how reverses work and why they should be avoided.

TEASERS

In this type of wager, a bettor gets extra points for his side but must pick more than one team against the spread. The most common teaser is the six-point teaser in which the bettor can adjust the point spread by six points in each of two different games. The bettor must usually give 6 to 5 odds on this bet, and both teams must win for the bettor to collect.

Here is an example of how teaser betting works. In Week 8 of the 2002 season, the Bills were seven point favorites over the Lions, while the Bucs were eight point favorites over the Panthers. Using a six-point teaser in these games, you could have teased the Bills down to one point favorites, or, if you liked the Lions, gotten 13 points on them. In the Bucs-Panthers game, you could have teased the Bucs down to two point favorites or the Panthers up to 14 point underdogs. Again, both picks had to win for you to win the teaser bet.

Other types of teaser bets are 6 1/2-point teasers (two teams and 13 to 10 odds given by the bettor); seven-point teasers (two teams and 7 to 5 odds given); and ten-point teasers (three teams—all must win—and 6 to 5 odds given by the bettor). Ties on two-team teaser bets usually void the whole ticket and result in a refund, like in Las Vegas, or no bet with the illegal bookies. On multi-game teasers, ties reduce the teaser bet to the games left in the teaser—for example, a five-team teaser automatically becomes a four-team teaser and so on, with the odds reduced accordingly. The exception is the ten-point teaser in which any tie causes the wager to lose.

The teaser bet is also a sucker bet and a great source of profit to the Las Vegas sports books. Novice bettors like to tease down favorites of 6 to 8 1/2 points to a small spread so that as long as the favorite wins the game, it is almost certain to cover the teaser price. When the underdog wins outright in such games, the Las Vegas sports books make a killing on teasers.

HOW THE LINE IS SET

At around 5:00 p.m. Pacific time every NFL Sunday a few men get together in the offices of Las Vegas Sports Consultants. These men know what happened in the NFL games played earlier that day. They have statistics from the games, as well as information concerning key injuries. They also have computer access to any well-known betting trends. Most importantly, they have a firm grip on the public's betting pulse and views of NFL teams. With this information in hand, they meet to set betting lines on the NFL games for the following week.

THE SEND-OUT

Before this critical meeting, each of the men not only has set his own line for each game, but is also ready to defend the number he chose. In this meeting each man states his line on each game and the reasons for it. Where there is a strong consensus on a number on a game, that number becomes the **send-out**, that is, the number that will be sent to the sports-book clients of Las Vegas Sports Consultants. On games where there is disagreement, each of the men makes his case until a consensus is reached. Only in rare instances does a consensus not come easily.

The teams that play on Sunday and Monday night—games that take place *after* this 5:00 p.m. Sunday meeting—are also evaluated at this meeting. However, the send-outs on these teams' games for the following week are subject to change after the Sunday and Monday night games are played. Most sports books don't post games involving the Monday night teams until Tuesday, after the Las Vegas Sports Consultants crew has had a chance to adjust the send-out number.

GOAL OF THE LINE

The mission of Las Vegas Sports Consultants is to come up with a number for each game that will make each club an equally attractive betting option. If they succeed, their sports book clients, as well as the hundreds of thousands of illegal bookies across America, will be very happy. If the betting action on games is equal, the books are assured of a profit because of the 11 to 10 odds bettors are almost always required to give on their wagers. An equal split on a game means that the books are guaranteed a 4.55 percent take of the money that bettors risk on it.

The ideal—equal money on both sides of a game—is very rarely achieved. Equal money on both sides of a game with back-and-forth line movement is also seldom achieved. What usually happens is that a sports book or bookie has more action on one team than the other. This means either that the line must move, giving bettors the possibility of a **middle** (winning both sides of the game) or a **side** (in which the bettor wins one side and pushes the other), or that a sports book or bookie will have more action on one team than the other and thus be rooting for one team to cover the spread. This situation is called **rooting for a decision**, and is what usually happens.

In recent years, several offshore books—mainly CRIS and Olympic—have also come out with numbers for the next weeks' games at around 5:00 p.m. Pacific time on Sundays. These books, as well as other offshore sports books, have their own handicappers and oddsmakers who make these lines. In fact, Olympic almost always comes out with numbers for their betting clients before any Las Vegas books do so.

Sports books (and successful bookies) usually have opinions on games—knowledgeable opinions. So what they generally aim for is a reasonable split of the action where a win on their opinion means significantly more than a loss. Let's say a sports book has $20,000 in bets on one side of a game and $15,000 on the other (ignoring the vig for a moment). A win in this contest for the sports book would net a $7,000 profit ($22,000 taken in from the losing bets—that is, $20,000 plus the $2,000 vig—minus the $15,000 paid out on wins). A loss in this contest would cost the sports book $3,500 (a loss of $20,000 paid to the winning bettors minus $16,500, or the $15,000 wagered by the losers plus their $1,500 vig). In this game a win is worth twice as much to the book as a loss. With their 11 to 10 edge, sports books would have to lose more than twice as many games like this than they win to start losing money. In this instance, the 11 to 10 edge becomes a 2 to 1 edge from the sports book's point of view.

So what Las Vegas Sports Consultants, as well as the offshore books that post early NFL numbers, is realistically trying to do, is come up with a number that won't move that much and will provide fairly close to even betting action. It doesn't matter what the result of the game is. If the betting is fairly equal on both sides and the line doesn't move much, especially through key numbers (more about these later), the Las Vegas Sports Consultants' crew of oddsmakers will have done a good job.

HOW THE LINE IS REALLY SET

Let's look at a few examples from the 1996 season to show how Las Vegas Sports Consultants came up with their numbers.

1) New England Patriots at New York Giants, Week 17

The original line on this game favored the Patriots by 8 1/2 points. How was that number derived?

In the last week of the season, the most important element in setting lines has to do with incentive. The teams that need a win to reach the playoffs or for playoff positioning will usually be giving more points—or getting fewer—than they normally would. Teams that have no playoff or other incentive often get more points or give fewer than they normally would.

Going into the last week of the season, the Patriots stood at 10 wins and 5 losses. They had clinched a berth in the AFC playoffs, but their positioning in the playoffs was uncertain as the oddsmakers met in the offices of Las

Vegas Sports Consultants on the eve of Sunday, December 15. One thing was certain: a Patriots win the next week would clinch the AFC East division for the Patriots and the number-two seed in the AFC playoff bracket. (The number-two seed gets a valuable week of rest after the end of the regular season.) Thus, the Patriots, in the eyes of the betting public, had incentive in this game. The Patriots would not be ensured of the number-two spot in the AFC before the kickoff the following Saturday against the Giants. A loss in that game and a Pittsburgh win the next day in Carolina would knock the Patriots out of the number-two spot.

For the Giants, the picture was entirely different. At 6 and 9, they were totally out of the playoff picture. They had clinched finishing in the basement of the NFC East, under .500. Thus, in terms of incentive in the standings, the Giants had none.

How teams have played in recent weeks is also very important to the oddsmaker. Here again, the Patriots seemed to have a big edge over the Giants. The Patriots had lost their last game, but it was a 12-6 war (all field goals) against a good Dallas team. In their previous three games, the Patriots had won handily—27-13 at home over the Colts, 45-7 in a road rout at San Diego in a nationally televised Sunday night game (viewed by more bettors than a normal game and thus weighted more heavily by Las Vegas Sports Consultants), and 34-10 at home over the Jets. In their last game, the Giants had lost by two touchdowns at home (3-17) against a 2-12 Saints team that had previously been winless on the road. In the two games before that, the Giants had won in Miami (17-7) and lost badly (0-24) in Philadelphia. Thus, in terms of recent play against other teams, the Patriots had shown a lot more than the Giants.

Against the spread, both teams sported 7 and 8 records, but the Patriots had been coming on before the last loss with three straight covers and lost by only one point to the spread as five-point underdogs in the 12-6 loss to Dallas. The Giants had lost four of their last six to the number. Thus, the betting public was even more likely to bet the Patriots than the Giants.

The spread had to be made richer than normal because the Patriots had more incentive and were a much better looking team in recent weeks.

Another factor that oddsmakers consider is injuries. In their loss to New Orleans, Giants quarterback Dave Brown was injured. It seemed probable that he would play the following week, but if he didn't, Danny Kanell would take his place. Kanell had had a poor outing against the Saints. With the New York ground game doing poorly in recent weeks, the Brown injury had to be considered in making the line.

The Giants did have one edge over the Patriots that needed to be considered. The Patriots had played in Dallas earlier that day. They would be playing on the road again in New York on the next Saturday—one day earlier than normal. As a result, the Patriots had a fatigue disadvantage in this game.

When oddsmakers make prices, or set lines, they are especially concerned about **key numbers**—the margins by which games are most frequently decided. The most frequent winning margin, by far, in the NFL is three. In nearly every season, that is the most frequent margin of victory, and 1996 was no exception as 32 of 251 games (12.7 percent) were decided by three points. In 1996, seven points was the second most frequent margin with 24 games ending up with that differential. Other key numbers are six, four, ten, and fourteen points.

Oddsmakers are concerned about these key numbers because they don't want their clients, the sports books, to sweat out middles. To use once again the 1996 Patriots-Giants game as an example, let's say the oddsmakers at Las Vegas Sports Consultants opened the Patriots as 6 1/2-point favorites. If the line went quickly to eight for the Patriots, the books could lose badly if the game "fell seven" (ended with the Patriots winning by seven), a not unlikely occurrence because seven is such a frequent margin. Early New England bettors would have given 6 1/2 points and won, and late New York bettors would have taken eight (or more) and *also won*—a middle. Las Vegas Sports Consultants has to think twice about setting games around seven and other key numbers.

Getting back now to the setting of the Patriots-Giants line, the Las Vegas Sports Consultants linesmakers looked at some recent prices for a sort of barometer reading on the game. Two weeks before, the Patriots had been favored by 13 at home (the closing line against the Jets) and covered easily (34-10). If that game were played again now, the Patriots (with their incentive) would have to be favored by about 17 points at home or 12 on the road. (There is usually a 4 1/2 or five-point difference between road and home spreads in order to account for the "home field advantage.") The Jets were about five points inferior to the Giants. Using the Jets as a barometer would make the Pats a seven-point favorite over the Giants.

The Giants, on the other hand, had been a 9 1/2-point home underdog to the Cowboys four weeks before and had won the game outright, 20-6. The Cowboys were considered a couple of points better than the Patriots, as shown by their having been five-point home favorites over the Pats the previous week—usually equal teams have the home team favored by 2 1/2 or three points. Using the Cowboys as a barometer made the Patriots again about a seven-point road favorite over the Giants.

The oddsmakers at Las Vegas Sports Consultants, however, felt that seven would be too low a number on this game. The betting at such a number would generate lots of action on the Patriots—who, remember, supposedly needed the game more—and virtually none on the Giants. The next key number is ten. That would be too high, as the Giants had won and covered at a lower number (+9 1/2) at home against a Dallas team that was better than New England.

The number 8 1/2 seemed a good compromise for the game. It would take into account the incentive for the Patriots and also the public tendency to bet a good team, like the Patriots, after a loss. New England money could be expected to come in—however, so should New York money since the Giants had shown some strength against good teams at home. Las Vegas Sports Consultants' crew felt it was extremely unlikely that the number on the game would hit seven or ten, the two key numbers it was placed between. Thus, Patriots minus 8 1/2 became the send-out number for this game.

2) Seattle Seahawks at Miami Dolphins, Week 6

Let's see how the betting line was formed on this game.

Going into this contest, the Seahawks were 1 and 4. They were coming off a 31-10 home loss to the Packers. This was their third home loss in as many home games; all were by double figures against good teams (the Broncos and Chiefs also beat the Seahawks in Seattle). The Seahawks were also just 1 and 4 against the betting line—with their one win a lucky come-from-behind, with two late touchdowns, 17-13 win in Tampa. The Seahawks were widely reported as disappointed in their quarterback, Rick Mirer. There had been speculation that a change to John Friesz would take place. The oddsmakers at Las Vegas Sports Consultants were aware of this speculation, as well as Mirer's recent poor play.

The Dolphins, on the other hand, were 3 and 1 (2 and 2 against the line). They were coming off a bye week, which meant that bettors would be favoring them as being better rested. However, thirteen days before the match with the Seahawks was to be played and six days before the Las Vegas Sports Consultants crew put a line on it, the Dolphins lost their starting quarterback, Dan Marino, to a broken ankle. He would be out from four to six weeks and would definitely miss the game against Seattle.

The oddsmakers at Las Vegas Sports Consultants had the especially tough job of deciding what price to put on Marino's value to his team. The Dolphins had lost a close 10-6 decision to Indianapolis in the game in which Marino was injured and decided to start recent acquisition, Craig Erickson, at quarterback. But Miami's offense—with the exception of the loss at Indianapolis—had run the ball well, while Seattle's run defense—with the exception of the win at Tampa Bay—had been porous against the run. Thus the betting public was likely to feel that Miami could cope without Marino—especially against a weak team like the Seahawks. The popular theory that a good team like Miami will play well after a loss also had to figure in the line set by the Las Vegas Sports Consultants oddsmakers.

Another key factor in the setting of a line is how the teams tend to do relative to each other in terms of drawing money. In games against other poor teams, the Dolphins had drawn money against Arizona and the New York Jets, then gone on to win by four touchdowns against Arizona while beating the Jets by only nine points (not covering). In Seattle's last two games, on the other hand, late money had come in *against* the Seahawks in both their loss to the Packers and their win over Tampa. Thus Miami, with its greater drawing power, had to be priced higher than it otherwise would have been.

OTHER NFL WAGERS

The previous week the Seahawks had been ten-point home underdogs against the Packers. If the same match-up were to be held this week in Green Bay, the line would now have to be more like 16 to account for the Pack's big win plus their large home field advantage. With Marino, the Dolphins would be about six points inferior to the Packers. Of course, Marino was out, but with the Miami running game doing well and the public's tendency to bet the Dolphins and not the Seahawks, the crew at Las Vegas Sports Consultants would penalize the Dolphins by only a field goal (three points) rather than the five or six they would normally have charged. Thus the Dolphins would be favored by ten points over the Seahawks *with* Marino and seven without him.

Another way to look at the game would be to make the Jets the barometer. The Jets had been 12 1/2-point consensus underdogs against the Dolphins three weeks earlier (there was a wide variation in the closing line in this game). The Seahawks were about a field goal better than the Jets. This price made the Dolphins 9 1/2-point home favorites over the Seahawks with Marino, and 6 1/2-point home favorites without him. Since they didn't want to risk having the game go *through* the key number of seven (those middles!), the oddsmakers at Las Vegas Sports Consultants—after much heated discussion—made the send-out line on this game exactly seven for the Dolphins.

3) Cincinnati Bengals at Jacksonville Jaguars, Week 14

Both teams came into this game with 5 and 7 records and had just come off wins: the Bengals having defeated the Falcons at home, 41-31, and the Jaguars having come from behind for a win over the Ravens on the road, 28-25 in overtime, their first road win of the season. The winner of this game would stay on the fringes of playoff contention at 6 and 7 while the loser would have its playoff hopes pretty much extinguished.

These teams had already played each other once during the season with the Bengals winning 28-21 at home five weeks before. The crew at Las Vegas Sports Consultants is sensitive about revenge games and often will adjust the spread against the team that wants revenge by raising their price if they are favorites or lowering the points they get if they are underdogs.

What kept the line down was that the Bengals had been playing well in recent weeks. After a 1 and 6 start, the Bengals—after replacing Dave Shula with Bruce Coslet at head coach—had won four of their last five. Their only loss in these five games was to the strong 9 and 3 Bills in Buffalo. One of the four wins in this stretch was a ten-point home win over the Pittsburgh Steelers, then in first place in the AFC Central.

Meanwhile, the Jaguars had won just two of their last five games. Both wins had come over the cellar dwellers of the AFC Central, the Baltimore Ravens. In both wins, the Jaguars had to overcome double-digit deficits in the fourth quarter.

In recent weeks, both teams had played the Ravens in Baltimore. Their results were similar, with both beating the Ravens by three points and overcoming large deficits to do it. The Bengals had been 3 1/2-point underdogs in Baltimore four weeks earlier, while the Jaguars had been three-point underdogs there in the game just played. For both the Jaguars and the Bengals, the wins in Baltimore were their only road wins of the season so far. The Bengals had improved in public perception since their win in Baltimore (with the win over Pittsburgh), while the loss—by 25 points—to the Steelers in Pittsburgh had worsened the public perception of the Jaguars. The big question for Las Vegas Sports Consultants was by how much.

In Jacksonville, the Jaguars would have been about four-point underdogs to the Steelers. (Pittsburgh had a large home field edge.) Thus, the Bengals were a much better team than the Jaguars by the Steelers barometer.

Without the Bengals' improvement in recent weeks and their better showing against the Steelers, this would have been considered a game between equal teams with wanting revenge being an extra Jaguars incentive. Such a game would have had the Jaguars at home about a four-point favorite, with revenge being weighted an extra point or maybe point and a half of the four.

But making the Jaguars a four-point favorite would have caused an avalanche of money to come in on the improving Bengals, as recent performances are foremost in the public mind. The number would have very possibly gone through the key number of three and left the book-makers worrying about being middled if the Jaguars won by three. Even making the Jaguars a three-point favorite would have brought unequal action on the Bengals.

After deliberation, Las Vegas Sports Consultants de-cided that the Bengals were seen by the public as the better of the two teams. With that in mind, the line was cut to 1 1/2 on the Jaguars. This number created a point and a half cushion between 1 1/2 and the key number of three, in case some money came in on the Jaguars. Thus the recent Bengal improvement was valued at 2 1/2 points by Las Vegas Sports Consultants.

WHAT HAPPENS TO THE SEND-OUT NUMBERS?

The number that Las Vegas Sports Consultants decides to use as the send-out is not necessarily the number that bettors—especially "normal" bettors—will see when they bet. Adjustments to these numbers take place both early on and during the week.

The first possible adjustments take place on Sunday night when the first Las Vegas sports books put up the numbers. These sports books have employees who are oddsmakers themselves and they may make adjustments to Las Vegas Sports Consultants' send-out numbers. Some sports books may offer the number to a couple of highly regarded bettors whose betting will cause adjustments in the line.

All Vegas sports books have their numbers posted by Monday morning. A number of these books do not use Las Vegas Sports Consultants' send-outs, but use other consultants or in-house staff to set their lines. This sometimes causes a variety of numbers to be available Sunday night and, especially, Monday morning. Shopping amongst these numbers can virtually wipe out the 11 to 10 odds that bettors must give. A number of professional bettors pounce on these early numbers. This early betting tends to force the number towards a "truer" line.

Adjustments on games are also made by illegal bookies. Often these bookmakers don't give the line to their customers until Thursday or even later—many bettors who rely on local bookies can't get in their bet until game day. Between Sunday night/Monday morning and the end of the week, these bookies watch how the money is coming in and adjust their prices accordingly. These bookies also monitor injuries and other team news before putting out numbers to their customers. For the typical bettor, this delay is a serious disadvantage. By not having access to the early numbers that are more vulnerable and varied than those given late in the week, most bettors have a very limited edge compared to those who have access to early numbers. A serious bettor must have access to betting lines on Sunday night or Monday morning at the latest.

For now, let's see what happened to the betting line and Las Vegas Sports Consultants' send-out numbers in the three examples above.

OTHER NFL WAGERS

1) Patriots at Giants

This game saw no immediate adjustments in the send-out number. The Las Vegas sports books that put out the number on Sunday night for the most part stayed at 8 1/2 for the Pats. The number remained at 8 1/2 throughout Monday.

But as the week went on, the number started to climb. By Thursday, the day that many bettors who use illegals first have access, the Patriots were favored by 9 1/2 nearly everywhere. There were two reasons why the line went up by a point. First, there were bettors, either in Vegas or with access to the Vegas lines, who felt that the Patriots' playoff incentive wasn't priced highly enough in the line. These bettors felt that giving 8 1/2 on the Patriots was a bargain.

Meanwhile, New York bettors decided to wait and hope that the line hit ten—a valuable key number. The other reason the number climbed was that a bunch of bettors took **leads**, which means that they expected the number to go up and hoped either to get the best of it or go for a middle (taking ten on the Giants later in the week).

Other people who took leads were the illegal bookies. These bookie-bettors hoped that their betting customers would be willing to give the higher number (9 1/2 or 10) later in the week. If this happened, the bookies would have laid off their bets with a point or a point-and-a-half edge. If the game ended with the Patriots winning by nine, these bookies would hit the jackpot. They would both win their early bets and beat their customers who gave the inferior number of 9 1/2 or higher.

Thus, for most bettors who wanted the Patriots, 9 1/2 was the cheapest line available. Most bettors wanted to bet the Patriots because of the playoff incentive plus their better recent play as compared with the Giants. They didn't realize that the playoff incentive had already been factored into the line. Indeed, it was perhaps over factored into the price! Later in the week in a few places, the price actually hit ten on the Patriots. This number finally brought out the money on the Giants, and the smart bettors going for a middle took the ten as well. All of this money sent the game back down to 9 1/2 on game day, Saturday. Bettors who were shut out both from the early number of 8 1/2 and the ten that was available the day before the game were thus taking far the worst of it in terms of betting the NFL. Yet millions of bettors do just that, all the while giving 11 to 10 odds: a major reason that the vast majority of bettors lose year after year betting the NFL.

The game itself was a wild one in which the underdog Giants got off to a 22-0 lead. The Patriots overcame that with a huge second-half rally to win by a point (23-22), scoring 20 of their points in the fourth quarter. Since the line went up during the week, the game was a winner for most of America's bookies—especially those in Vegas. Even the New England teaser bets—those who teased down the Patriots by six or even seven points—did not win. The Patriots gained the number-two spot in the AFC playoff seeding, but showed that even a team with strong incentive does not necessarily cover the point spread— something that bettors forget every year.

2) Seahawks at Dolphins

The sports books that posted the early lines, fearing a siding, mostly disagreed with Las Vegas Sports Consultants on this game and put up a consensus number of 7 1/2 (instead of seven) for the Dolphins. These books felt that the public would come in strong giving "just" seven points on the Dolphins—even in Dan Marino's absence. If the line went up and then the Dolphins went on to win by seven, early Miami bettors would get a push while later Seattle bettors would win with 7 1/2 points or more. Some eights also appeared on Sunday night and Monday morning on this game. By late Monday, the predominant number on this game was 7 1/2, but eight was around.

By Tuesday and Wednesday, however, the 7 1/2 had mostly disappeared and eight was almost all that was available. Even 8 1/2 began to appear in some places, but was quickly taken by Seattle bettors who felt that the line would not go higher and certainly would not hit ten, the next key number. Eight was the predominant number available on the Seahawks-Dolphins game by the time "normal" bettors called their bookies on Thursday for the "opening" line.

Late in the week—mostly on Sunday—the line came back down to 7 1/2. The late-week consensus was that eight points was too many for the Dan Marino-less Dolphins to be spotting, even to a 1 and 4 Seattle road team that was being outscored by over 13 points a contest.

So, the average bettor had the option of giving 7 1/2 on the Dolphins on Sunday, or maybe taking eight points on the Seahawks (earlier in the week) in this game. In the game itself, the Seahawks used three long scoring passes by new quarterback John Friesz, the last one an 80-yarder with 2:03 left, to win 22-15. The Miami running game went just 32 carries for 85 yards, mostly because of a good performance by the Seattle defense against the run.

A significant thing about the betting on this game is that a lot of six- and seven-point teaser bettors lost (teasing the Dolphins down to under three-point favorites—where an outright win would clinch the bet) on the Dolphins. On the straight-betting side, the Las Vegas line opened and closed at 7 1/2, which meant that the sports books won the vig on the game. Outside of Las Vegas, the illegals lost a small amount as most of them went from eight to 7 1/2 on the game.

And once again, the line had no bearing on winning or losing a bet on this game. All Seattle bets won and all Miami bets lost, at every price.

3) Bengals at Jaguars

The sports books that posted Sunday night lines had a *huge* disagreement with Las Vegas Sports Consultants' send-out number of 1 1/2 on the Jaguars. The sports books felt that the Jaguars' revenge motive was not factored in enough. They also felt that the Bengals' 1 and 5 road record was a poor match against the Jaguars 4 and 1 record at home. The early line posted by these sports books favored the Jaguars not by Las Vegas Sports Consultants' 1 1/2 points, but by *three*: a significant difference since so many games are decided by three points in the NFL.

By Monday morning the line on the Bengals-Jaguars game was split between 2 1/2 and three. But as Monday progressed, the threes disappeared and the line became 2 1/2 with an occasional two sprinkled in. Cincinnati bettors, feeling that the line would not go higher than three, had decided to pounce on that key number.

The 2 1/2 remained for the rest of the week, with an occasional move down to two. But these moves were balanced by quick counter moves back up to 2 1/2. The average bettor in this country basically got just one price on this game: Jaguars by 2 1/2. Bettors with good access, on the other hand, were able to give two points on the Jaguars or take three on the Bengals.

The game itself was a thriller with four lead changes. With 2:07 left, the Jaguars hit a 20-yard field goal that put them up by a 30-20 count. That clinched the outright result. But with 15 seconds left in the game, the Bengals scored on a 25-yard touchdown pass. The point-after brought the final score to 30-27 in the Jaguars' favor.

For most of the illegal bookies, the equal action on the game at 2 1/2 made them a modest profit. For a number of the Vegas sports books, the game was a mini-disaster. All Jaguar bettors won, while a number of Bengal bettors escaped with a tie by getting the three points early in the week. In other words, these sports books got sided.

OTHER NFL WAGERS

For most bettors, the game was a 1/2-point win for those who gave the 2 1/2 on the Jaguars or a tough 1/2-point loss for those who took 2 1/2 on the Bengals. Most losing bettors around America gave the game no more thought. However, those bettors who liked the Bengals and had early-week access were able to take three points and get a tie on their bets.

Unfortunately, those bettors are in the extreme minority. Most bettors don't care that they are taking the worst of it by missing the early line moves, and they pay the price for that indifference on games such as this. Since bettors give 11 to 10 odds, getting a tie versus a loss on a bet is 10 percent more important than getting a win versus a tie. Thus getting a tie in a game like this is very important to your success as a sports bettor. A few such results like this—and nearly all NFL seasons have more than a few such results—can turn a break-even season into a decent winning one for a bettor. They can even turn an overall losing bettor into an overall winning one.

I cannot overstate the importance of access and good shopping. In 1997, I ended up between six and seven bets ahead mainly because of my access to the early and late numbers. Without this access, I would have lost money that season. In 2004, there were seven games where my access to great numbers made a difference in my betting results, as you will see in Appendix Two, where I discuss in full that season's bets. In one of these games, I won rather than lost. In three games, I tied rather than lost. In three other games, I won rather than tied. My access to great numbers made that difficult season a winning one for me, and careful shopping will make a big difference to you as well.

But finding the best numbers is not the only challenge you will face as a winning sports bettor. Part Two of this book begins with other obstacles in the winning bettor's path.

6

Obstacles in the Bettor's Path

Being shut out of the early week betting action and going against tough lines are just two of the obstacles that a bettor has to overcome in wagering on the NFL. Other major obstacles you'll have to deal with include:

1) How American society views sports wagering
2) How the media often cost normal bettors money
3) NFL Touts
4) Sucker Bets

AMERICAN SOCIETY & SPORTS WAGERING

THE STIGMA

Even though wagering—especially casino wagering and lotteries—is becoming much more widespread in the United States, there is still a stigma attached to betting. This stigma applies especially to sports betting.

In 1986, *Sports Illustrated* magazine did a story on sports betting as an evil in society. Most big bettors, the story went, were looking for edges like fixed games.

There are others who believe that wagering on sports is the ultimate something-for-nothing activity. They think no real work is involved and that nothing of value is produced by professional bettors.

Anti-betting people also point out that sports betting (outside Nevada) is illegal. Betting on sports, say these people, contributes to the growth of the underworld.

Many other people think it is impossible for a normal person to win money by wagering and that all bettors wind up broke. The media like to run stories about people, now in Gamblers Anonymous, who went through financial and personal hell because of wagering. Football betting is mentioned a lot in these stories.

THE ALLEGED FIX

Recently, a book about the National Basketball Association called *Money Players*, by Armen Keteyian and Harvey Araton, alleged that Isiah Thomas and James Edwards shaved points for the Detroit Pistons in the 1989-1990 season. Two games that were mentioned were matches against the Milwaukee Bucks and the Golden State Warriors. As favorites, the Pistons lost both games. What wasn't mentioned in the book was that the closing line on the Bucks game (Pistons -10) stayed the same all day and that the closing line on the Warriors game (Pistons -3 1/2) actually came up from three during the day. In major fixes, the line would *always* move in the direction of the fix.

Thomas's poor performance against the Bucks, scoring just three points, was used as evidence. What the authors didn't mention was that Thomas was coming off an injury that took place the game before. In short, there was absolutely no evidence that these games were fixed.

THE STRAIGHT DEAL

I don't believe that NFL games are fixed and here's why.

First, over the course of my handicapping career I have consistently won money betting the NFL. If the games weren't honest, I don't believe I could have won because handicapping would be irrelevant. If, in addition to giving 11 to 10 odds, I had to overcome players who were dumping or shaving points, the odds against me would simply be too great to beat.

Second, in order for a game to be fixed, two events have to happen. The fixer must be able to get some important players in on the fix and he must also be able to bet enough money to overcome the payments he has made to the crooked players.

Over the last twenty-five years, NFL salaries have skyrocketed. The average player now makes well into the seven figures a year. The important players—who would have to be in on the fix to make it work—make in the upper seven figures or low eight figures (tens of millions plus) each season. It would cost a lot of money to get to such players. These players would also know that if they entered a fixing pact, the fixer would forever have a blackmail hold on them. This hold would not only keep the player's career in perpetual jeopardy but all outside earning sources (advertisements, endorsements, etc.) in jeopardy as well. To be willing to go along with all that and agree to such a permanent risk, a player would probably have to be paid about ten million dollars to fix a game. And to be sure that the game would go according to plan, several players would have to bought. The total cost of a fix would probably be about $30 million or more a game!

OBSTACLES IN THE BETTOR'S PATH

The fixer would then have to be able to bet enough on the game to turn a profit on the deal. The Vegas sports books would probably have to be avoided since all bets over $10,000 made there have to be reported to the IRS—something a fixer does not want to do. It is tough to bet over $25,000 a game with an illegal bookmaker—and you will be allowed to bet even that much only if the bookmaker knows you well. A fixer could try to spread his bet all over the country and off shore, but he would have to use hundreds or thousands of bookmakers.

Bookmakers would definitely notice when they saw this tidal wave of money coming in on one team. As the money came in from all over the country, bookmakers would be in a race to lay off the money with other book-makers. When huge money comes in from seemingly nowhere it is called unnatural money, and bookmakers are always suspicious about it. With over thirty million coming in, suspicion would quickly be rampant.

When bookmakers get suspicious, they sometimes take games off the board, meaning no one can bet on the game, until they know the reason for this unnatural money. And there is *always* a reasonable explanation. Sometimes it's an injury that comes to light, sometimes a big name in betting likes the team. Such moves can even come from some tout service calling the game a **can't lose lock** (another type of nonsense I'll get into later).

Bookmakers, who themselves depend on accurate handicapping, know that the only way they can survive is for the NFL games to be honest. Coups, such as the ones that have tarnished college basketball from time to time, could wipe them out. Bookmakers would be the first to turn in anyone who tried to fix a game. I don't think any-one even tries with pro football players these days.

Other participants that have been pointed to as pos-sible culprits in fixes have been the referees. Since referees make far less money than players and can exert great control over a game, this could be feasible except for two reasons.

First, the NFL does a *very* close background check when potential referees apply for a job. If they are allowed to ref NFL games, a lot of solid sources have to consider them bribe-proof.

Second, sources in Las Vegas—back to the time that Bob Martin set the opening NFL line (1967-1980)—keep records on what referees work what games and correlate that with any big money that comes in on a game. If any suspicious correlation between a particular ref and unnatural money turned up, they would report this data to the NFL.

Still, now and again, people make accusations about fixes by referees. In the 1989 book, *Interference*, by Dan E. Moldea, it was implied that eight NFL games were fixed during the 1979 season. Two referees were supposedly involved in these fixes.

What made the allegations dubious to me were that Moldea never named the referees in the book, and six of the games were Monday or Thursday night nationally telecast games played within a six-week period. The NFL rotates the referees who work the nationally telecast games, especially within such a short time period. I doubt very much that any two referees could have covered each of these six games. Again, the refs were conveniently not named.

What I have noticed about football bettors who believe games are fixed is that they are overwhelmingly *losing* bettors. Crying "fix" is an easy way to dodge the real problem—that they don't know how to handicap games.

But fixes are only one of the myths that make American society so hostile to sports betting. Another myth that hinders the bettor is the one that says all gambling is a vice without any benefit that inevitably leads gamblers to going broke.

BETTING AND THE REALITY

It is a reality that most people, though certainly not all, lose money betting the NFL over the long term. However, what most of these bettors get in return is excitement and the challenge of trying to buck the odds.

It is a reality that some people who bet the NFL are gambling addicts who need help. However, in almost any activity there is a possibility of addiction. Just a few of these activities are drinking, working, eating, and sex. In all of these activities—as in betting the NFL—the truly addicted person is in the extreme minority. But few people want to outlaw drinking, working, eating, or sex, because attempts to ban such activities have historically been notorious failures. It's just as misguided to outlaw betting on the NFL because of the slim possibility of a bettor's becoming a gambling addict. For most people who bet the NFL, it is one of a large number of activities they take part in over the course of a typical week. Losses are usually affordable and bettors pay them because they're having fun.

Outlawing NFL betting outside of Nevada is silly and hypocritical. The real reason that NFL betting is illegal outside of Nevada is that the illegal sports bookies provide a service that the government probably couldn't compete with if their agencies became the bookmakers.

What the government would have to compete with would be an outlet where someone could bet right up to kickoff, on credit, giving just 11 to 10 odds, and where taxes on the winnings of the normal bettor would likely never be collected, though professionals like myself do pay taxes on betting winnings. Since the government can't compete with the illegal bookies, they outlaw them.

Licensing bookmakers would also be expensive. Many years ago in Nevada, the legal sports books took out a 10 percent gaming tax in addition to the 11 to 10 the bettor gave. A $100 bet had to be paid for with $121 up front (11 to 10 on $100 was $110 and ten percent of $110 was an additional $11). During this time the illegal bookies in Nevada thrived since bettors had to lay only the normal 11 to 10 with them. Eventually the state lowered the gaming tax to .25 percent (one quarter of one percent) and had the sports books, and not the bettors, pay it. I doubt that other states would be that smart. Thus if bookies were licensed, the states' heavy taxes would drive those bettors right back to the illegals.

Many people who spout off about the evils of illegal betting sing a different tune when it becomes legal. Before the numbers game—a sucker bet in which the bettor is going against huge and unassailable odds of 40 percent and up—became legal as the state lottery, I knew a reporter who wrote a police beat column who liked to do pieces on police busts of illegal numbers operations. This reporter often said how evil numbers betting was—until it became legal. Since then, this reporter has often chided me for not betting the numbers, saying "you have to be in it to win it."

The fact is that NFL betting affects virtually no one except the people placing and receiving the bets. The one company that does probably prosper from football betting is the telephone company, since so many wagers are placed via phone.

As for the idea that illegal football betting contributes to the underworld—it's mostly fantasy. Most bookmakers I've known are hard-working solid-citizen types trying to use the 11 to 10 edge to make a decent living. If anything, they are more honest than most, because the bookie's word is truly his bond. Extremely few bookies are directly connected to the Mafia or other organized crime. Proof of this is that very few bettors who welsh on bets are physically beaten or threatened. The main punishment for people who try to not pay betting losses is the loss of reputation in the betting community. This loss of reputation soon makes it impossible for these bettors to place bets.

Another reality is that NFL betting is one of the purest activities around, with lines moving up and down with all the impartiality of the free market. There is no government agency or regulatory board that sets prices on NFL games. Lines move because of the money bet into them. If the betting public decides that the line is too low on a favorite, they will bet it. Those who missed the early bargain and still want to bet the favorite will then have to pay a higher price—supply and demand. It is the same for a bargain underdog. If the betting public feels the price is high enough, they bet it and push the line down.

NFL betting is an equal-opportunity activity with relatively low start-up costs, where over the long run, hard work really can pay off. Seniority will not keep some out while saving others from a red bottom line—anyone can bet the NFL, and if they bet losers, it will cost them money. But if you are a competent handicapper and have access to a decent number of lines, in the end you will profit.

HOW THE MEDIA HURTS BETTORS

Earlier, I wrote that the media cover the NFL very thoroughly. This is true from both a wagering and nonwagering point of view, and some of the information you can get from the media will be essential to your handicapping success. But other media coverage of the NFL tends to *cost* the average bettor in terms of bets won and lost. This is the type of coverage we'll go over here.

The game of football can be made to appear very complex. How many people can really define what a "West Coast offense" is? How many can accurately identify a "zone blitz"? What about "nickel" and "dime" defenses? How many bettors are at a loss when starters are posted early in the game? What about when a quarterback goes down and is replaced by someone virtually unknown?

NFL analysts in the newspapers and media have quick answers to all of the above questions. They have a listing of every player and his NFL experience at their fingertips. They have staff-written copy on hand to explain all types of offenses and defenses. They have formidable arrays of statistics available to cover any play or situation.

Hearing all of these terms, facts, and statistics can be intimidating to a beginner at betting. Part of you asks, "How can I bet these games when there's so much information I don't know?" It can be especially intimidating when a media authority makes a selection on a game that goes against yours.

What the beginning bettor doesn't realize is that it is one thing to describe what has happened and to pin statistics on it. However, it is something else entirely to try to predict that which has yet to take place. And that is what handicappers try to do.

There is no question that the media do an excellent job of reporting that which has already happened.

The televising of the NFL is excellent. Very seldom are camera people out of position. On many plays—including all of the key ones—they show replays. After you watch a game, you know exactly what happened in it. You have seen all of the turning points and key plays. You know how well each team ran and passed the ball, as well as how well each team defended against the run and pass.

It is true that a number of the NFL announcers leave something to be desired. Sometimes they overemphasize a play and other times they seem to miss the importance of one. Often, announcers will overreact to the game itself.

Still the coverage of the games is excellent. If there were a way that I could closely view all sixteen games every weekend, I would do it. Since this is not possible, I try to concentrate on three games in each time slot (one on regular TV, two on satellite dish) every Sunday. I believe it is better to know fully what happened in six games than to know just bits and snatches of fourteen, which is the usual number of Sunday afternoon games. I also watch the Sunday night and Monday night games as closely as possible.

Even with games you do not see, you can get good ideas of what happened from other sources. ESPN has an online service that shows every drive in each game. The Monday *USA Today* carries complete statistical pictures of each game as well as summaries of every scoring drive. With the Internet you can read papers in every NFL city for a detailed picture of the games played the day before. And both the print and televised media provide good coverage of injuries, roster changes, and other developments that occur during the week.

Thus the NFL is a sport of virtually no hidden information. The key to making winning bets—predicting that which has yet to happen—is how to process this information. When the media try to predict that which has yet to happen, they tend to do poorly. Living in New York City, I read, see, and hear a number of media point spread prognosticators. Some of them are:

1) The New York Post

Every Friday, eleven handicappers in the *Post* make predictions on all NFL games against the spread. I've never seen one of these handicappers consistently pick the 52.4 percent winners needed to beat the 11 to 10 odds. In fact, virtually every year for the past twenty-plus years the consensus in the *Post* has finished below 50 percent. Of course, picking *every* game against the spread is tough. However, the *Post's* record in selections has been especially poor on the best-bet picks, or the three top selections, of the handicappers. It is a rare year when the consensus best-bets finish above 50 percent, and I can't remember any year that they overcame the 11 to 10.

Since 1977, the Friday *Post* has shown that just because someone follows the games closely, as reporters do, doesn't mean that he can pick winners.

Then the *Post* brought in a special handicapping writer named Dave Blezow. He often mentions trends in his handicapping analysis on Friday. However, Blezow over the years has often done his best when he's gone *against* a trend he has mentioned. In the Sunday *Post*, Blezow has made available to his readers a huge variety of trends meant to cover every game: how teams do at home, on the road, on grass, on turf, as favorites, and as underdogs, as well as other circumstances.

Years ago I used to compile and use data of the type Blezow uses. I now know that trends are mostly useless since teams change so quickly due to free agency. For example, a team may be 12 and 4 on road turf for the last five years, but how relevant is that if only three of its players have been there that long?

Moreover, whenever some trend does make sense, you can be sure that Las Vegas Sports Consultants has already taken account of it in the line, though their official position is that "history [trends] means nothing"—a quote

I take with reservations. Trends have a limited place in handicapping since most long-term ones make it into the price. And occasionally they can help more when they are recent and have taken place with most of the current roster around.

In 2001, the *New York Post* brought in someone named The Wild Cat. This guest handicapper picks just a couple of games every week. The Wild Cat has compiled a winning record every year thus far. He wins about 57 percent. Like me, he selects almost all underdogs and like me he looks closely at the psychological aspects of a game. The Wild Cat is definitely the exception to the rule with media selectors.

On the negative side, The Wild Cat doesn't add the vig (the 11-10 charged on losses) into his record. A 1-1 week is treated as a break-even week, not a week where a tenth of a unit was lost.

2) WFAN's Mike Francesa and Chris Russo

Every Friday Francesa and Russo make predictions against the spread. The normal format is for each to announce three best bets for the week and explain the reasons for his choices.

Russo and especially Francesa often make the beginner's mistake of picking favorites to cover simply because they are the better team. They don't seem to realize that just because a team is better doesn't mean it will cover the point spread.

And, like many other reporters who try to pick games, Francesa tends to use over-simplified cause and effect. For instance, he may decide that if a team has a good passing game and the other team "can't defend" against the pass that the passing team will pile up points and thus cover. However, oftentimes the team with the seeming disadvantage will make adjustments for one game, especially if the team with the disadvantage has an *emotional edge* in the game. In addition, the advantage of one team over another is almost always already put into the line.

One of the most important things for a sports bettor to realize is that the NFL has very strong parity. If you were to rank all football players in the country, with zero being the worst and 100 being the best, the worst NFL players would rate about a 95 or 96. The best players would, of course, rate a 100. This small difference means that the scales can be tipped the other way on any given Sunday or Monday. This is far different from college football, where the best player would be a 96 or 97 and the worst might be a 70. College football, of course, has much less parity than the NFL and plays more to form.

Francesa and Russo seldom pick the 52.4 percent winners needed to beat the 11 to 10. To cover this, they often talk about their records in relation to the .500 mark. The 11-10 vig seems not to exist in the world of WFAN, but it definitely *does* exist in the world of the people who follow Francesa and Russo's selections when they call their bookmakers.

Occasionally Francesa has done something that I think encourages especially dangerous behavior in listeners who bet. In the mid-'90s, after getting off to several very bad season starts picking three games a week, around the middle of those seasons he started picking lots of games—often ten or more a week. That is like encouraging bettors to plunge when losing—the worst type of betting behavior to encourage. Bettors who go for broke after losses are likely to suffer disastrous consequences in the long run.

In 1997, Francesa finished at 58-64 against the spread, which represented over a ten-unit loss for anyone who backed his selections with real money, assuming that all bets were for the same amount. That same year Russo finished at 31-28-3 for a .525 winning record. This would have represented a microscopic profit (two-tenths of a bet ahead if all bets had been the same) for someone who bet Russo's selections. At the time of publication of this book, Francesca had beaten the 11 to 10 odds in two years of seven since 1997.

Francesa has also on occasion set a different kind of bad example for bettors; he let his personal favorites dictate his selections. For a couple of years in the early '90s Francesa did a television show with Bill Parcells. The two became friendly on this show. Afterward, in the four years that Parcells coached the Patriots, Francesa would never pick against the Pats.

Then, in the 1997 season, when Bill Parcells started coaching the Jets, Francesa would never pick against the Jets and often picked them.

3) Pro Football Weekly

Each week eight of the writers at *Pro Football Weekly* select all of the games against the point spread. The consensus went under .500 for years, except for Dan Arkush, who beat the 11 to 10 in 1995 and 1996. Unfortunately, Arkush hasn't beaten the 11 to 10 since then, and Hub Arkush, the publisher of *Pro Football Weekly*, has beaten the 11 to 10 just one season since 1996. None of the other predictors there has won consistently, either.

4) ESPN

Pete Axthelm was on-air point spread selector at the network the first four years they televised the NFL (1987-1990). He beat the 11 to 10 in three of those years, usually picking five games a week.

Pete beat the 11 to 10 following my selections in those years despite a major disadvantage in handicapping: the movement in the lines caused by the huge bets of my followers.

After Pete passed away, ESPN hired Norm Hitzges. He turned in three disgraceful years in which he finished far under .500. He never beat the 11 to 10 in any of the three years he was there.

After Hitzges, ESPN brought in Hank Goldberg. Goldberg uses trends in selecting, and at least relates them to the current forms of the teams. He was an improvement, even though he has beaten the 11 to 10 in only four of the eleven years he's been there. In 1996, Goldberg's third season on ESPN, he did very well, going 55-33 against the spread. Unfortunately, in 1997, he finished more than ten games under .500 in his selections. Goldberg, to his credit, beat the 11 to 10 each season from 2001-2003. Still, over the long run of eleven years, he is an overall loser against the 11 to 10.

Like WFAN, ESPN makes a big deal about the .500 mark in selections. But beating the point spread 50 percent of the time is absolutely nothing to be proud of. It simply is not enough when going against the 11 to 10. I am sure ESPN realizes that many thousands of bettors are watching when point spread picks are made. I am also sure that ESPN realizes that bettors have to give 11 to 10 odds.

5) Gerald Strine of Newsday

Though Strine left *Newsday* after the 1995 season, I still feel his record deserves mention here because of the lesson it teaches in handicapping. On the positive side, Strine was among the first people to make NFL spread selections in major newspapers.

He started in 1974 and hit better than 60 percent over his first four seasons in the media, mostly at the *Washington Post*. From 1974-77, Strine's method of handicapping—comparing offensive lines against defensive lines—brought him success.

However, in 1978, there were big rules changes in the NFL, which totally changed the handicapping game. The rules permitted offensive linemen much greater arm movement in holding out defensive linemen—basically allowing holding—and no longer permitted pass defenders to bump pass receivers except for once in the first five yards from scrimmage. Also, pass interference was interpreted much more strictly.

These rules created much greater parity in the NFL and negated the advantages that defensive lines formerly had over offensive lines. The rules also made the passing game more important than it had been. Strine, unfortunately, appears never to have really figured out that the importance of scrimmage play to winning NFL handicapping has decreased greatly since 1978 while the importance of emotional intensity (or lack of it) has soared. As a result, his winning percentage suffered badly.

What kept Strine in the black for many seasons after 1977 were plunge bets that he made on games in the late season, playoffs, or Super Bowl. Sometimes his bets went as high as $3,000—after a season of betting $250 a game. This, again, can encourage readers to go for broke—a dangerous thing.

In 1990, Strine was behind $1,950 going into the Giant-Bills Super Bowl. He risked $2,200 (to win $2,000) on the Bills in the game. As 6 1/2-point favorites, they lost, 20-19. That made Strine's losses for the year $4,150—equal to several of his winning seasons.

In 1997, Strine had a winning season, but again did something that gave the wrong idea to readers. After building up a nice early season profit, Strine then started to wager $100 on most games, as opposed to his usual $250. A good handicapper would never cut back in this

CARDOZA PUBLISHING • DAN GORDON

way—he would know that on these subsequent games he would continue to have the same chance of winning.

Plunging in newspaper columns, by the way, is not that unusual. As I will soon relate, an editor once pressured *me* to do this.

OTHER POINTS ABOUT MEDIA PROGNOSTICATORS

Years ago, the Castaways Sports Book in Las Vegas held a contest every week in which contestants had to pick every NFL game of the week against the point spread. I never entered this contest because, as I will show, when you must pick too many games against a single line, your results will depend too much on luck. For the same reason, media prognosticators who pick too many games are going to have results based mainly on luck.

Here's why. In an average week, I will bet four or five games, selecting among a wide variety of lines. That leaves ten or eleven games that I don't bet because their lines everywhere are basically "right"—that is, their lines are at a level that achieves parity between the two teams. Trying to predict the results of these games against the point spread is like trying to predict the results of a coin toss: the results are equally likely to go either way. Because you are as likely to lose as win on these bets, you can't make money in the long run on them going against the bookmakers' 11 to 10 odds.

When media people select games against the spread, it is always against one number—shopping is not allowed. Since shopping for prices is a key factor in finding "wrong" lines, a media selector should make only those selections that are appropriate for the numbers he is actually picking against. In addition, a media point spread selector should tell his readers or viewers what he would do on other games if certain other prices became

76

available. This would be a true handicapping service for the betting public.

I got to do that for one season in one of my publications. In my second (and final) season writing for the *New York Daily News*, in 1986, I was asked to provide leans—that is, the team I was leaning toward at a given price. The reason that Vic Ziegel and the *News* wanted me to do this was to make me a more "normal" point spread selector by giving out more games. What I did instead was tell readers at what price a game would be a bet. In this second season with the *News* I won on both my picks and on my leans.

Often writers make three selections they call "best bets." But any format that requires a specific number of picks is too restrictive. Suppose a handicapping writer likes just two games for the week. He has to include another game to go with the format. Suppose he likes five. Then he has to leave out two games. Either way, the reader/bettor is getting cheated.

On ESPN, Hank Goldberg selects six games—five Sunday games and the Monday night game. He is certain in such a format to be giving the public games that should not be included.

MY EXPERIENCES WITH THE MEDIA

In the 1985 season, I got off to a good start. I was writing for the *Daily News* and the *San Francisco Examiner* and in the first two weeks of the season, all three of my selections in my newspaper columns won. And not only did all of them win against the point spread, but all were underdogs that won straight up. In fact, my selections had never even trailed on the scoreboard in these games.

Then, shortly after the second week's games, Bob Decker, the assistant editor at the *Daily News* at the time, asked, "Why don't you pick more games?"

It was a refrain I was to hear again and again in my media sports-picking career. I had thought that my 3 and 0 record would make both my readers and editors happy, but it turned out not to be the case.

Other people in the media were also pushing for me to pick more games. Finally, in 1988, I felt under enough pressure that I did—with disastrous results.

Meanwhile, back in 1985, things had taken a turn for the worse and I realized I was probably going to have my first losing season in the media. That's when Vic Ziegel, my editor at the *Daily News*, urged me to make plunge bets in the playoffs. When I protested, he attempted to compromise by agreeing that I could tell my readers NOT to make plunge bets. This inconsistent behavior would be rationalized by telling readers that I was using "newspaper" money rather than "real" money. He didn't appear to give much thought to the real message the readers would receive.

I didn't plunge and two years later I was released from the *News*.

During my time in the media, I came to see how most editors viewed sports handicapping as entertainment rather than as reportage that should meet the same journalistic standards upheld for other sections. That's why you, as a serious handicapper, should take all media predictions with a big grain of salt.

7

NFL Touts

As NFL betting has grown, so has the tout business. A **tout** is someone who gets paid to help the bettor make money betting the NFL.

The question I hear many bettors ask, even about legitimate handicappers, is why don't these guys, if they know what they're doing, just bet for themselves and make tons of money? Why do they take on the aggravation of running an advice business?

FINANCIAL REALITIES

The answer is that they couldn't afford to. Supporting yourself just betting on the NFL takes a huge financial stake because your edge is relatively small. Finishing twenty bets ahead after the 11 to 10 is tough over the course of an NFL season. But even if you could win at this rate every year, you'd have to have an average bet of about $3,000 per game to make a $60,000-a-year living.

Since even the best handicappers can lose—even have a losing *season*— because of bad luck over the short term, you have to be prepared to ride out losses, meaning you need a stake of many multiples of your bet to avoid losing it all. The exact amount depends on your winning percentage, the number of games you bet, and other things, but for a pro who depends on his bankroll for his living and has no other way than sports-betting to replenish it, a very substantial betting stake is required.

To make a decent living, there is nothing wrong or inconsistent with a capable handicapper selling his selections to those who prefer others to do their handicapping.

WINNING EXPECTATIONS

I have done touting myself, though I found it a tough way to make money. Most bettors expect the tout to win a huge percentage of the time. They don't like to hear that realistic long-term win percentages will be in the 55 to 60 percent range. This is despite the fact that virtually every handicapping tournament shows that the best anyone can do selecting NFL games over the course of one season is in the low to middle 60 percent range.

I know of no service that has done better than about 60 percent over a number of seasons. And those that consistently reach 60 percent are very few. Yet, despite all the evidence available, customers still want someone who claims to win 75 or 80 percent against the point spread. Many are turned off and away when I tell them not to expect those percentages from me, especially when other services out there are making those claims. But just remember this: if someone knew he would win 80 of his next 100 bets, he could turn $1,000 into $15 billion by proper proportional betting—all over the course of one season! Of course, this huge "winner" would run into problems with bookmaker limits that would cut down on his winnings!

Other would-be customers are often underfinanced. This doesn't mean that I pick more losers than winners, but that these bettors are not ready for the long haul—some of which will contain losing streaks.

Let's use dollar amounts to show what I mean. Let's say I charge $400 for an NFL season. Say my customer does well that year, going 46-34 (a good .575 percentage). To keep things simple, let's also say that all my customer's bets are for the same amount, which in reality, they wouldn't be. This would mean that the customer ended up 8.6 units ahead. If my customer was betting $100 a game, he ended up making $860 minus the $400 for my fee.

Over the course of the season, I would have to end up four bets ahead just to cover what this person paid me. Over 80 bets, I would have to win 55 percent (44-36) before this person saw any profit. This person is betting far too little to be following me.

KEEPING THE ACTION UNDER CONTROL

I remember one year in the NBA playoffs where I lost nine bets in a row. Because I had the money to continue betting, I ended up hitting just over 60 percent for the playoffs and won about nine units. However, if I had used too large a betting unit, I would have tapped out.

In 1997, I had one week where I went 0-5. Despite this horrendous week, I ended up the season a winner (55 percent against the spread). Someone who was underfinanced, however, might have tapped out that week and never seen the profits.

What's even worse is that it is not at all a sure thing that I—or any other handicapper—will come out ahead over the course of a single NFL season. Many bettors don't want to hear about the possibility of losing over the course of a season, but not wanting to hear it doesn't make the possibility of its happening go away.

Other potential customers are hampered by not having access to early- and late-week lines. The lines are most vulnerable early in the week when professional bettors are pouncing on mistakes made by the odds makers in their attempt to read the betting public. Unfortunately, most bettors who follow touts like to bet at the end of the week, and often have betting access only then. Not betting early takes away early-week plays for bettors following me, and will often cost them wins. What's even worse is when they bet the games against my advice even after the early numbers have changed. This may not only deny them wins, but turn those wins into losses.

I remember a time I gave a bettor just one selection for the week. It was the Falcons +6 over the Bengals. I told him not to take less than six points on the Falcons. He followed my advice and took six points early in the week.

However, as the week went on this man craved more action. But no matter how many times he called me for more picks, I kept telling him that the rest of the games that weekend were not good investments. Still, at the end of the week he bet more. First, he increased his bet on the Falcons. However, now he was taking 4 1/2 points instead of six. Then, he bet two games that were on television. You can probably guess what happened. The Falcons lost by exactly six points and the two television game bets lost. A week that should have ended with a push bet ended up 0-3 for him.

I have noticed through the years that many bettors who use touts crave action. To get it, they are willing to take the worst of the betting line after it has changed during the week. Giving up the 11 to 10, betting with the moves, and taking the worst of it cost money. Passing on games that aren't worth giving 11 to 10 odds saves money.

I know many NFL touts. Some are able to win but most of them have been consistent losers when they bet.

Many have actually gone broke betting and are looking to get money from others to make up for their poor selections.

There is one well-known sports service owner in New York who lost so much to a bookmaker (especially in college basketball) that it was rumored his losses provided the bookmaker's children with their college educations.

OTHER POINTS ABOUT TOUTS

Many touts have multiple services within one service. This way they can almost always truthfully claim that at least one of their services is doing well. For instance, a tout may operate the following services:

A) An early-week newsletter, giving selections on each game, emphasizing two or three

B) A midweek newsletter, giving selections based on "new" information

C) A weekend phone service, giving selections over the weekend

D) A late phone service, giving selections in the two hours before game time that have the latest "inside" information

E) An exclusive phone service, giving the absolute top picks within a half-hour of game time

Typically, the last option would cost bettors the most and the first would cost bettors the least. Also, as the week goes on, the tout would generally switch sides on some games because of "new" information. In this way, the tout can truthfully advertise that one of his services had the winner of the game. In addition, at least one of the five services will almost always have a good week.

CARDOZA PUBLISHING • DAN GORDON

That the exclusive phone service, charging $200 a week, might go 1-4 one week, while the cheap newsletter that costs $75 for the whole season might go 3-0 is of no concern to the tout. In his next early-week newsletter, he will chirp about going 3-0 the week before.

If, on the other hand, the exclusive phone service has done the best, the tout advertises the phone line's great week to the customers of its other services to try to get them to upgrade.

To top it off, some tout services are owned by others. For instance, Jim Feist not only owns his own service (which has many services under his name), but he also has a piece of Larry Ness (formerly Top Play) and Wayne Alan Root. If one service of the empire is doing poorly, another within it that is doing well can mail a flier to the disgruntled customers of the poorly performing service.

Other sports services give out selections on 900 numbers. With these services, there is a charge-per-call that can vary from as little as $5 to as much as $50. Sometimes there are additional charges for extra minutes.

Sports services use the 900 numbers in various ways. On a five-dollar call, they may offer just one selection and tell the caller to call back in ten minutes for another selection. These calls can add up to much more money than the caller might realize. An average Sunday might mean six calls to the 900 number, turning a five-dollar call into a total charge of $30, or three $50 calls into a $150 charge.

BETTING LOCKS

Other services have a practice that might be called "withholding the best." Touts who offer several different levels of services frequently call one a "best-bet" service. On their other, less-expensive services, they give out their "regular" selections (without the best bet). In effect, "regular" customers are paying for not getting the best game(s).

Sports services realize that most people who sign up with them are insecure and believe they don't really know what is happening in the NFL. To try to bamboozle potential customers, many services make claims about having scouts all over that give them inside information. A number of the more aggressive services even make veiled, and sometimes, not-so-veiled, references to fixed games. This usually sounds good to the customer until the service loses a few "sure things." When this happens, the service always has another, better "sure thing" coming up.

One sports service claimed to me that they could not only pick winners but could call the *exact score on games*! They wanted a lot of money for this service. I cooled off this tout by telling him that I would give him huge odds on a large bet—I had other people also willing to pay huge bucks—if he could call just three exact scores for the rest of the NFL season (the season was in its fourth week then). He could pick any three of the remaining games. The tout hung up the phone after I made this offer.

Other services advertise **lock games**, meaning games that can't lose. How they can sell such games is beyond me. It would seem to me that if someone had a game that could not lose, rather than share it with many others through a sports service, he should bet it himself and put on it everything he owns. Since the game "can't lose," this would not be over betting!

Anyone who has watched sports for about a month realizes that the difference between winning and losing, especially against the spread, can be infinitesimally small. In the NFL, a game will often be totally turned around by one or two plays, or even a single penalty call. There are an almost infinite number of scenarios that can happen in a single NFL game. The best anyone can do in handicapping is come up with a side that has a slightly better than 60 percent chance of covering the spread. This still means that almost four times in ten the game will lose—which makes any talk of a lock complete nonsense.

In 2003, there was a Monday Night game between the Colts and the Bucs. The Bucs—four point favorites—scored a touchdown with under five minutes left to go up 35-14. For many betting the Bucs, they must certainly have looked like a lock at this point. Any Buc bettor would have liked to increase his bet on the game at this point. In fact, if given the opportunity, some Buc bettors would have bet everything they had if they could have given only 4 points on the Bucs at this time. However, the Colts then scored three touchdowns to tie the game, and eventually won in overtime 38-35.

To summarize, the only locks that exist are those that need keys to open them.

INSIDE SCOOP ON TOUTING

The business of touting actually tends to worsen the quality of selections because of customer pressure to make or avoid certain picks. I remember when, in 1983, I was on a Las Vegas radio show on which I gave selections. One week I liked Tampa Bay as a 5 1/2-point underdog at Green Bay. The Bucs got killed in the game, 55-14. In fact, the Packers scored 49 points in the first half—still an NFL record.

The next week Tampa Bay played in Dallas. They were 14-point underdogs. I thought the Bucs were an outstanding bet in this game. Someone else on the radio show also liked the Bucs, but said he couldn't give them out as a selection with his sports service. Why? Because he had given them out the last week against the Packers and his customers "wouldn't stand" for being given them again. This handicapper had to pass up an excellent value for his customers because of the abnormal result of the previous week. In this game, Tampa Bay lost to Dallas by three in overtime but more than covered the spread.

I remember another example early in the 1996 season. In Week 5, the Packers were playing at Seattle. They were coming off their first loss the previous week in Minnesota. To me, a bounce-back seemed likely.

But another tout I knew said he couldn't give out the Packers since they were "too easy." What he meant was that his customers could come up with this selection on their own. What they expected from him were tips that were more "creative."

This tout's creativity led him to pick the Seahawks in this game. The Packers won and covered, 31-10.

Some of the more laughable tout ads are those that are printed a month or more ahead of time. These are often found in NFL betting schedules. The ads will claim that this service has winners in games that are to be played a month or more after the ads were placed. But there is no way to know that far ahead whether the right factors will be in place to make a particular game a good bet.

An ad by tout Kevin Duffy in the *New York Daily News* went even further on claims for an NCAA tournament. The ad claimed that Duffy had gone 6-0 in the previous round. But the round in question wasn't even played until long *after* the ad had been written up and submitted to the paper!

In summary, the only touts you should even consider using are those who talk about the long haul and realistic winning percentages, which are in the upper 50 percent to lower 60 percent range. However, you will be hard pressed to find any touts who act this way and survive for long in this field.

8

Sucker Bets and Their Allure

The usual way to bet the NFL is to bet one game at a time and give 11 to 10 odds. Usually the bet is a bet on one team (or side) against the point spread, though some bettors wager on the over-under (total) of a game. However, bookies also offer other types of bets. What makes these bets alluring is that they seem to pay bonuses that don't exist on straight one-game-at-a-time bets. But in reality, these exotic bets usually *cost* you. Let's take a look.

PARLAYS AND PARLAY CARDS

Parlays are usually bet in two- or three-game groups. On a two-game parlay, a bettor usually gets 13 to 5 odds if he wins both games. For a small investment, the payoff seems big—on a $50 wager, a payoff of $130. On a straight bet, by contrast, a bettor must risk $143 ($130 plus the $13 vig) to win $130. And if he is going to bet two games at $50 each, he must risk $110 to win only $100. So why not bet parlays?

SUCKER BETS AND THEIR ALLURE

The problem is that the odds of winning two of two bets (with only 50 percent picking ability) is 3 to 1 against. You arrive at this figure by multiplying the theoretical chance of winning one game (1 of 2, or 1/2) by the theoretical chance of winning the second game (again 1 of 2, or 1/2) for a result of 1/4. This equals one chance in four of winning two games, or 3 to 1 against. If the odds are 3 to 1 against going two for two, the fair payout odds should also be 3 to 1(or 15 to 5). But they aren't. Instead, they are only 13 to 5.

Another way of looking at this is that there are four possibilities for what can happen on a $50 parlay. One is that the bettor wins both games. In that case he wins $130. Or, he can split the two games two ways—win the first and lose the second or win the second and lose the first—in either case, he will lose $50. The final possibility is that the bettor will lose both games. In that case, too, he will lose $50. There are thus three ways to lose $50 and one way to win $130. With a total of $200 risked (4 x $50), the two-team parlay bettor will, in the long run, lose $20 of each $200 risked—a 10 percent disadvantage. This disadvantage is over twice the 4.5 percent disadvantage that a bettor faces betting one game at a time giving 11 to 10 odds.

In addition, the bettor must bet both games with the same bookie or sports book, so he is stuck on both games with that book's lines. This tends to cut down on the edge he can get by shopping for the best price.

A three-team parlay usually pays off at odds of 6 to 1. Here a $50 bettor receives $300 on a $50 investment. Sounds great, doesn't it?

However, the odds of cashing that three-team parlay ticket (with 50 percent picking ability) are only 1 in 8. To calculate this for yourself, multiply 1/2 by 1/2 by 1/2 (each being the chance of a positive result on a game).

The result is 1/8, or 7 to 1 against.

To say this another way, there are eight possible outcomes with a three-team parlay. The bettor can win all three bets, can win two of three (three different ways), can win one of three (three different ways), or can lose all three. If the bettor wins two, one, or none of his games, he loses the $50. There are seven ways that can happen. Only on the eighth possibility—going three for three—will the bettor cash the ticket.

Wagering $50 eight times (once for each possible outcome), he will lose $50 seven times (for a $350 total loss) and win $300 once. That adds up to a total loss of $50 for a total of $400 bet, which means that a bettor is going against 12.5 percent odds when betting a three-team parlay. The odds a bettor is bucking on a three-team parlay are thus stiffer than those on a two-team parlay even though the payoff sounds so much better.

And once again, the bettor is limited in his shopping, since the lines for each game of the parlay bet must be gotten from the same sports book.

Another form of parlay is the parlay card, or sheet. On these, the payoff odds are even worse than on straight parlays. On parlay cards, a bettor must choose at least three games and the payoffs are worse—usually 5 to 1 for three games rather than the 6 to 1 on a normal three-game parlay. That means the house has a 25 percent edge on this wager. Four-teamers usually pay 10 to 1, which gives the house a 31.25 percent edge. A ten-teamer might pay 500 to 1, which sounds good until you realize that the real odds against going 10 for 10 are 1,023 to 1, which means that the house has over a fifty percent edge on that proposition.

Even worse, a tie on a sheet usually counts as a loss. So, if you have three winners and a tie, it is the same as going zero for four! Realizing this, sheet operators try to give likely game margins, lines of three, six, and seven, as often as possible. That way, the house edge is even greater.

Yet millions of people continue to bet cards or sheets. Years ago, I helped a bookmaker distribute some sheets. The hundreds of people I gave them to—almost without exception—said they won on these sheets several times a year. But the year that I distributed sheets there were just three winners the whole season. And those winners all went three for three—the minimum number of games, with the lowest payout.

In Las Vegas, most sports books put out parlay cards. Here bettors have fewer disadvantages than bettors who play the illegal sheets. At some sports books, ties win. And at most the payouts are higher. Three-teamers, for example, pay off at 6 to 1 odds, the normal payout on a three-team parlay.

There is one edge worth mentioning that brings some professional bettors to bet parlay cards in Las Vegas. This edge is that games can frequently have different lines at different sports books. Smart bettors can take advantage of this by shopping for middles on these cards. This can be especially helpful if ties win. A bettor can find the favorite at -2 1/2 on one card and the underdog in the same game at +4 on the card at another sports book. If the game falls three or four and ties win, the bettor wins the game on both cards.

What professional bettors do is find three or four games with widely varying lines that go through key numbers (especially three, four, six, seven, or ten). They then bet *every* possible way on these three or four games (it takes either eight or 16 cards) and hope to hit one or more middles that will make the week a winning one. Making money from middling sheets requires serious leg-work and discipline: consistently checking every sports book in town and every game on every card. However, there are some serious bettors who do it and turn a profit in most years. A bankroll and patience are what's needed to make money this way. Las Vegas is probably the only place where you can make a profit using parlay cards.

Another type of parlay that can be a big winner for smart bettors is a parlay called the **correlated parlay**. Almost all parlays are non-correlated, which means that one result has no bearing on another result. But there are exceptions, mostly in some Nevada sports books. For example, in the 2005 Super Bowl one could bet a parlay of under 3 1/2 field goals made, with under four field goals attempted. Obviously if under four field goals are attempted, one has to win the other part of the parlay of under 3 1/2 field goals made!

REVERSES AND OTHER STRANGE BETS

In a reverse bet, remember, a bettor picks two games. On a $100 reverse, he wins $400 if both games win; loses $120 if one game wins and the other loses; and loses $220 if both games lose.

Winning $400 is the lure that gets people to bet reverses. This 4 to 1 payout for going two for two is better than the true odds of going two for two, which are 3 to 1. However, these winnings are outweighed by what happens when you lose.

First, if you split on a reverse bet, you lose $120. That's $110 more than the $10 you lose if you split on two regular bets (making $100 on the winner and losing $110 on the loser).

Second, if you lose both games, you lose $220. That is the same as losing two straight bets (losing $110 twice). Since on every $100 reverse bet you have two chances of splitting (for a total loss of $120 + $120, or $240), one chance of losing both games (for a loss of $220), and one chance of winning (for a profit of $400), four $100 reverse bets add up to a $60 loss ($400 in wins minus $460 in losses).

This $60 loss on a total of $880 risked (4 x $220) means the odds against you are 6.8 percent. This is nearly 50 percent greater than the odds being bucked when betting one game at a time (4.55 percent). Also, once again, since you must bet the whole reverse with one bookie, the edge you can get from shopping for the best price is restricted.

Another type of two-game bet is the **"if" bet**. On "if" bets, you specify which team you want to bet "on top." If that game loses, the second game becomes a non-bet. However, if the game "on top" wins, the second game is automatically bet. "If" bets don't have to be for the same amount. However, like reverse bets, these bets increase the edge of the bookmaker.

Here's how. Consider an "if" bet in which you have bet both teams for the same amount. Let's say the bet is Giants for $100, *if* Jets $100. If you lose the Giants game, the Jets bet doesn't count. In this case, you lose $110 (laying 11 to 10 on both games, as usual). If the Giants win, on the other hand, then your bet goes through on the Jets game. If you win the Jets game, you win $200 ($100 plus $100). If you lose the Jets game, you lose $10 (your $100 win on the Giants minus your $110 loss on the Jets).

On your Giants/Jets "if" bet you have two chances of losing $110 (Giants loss with Jets win or Giants loss with Jets loss), one chance of winning $200 (both Giants and Jets win), and one chance of losing $10 (Giants win and Jets lose). With a total risk of $440 on the four possible outcomes, you can thus expect to lose $30 ($200 minus $110 minus $110 minus $10 = negative $30). The house edge on this bet is again 6.8 percent—again nearly 50 percent worse than betting one game at a time.

Let's also consider an "if" bet in which the game "on top" is bet more heavily. Let's say the bet is Giants $200 if Jets $100. If the Giants lose or both the Giants and Jets lose, you lose $220. If the Giants win but the Jets lose, you make $90 ($200 minus $110). If both the Giants and Jets win, you make $300 ($200 plus $100). In this case, with a total risk of $880 on the four possible outcomes, you can expect to lose $50 or almost 5.7 percent—over a full percent greater than if you had bet one game at a time.

And what if, instead, you bet the game "on top" lighter? Let's say the bet is Giants $100 *if* Jets $200. If the Giants lose, you lose $110 (two possibilities). If the Giants win and the Jets lose, you lose $120 ($100 minus $220). If both the Giants and Jets win, you win $300 ($100 plus $200). In this case, with a total risk on the four possible outcomes of $440, you can expect to lose $40, or a whopping 9.1 percent. This makes the odds against you about double what they'd be if you bet one game at a time.

TEASER BETS

The name of this bet should be enough to keep smart bettors away. However, every year the number of bettors who wager on teaser bets grows.

What gets bettors to bet teasers? The games they remember losing by "just a point or two." Since so many games seem to fall so close to the number, the lure of getting extra points on games becomes too much for many bettors to pass up. There are four main types of teaser bets:

1) There is the two-team teaser where a bettor gets six points on each of two games. The price of these extra points is giving 6 to 5 odds on the bet. In two-team teasers, both games must

win for the bettor to get paid. Also, in all two-team teasers, if any game ends in a tie on the adjusted price, the teaser is considered no bet. This "non bet" is regardless of how the other game did. On multi-game teasers, ties reduce the teaser bet to the games left in the teaser—for example, a five-team teaser automatically becomes a four-team teaser and so on, with the odds reduced accordingly. The exception is the ten-point teaser in which any tie causes the wager to lose.

2) Another type of two-team teaser is one in which a bettor gets 6 1/2 points on each of two games. The bettor must give 13 to 10 odds on this bet.

3) The third type of two-team teaser is one in which a bettor gets seven points on each of two games. Here, a bettor must give 7 to 5 (14 to 10) odds.

4) Another common type of teaser is the three-team teaser where a bettor gets ten points on each of the games. The bettor gives 6 to 5 odds for this teaser, and again, a tie loses this bet.

Over the 2001 and 2002 seasons, 197 of the 526 games played fell within 5 1/2 points of the closing line. All of those games would have been wins regardless of which side of the teaser you bet. In 23 games, the game fell exactly six points from the closing line. Giving the bettor the benefit of the extra game, (s)he would have won 12 of these games and tied 11.

All in all, a bettor would have had a 70.291 percent winning record on six-point *individual*-game teaser bets in those seasons. However, you must win *two* games to win the six-point teaser bet. By squaring the 70.291 percent winning record, we find that you would have won just 49.408 percent of the real-life two-game teasers. Laying 6 to 5 odds means you must win 54.545 percent of the two-team teasers just to break even. Overall, the house had a gigantic 10.4 percent edge on six-point teaser bets those two seasons.

On the other teaser bets, the picture is just as bleak. On 6 1/2 point teasers, just 50.286 percent of the two teamers came in. Giving 13 to 10 odds (56.522 percent) means that the house edge on these teasers was 11.03 percent.

On the seven-point teaser, bettors won 51.37 percent of the time. However, 58.333 percent is needed to break even against the 7 to 5 odds. The house had a huge 11.93 percent edge on these bets.

On the rarely seen ten-point teasers, you have to win 81.706 percent (the cube root of 54.545 percent) of your individual bets to break even. But just 77.776 percent of the games in the 2001 and 2002 seasons would have been winners taking 9 1/2 additional points. Remember, on the ten-point teaser, ties lose. This means just 47.018 percent (77.776 percent to the third power) of three-team teasers came in. Going against 6 to 5 odds means that the ten-point teaser bettor is bucking 13.80 percent odds—over three times what he is bucking on regular bets.

Teaser bets are a key source of income for the Las Vegas sports books. On a volume basis, sports books make more money per dollar bet on teasers than they do on straight bets and even more than they do on some parlay bets. Thus, teasers are a good bet to avoid. The extra points you get are more than eaten up by the odds you must give on these sucker propositions.

One last word about teaser bets. Though it may seem that many games fall close to the number, fewer do than you might think. Remember, the task of the odds maker in making prices is not to predict the likeliest outcome, but to gauge the betting public. In fact, with the volume of teaser action at sports books, one can be sure that the odds makers are happy to see games fall far from the line on the final score.

FINAL WORD

For very skilled handicappers, with a proven track record and high-enough win percentage to beat the odds against you on these bets, there can, at least in theory, be value in betting parlays and other exotics.

As for me, the best bet in the NFL is betting the point spread or over/under on individual games. Giving 11 to 10 odds is almost always the cheapest price you can give. For now, you should take advantage of that fact and stay away from the "juicy" bets just mentioned.

9

The Winning Foundation

MENTAL ATTITUDE

Before going into the basics of my winning approach to betting pro football, it is important to say something about the mental attitude you must have in this venture.

Betting pro football to win is a business and should be treated like any other business venture. The basics of making money at this business are that the lines put out by the oddsmakers are made not to predict the actual outcomes of games, nor to educate the public about the relative strengths of the teams, but to try to split the betting public by making one team as attractive as the other. The public's view of a match-up is occasionally incorrect.

A line can also be vulnerable because it is partly set by "feel."

A professional bettor looks for lines that are inaccurate in terms of the *real* differences between the two teams. When he finds such lines he wagers on them—and that is the *only* time he wagers.

THE WINNING FOUNDATION

While good oddsmakers have to tie their lines to public sentiment, the professional maintains a distance from such sentiment in order to be able to recognize those games where public sentiment is incorrect. A professional bettor has to be very patient. He has to wait for incorrect lines without being tempted to bet just for the sake of action. This waiting and passing on the majority of games is a necessity since a bettor must give 11 to 10 odds on his bets. The winning bettor must have an edge greater than 11 to 10, or 52.4 percent, in his favor to make a wager.

Many people bet pro football for reasons other than making money. Some bettors like the feeling of being in action. Others like to feel that they are experts on football. Some bettors bet pro football for the ego gratification it gives them when they win and can boast to others. Still others like to give themselves an extra incentive when they root for the home team. In the long run, betting pro football for any of these reasons will show a loss. You lose because you can't be objective in your handicapping when you are emotionally involved.

Betting pro football successfully does require confidence, but the ego must be kept under very tight control. The professional handicapper must be able to admit to himself when he has made mistakes handicapping a game, and must be ready to make the necessary adjustments for the next one. Not all losing bets are the result of bad luck.

A professional handicapper must be willing to work hard and keep up with day-by-day changes even on those teams he didn't wager on that week. A handicapper's view of each team is constantly becoming obsolete.

Early in the 2002 season, it quickly became apparent that I had overrated the St. Louis Rams. I had them rated as a B+ team (more on letter power ratings later) when the season began. In their season opener at Denver, I power rated the Rams four points over the Broncos and favored them though didn't bet them (since I don't bet favorites the first four games). But the Rams offense looked very out of sync in that game, as they scored just 16 points in a 23-16 loss. I pushed the Rams down 2 1/2 points in my power ratings after this game.

In their next three games, I bet against the Rams every game. I took 14 points with the Giants in Week 2 (I had power rated the game at 10 1/2), 3 1/2 with the Bucs in Week 3 (I had power rated the game Rams by one), and 13 with the Cowboys in Week 4 (I had power rated the game at 9). The Rams lost outright every game. The oddsmakers, who were tied into public perception, took a month before they caught up to the fact that the Rams were inferior to the team that had gone to two of the last three Super Bowls. Until that time, there was value betting against them.

What does a bettor with the right mental attitude *do* when wagering on the NFL?

First, as we've discussed, he wagers only when he has an edge. That is, he bets *only* when he has reason to believe a line is incorrect.

Second, he has respect for his betting money, and properly deploys it. He never overbets his bank and edge, nor allows himself to start **betting scared**, or betting less than he should because he's afraid of losing.

He shops for the best possible number on a game, always fighting for the greatest edge he can get. A tip: in shopping for the best possible number, you should never bet at a number that's worse than the opening line—that is, the consensus line on late Monday. In my experience, betting at worse than the opening line costs money in the long run. If a game opens with a team favored by four points, you should never give more than four points on the favorite or take less than four points on the underdog.

10

Beating the Point Spread

Before revealing the specific wagering situations I look for, I want to mention three points about how I view the NFL.

First, the league, like the rest of pro sports, has become one of big contracts and big money. It's my impression that this causes players and even coaches to become, at times, mentally fat. If a game or two has been played well and won, details might not seem that important for the next game. Letdowns happen more now than in the days when players were not paid as well and when today's job security and guaranteed money did not exist. This doesn't mean that the game was better in the old days. It just means that it was different to handicap. Teams tended to play more true to form in those days.

What big money and big contracts also mean now is that when teams perform beyond their capabilities for a game or two, one is more likely to see a bounce-back than in years past. For a handicapper this means that it is important to track and be ready to pounce on situations where such bounce-backs are likely to occur.

Second, there is tremendous parity in the league. As mentioned previously, there is not much difference between the best player at a position and the worst. When a team of slightly worse players is more motivated than a team of slightly better players, an outright upset is possible. Most certainly it's possible for the inferior team to cover the point spread.

Third, the point spread tends to nullify any obvious scrimmage edge (skill or power advantage) a team has over its opponent. In the 2001 and 2002 seasons, for example, there were 147 games in which the point spread was seven or more points. These were games where one team was perceived to have a big edge over its opponent at the line of scrimmage. While the underdog won just 37 of these 147 games outright (25.2 percent), the underdog covered the point spread in 78 of the games (while tying it in six)—a success rate of 55.3 percent. In 2004, there were 82 games with a spread of seven or more points. The underdog won just 19 of these games (23.2 percent) outright but had a winning 45-37-1 spread record (54.9 percent) in these high priced games. Again, winning the game doesn't mean that a team will cover the spread.

Also, as I shall demonstrate shortly, the difference between teams in the middle of the league is not as great as most bettors think. The difference, for example, between a 10 and 6 team and an 8 and 8 team is just three points on a neutral field.

In summary, the team that most bettors think is the better team may in fact be better. However, the point spread usually more than nullifies that edge. Thus, bettors who bet favorites are often betting poor value.

On the other hand, sometimes a team will perform very well or very poorly for just a game or two, and these short-term performances will give the public a false reading of the team. The oddsmakers mirror this public reading with their numbers. At this time anyone betting on an overrated team or against an underrated team is again betting poor value. How can you tell if a team is overrated or underrated? This is where the use of power ratings comes into play.

POWER RATINGS

In their strictest sense, **power ratings** are values given to each club that tell where that club stands in skill and strength in relation to every other club. The difference between one team and another in my power ratings tells me what should happen in a game between the two clubs on a neutral field with everyone healthy.

Of course, teams don't play on neutral fields in the NFL, but we'll deal with that later. In the meantime, when the rest of the betting public is blown astray by what happened in the last game, power ratings are my guide to the real strengths or weaknesses of a team.

Some handicappers rely mainly on objective factors, like scores and other statistics, to set their power ratings. Other handicappers rely mainly on subjective factors—their own feeling about a team based on certain team types of behavior.

Through my experience in twenty years of handicapping, I have come to use both—two sets of power ratings. I have devised these two ratings to reflect both my judgment about teams' strengths and their performance as measured by scores.

THE LETTER POWER RATINGS

The first rating is a letter power rating in which each team is ranked someplace between A+ (the best possible rating) and E- (the worst). These letter rankings correspond to how I feel a team is playing presently, and are meant to reflect how a team's record would look after a 16-game season playing at this level, assuming that their competition was average.

For example, if a team is playing like an 8-8 team, I give them a ranking of C—right in the middle of my range and in the middle of the league. A team playing like a 10 and 6 team would get a B- rating—two spots above a C rating. A team playing like the Denver Broncos did in much of 1998 (they ended up 14 and 2 and won the Super Bowl) gets an A rating—six spots above a C and four spots above a B- team. (Note that 14 and 2 is six games better than 8 and 8 and four games better than 10 and 6.) The 2004 Patriots at the end of the season were the first team since the 2001 Rams to be rated higher in my letter power ratings than B+.

For teams on the other end of the scale, a 6 and 10 team would be given a rating of D+— two spots (or games) behind the C rating of an 8 and 8 team. A team playing at a 4 and 12 tail-ender rate would be given a D- rating.

At the very top (A+) of my ratings would be both 15 and 1 and 16 and 0 teams, while at the very bottom (E-) would be any 1 and 15 or 0 and 16 teams. Only the 1985 Chicago Bears ever made it to A+ in my ratings. No team has ever sunk to E-.

Because they reflect a team's current performance, letter power ratings are updated continually throughout the season. And, in my letter power ratings, teams don't always end up ranked according to their actual record. This is because their actual wins and losses may involve an unusually easy or tough schedule, or unusually good or bad luck. Instead, I look closely at the games teams have played to put a "team picture" together.

CHART 1: POWER RATINGS	
Letter Power Rating	**Projected Record**
A+	15-1 or 16-0
A	14-2
A-	13-3
B+	12-4
B	11-5
B-	10-6
C+	9-7
C	8-8
C-	7-9
D+	6-10
D	5-11
D-	4-12
E+	3-13
E	2-14
E-	1-15 or 0-16

ment of the rater. One way to check your power ratings is to compare your ratings to those of other respected handicappers. *The Gold Sheet* and *Power Sweep* are among the publications with respected power ratings in them.

However, if power ratings were a completely objective thing, all handicappers would be betting the same games. They're not. Different winning handicappers can be looking at different things. Ultimately your ability to find value in a line (and make winning bets!) will depend on your developing your own skills.

Once I have assigned letter power ratings, I use a simple chart (see Chart 3, p. 50) to assign corresponding points by which to separate various teams. I've arrived at these point assignments through twenty years' study of how NFL teams do in pointwise ratio—that is, points scored versus points given up.

My study shows that when a team goes 8 and 8, it gives up and scores the same number of points on average over a season. When a team goes 9 and 7, it outscores teams by 1 1/2 points per game on average. When a team is 7 and 9, it is outscored by 1 1/2 points per game. Thus, the difference between a C- (7 and 9) kind of team and a C (8 and 8) kind of team is 1 1/2 points. The jump from C to C+ (a 9-7 team) is also 1 1/2 points. The jump from C- to C+ (two steps) is three points. This means that if a C+ team plays a C- team, a C+ team will be three points superior on average on a neutral field.

The jump from C+ to B- (a 10 and 6 team) is also 1 1/2 points, as is the jump down from C- to D+ (a 6 and 10 team). A 10 and 6 team outscores its opponents by three points a game on average, while 6 and 10 teams tend to be outscored by three points a game.

In my letter power ratings, I list the majority of NFL teams someplace between B- and D+. Chart 2 contains my power ratings for the start of the 2004 season.

CHART 2:
PRESEASON NFL POWER RATINGS, 2004

B+ Patriots

B Vikings, Colts

B- Packers, Seahawks, Broncos, Chiefs

C+ Eagles, Bucs, Bills, Ravens, Texans, Jaguars

C Cowboys, Saints, Rams, Dolphins, Jets, Steelers, Titans

C- Redskins, Falcons, Panthers, Bengals, Browns, Raiders

D+ Bears, Lions

D Giants

D- 49ers, Chargers

E+ Cards

Just seven of the 32 teams were outside the D+ to B- range at the start of the 2004 season.

By the end of the 2004 season, just six of the 32 teams fell outside of the B- to D+ range. The Patriots and Steelers were B+ teams, the Colts and Eagles (no Terrell Owens) were B teams, the Bears were a D team and the 49ers were an E+ team.

When the ratings move above B- and below D+, the equivalent point values get bigger (see Chart 3). Teams above the B- class outscore their opponents by more and in larger jumps per class than those that are rated between D+ and B-. Teams below D+ tend to be outscored by more and in larger jumps per class than the teams in the D+ to B- range. The jump from both B- (a 10 and 6 team) to B (an 11 and 5 team) and from D+ (a 6 and 10 team) to D (a 5 and 11 team) is 2 1/2 points. An 11 and 5 team tends to outscore opponents by 5 1/2 points a game, while a 5 and 11 team tends to be outscored by 5 1/2 points a game.

The jumps from B to B+ (a 12 and 4 team), B+ to A- (a 13 and 3 team), and A- to A (a 14 and 2 team) are also each worth an additional 2 1/2 points. The jumps downward from D to D- (a 4 and 12 team), D- to E+ (a 3 and 13 team), and E+ to E (a 2 and 14 team) are also each worth 2 1/2 points.

Thus, a B+ team will outscore an average (8 and 8) team by eight points a game, which is the same as saying it will outscore all opponents, on average, by eight points a game. Teams that are rated A- will have a 10 1/2-point-per-game edge, while A teams will have, on average, a 13-point-per-game edge. Meanwhile a D- team will be outscored by eight points per game; an E+ team will be outscored by 10 1/2 points per game; and an E team will be outscored by 13 points per game.

Finally the jump from A to A+ (a 15 and 1 or 16 and 0 team) is worth four points and the jump down from E to

E- (a 1 and 15 or 0 and 16 team) is also worth four points. That means an A+ team will outscore opponents by 17 points a game on average, while an E- team will be outscored by 17 points per game.

Thus, at least in the world of power ratings, if an A+ team plays an E- team, the A+ team should be ranked 34 points better on a neutral field.

However, since most NFL teams are ranked between D+ and B-, with a difference between these two letter rankings of only six points, the teams in this area of my letter power ratings are very close to even. It is in this area that I concentrate my handicapping. I believe that emotional edges mean more when the teams are fairly close to even—or between the B- and D+ letter levels.

When I wager on a team below the D+ level, I am careful to make sure they have shown something I call **coping ability** with the level of opponent they are facing—or a history of competing well against teams of similar class. I am also careful about going against a team that is above the B- level.

CHART 3: THE POWER RATING EDGE			
Letter Rating			
Point Differences		**Average Edge***	
A to A+	4	A+	17 points
A- to A	2 1/2	A	13
B+ to A-	2 1/2	A-	10 1/2
B to B+	2 1/2	B+	8
B- to B	2 1/2	B	5 1/2
C+ to B-	1 1/2	B-	3
C to C+	1 1/2	C+	1 _
C- to C	1 1/2	C	0
D+ to C-	1 1/2	C-	-1 _
D to D+	2 1/2	D+	-3
D- to D	2 1/2	D	-5 1/2
E+ to D-	2 1/2	D-	-8
E to E+	2 1/2	E+	-10 _
E- to E	4	E	-13
		E-	-17

* The average number of points by which each rank will outscore opponents or be outscored by opponents.

Injuries in Power Ratings

If a team has some key injuries, I will sometimes make adjustments in my letter power ratings. For instance, in Weeks 16 and 17 of the 2002 season, the Bucs were without their starting quarterback, Brad Johnson. Shaun King and Rob Johnson were step downs at that key position. I thus moved the Bucs from B- to C+ in the two weeks they were without Brad Johnson and moved them back to B- when he came back for the start of the playoffs. In 2004, the Eagles were pushed down to B from B+ when they were without wide receiver Terrell Owens. If I had known that Owens would be effective in the Super Bowl, I would have moved the Eagles back up to B+ and they would have been a bet. However, I could not know *before* the game that Owens would be effective. In general, however, injuries are overrated, as I will discuss later.

After each game I judge how each team played and decide whether to keep them at the same letter rating or move them up or down. I usually don't let a single game, which might be an aberration, cause a change. Usually a team has to prove to me that they deserve a higher letter rating, or show me two or more under performances to convince me that they need to be lowered. When I move a team, I virtually never move them more than one grade, and I can't recall ever having moved a team more than two.

Letter Power Ratings in the Playoffs

For the playoffs, I change the point differences between the letter power ratings. From D+ to B-, I raise the difference between ratings to 2 1/2 points from the 1 1/2 of the regular season. From B- to A the distance between ratings goes up to 3 1/2 from the regular season's 2 1/2. From D+ to E (almost never used since teams that far down in the power ratings virtually never reach the playoffs) the jump is 3 1/2 points between levels. The difference between A+ and A becomes five points, a point higher than the four used during the regular season.

The reason for these adjustments is that in playoff games differences between teams tend to show up more on the scoreboard than in the regular season. In playoff games there is statistically less parity, and scrimmage edges add up to bigger differences than in regular season games.

Number Power Ratings

At the beginning of every season, I also assign each team a **number power rating**, a more objective rating wholly controlled in its movement by team scores. Number power ratings provide a kind of balance against the subjectivity of my letter power ratings. They are also used as important indicators that a team is "due up" or "due down"—but more about that later.

To assign each team a number power rating at the start of the season, I mathematically play out the season using my letter power ratings, which I convert into projected point spreads using my Letter Rating Point Differences chart (see Chart 3). In addition, for my projected point spreads, every home club gets 2 1/2 points.

After projecting point spreads for each game, I convert the point spreads into decimal numbers (see Chart 4), which are then added to project each team's number of wins. As with my letter power rating point equivalents, I've arrived at these decimal number equivalents for point spreads through my own research.

CHART 4: SPREADS AS DECIMALS

Point Spread	Decimal Equivalent
1/2 or 1	.507
1 1/2	.512
2	.519
2 1/2	.524
3	.600
3 1/2	.615
4	.630
4 1/2	.643
5	.655
5 1/2	.667
6	.688
6 1/2	.706
7	.722
7 1/2	.737
8	.750
8 1/2	.762
9	.773
9 1/2	.783
10	.792
10 1/2	.800
11	.810
11 1/2	.818
12	.833
12 1/2	.846
13	.857
13 1/2	.875
14	.889
14 1/2	.900
15	.917
15 1/2	.933
16	.944
16 1/2	.952
17	.962
17 1/2 and more	.968

BEATING THE POINT SPREAD

Before the 2004 season began, for example, I rated the Packers as a B- team, a letter power rating that translates to ten wins against an *average* schedule. However, teams seldom have a totally average or neutral schedule. So I mathematically played out their season to see what number power rating I should give them to begin the season.

In their first game, the Packers were to play at the Panthers, a C- team. Since there is a 4 1/2 point difference between a B- and a C- team, and the Panthers got 2 1/2 points for their home field advantage, the Packers were two point favorites in my letter power ratings (4 1/2 points minus 2 1/2 points), which corresponded to a decimal (money line equivalent) of .52 for the Packers.

In their second game, the Packers were to play the Bears at home, a D+ team. That meant the Packers were six points better than the Bears. Add in 2 1/2 points for the Packers' home field advantage, and they were an 8 1/2 point favorite in my letter power ratings at home. This corresponded to a decimal of .76 for this game.

In their third game, the Packers would play at the Colts, a B team. The Colts were 2 1/2 points better than the Packers (remember, the jump from B- to B is 2 1/2 points), which made them a five point favorite, with home advantage, in my power rating, and a decimal equivalent of .65. This gave the Packers a decimal equivalent of .35 for this game. Below you will find the complete Packers schedule, and projected wins, for the 2004 season.

CHART 5: PACKERS SCHEDULE AND SEASON PROJECTION RATING

Game	Location/Opponent	Gap	Projected Line	Decimal Equivalent
1.	Packers (B-) at Panthers (C-)	+4 1/2	-2	.52
2.	Packers (B-) host Bears (D+)*	+6	-8 1/2	.76
3.	Packers (B-) at Colts (B)	-2 1/2	+5	.35
4.	Packers (B-) host Giants (D)*	+8 1/2	-11	.81
5.	Packers (B-) host Titans (C)*	+3	-5 1/2	.67
6.	Packers (B-) at Lions (D+)	+6	-3 1/2	.61
7.	Packers (B-) host Cowboys (C)*	+3	-5 1/2	.67
8.	Packers (B-) at Redskins (C-)	+4 1/2	-2	.52
9.	Packers (B-) host Vikings (B)*	-2 1/2	0	.50
10.	Packers (B-) at Texans (C+)	+1 1/2	+1	.49
11.	Packers (B-) host Rams (C)*	+3	-5 1/2	.67
12.	Packers (B-) at Eagles (C+)	+1 1/2	+1	.49
13.	Packers (B-) host Lions (C-)*	+4 1/2	-7	.72
14.	Packers (B-) host Jaguars (C+)*	+1 1/2	-4	.63
15.	Packers (B-) at Vikings (B)	-2 1/2	+5	.35
16.	Packers (B-) at Bears (C-)	+4 1/2	-2	.52
				9.28 wins

*Home games. At home, the Packers get an additional 2 1/2 points for home advantage. On the road, they get a -2 1/2 points road disadvantage.

Note: The Lions (Week 13) and Bears (Week 16) were higher rated than my pre-season ratings for them (p. 50). That was because I projected improvement for them in the second half of the season.

In the end, adding up the decimal numbers for all sixteen games of the regular season (.52 + .76 + .35 +... and so on), I projected 9.28 wins for the Packers.

PROJECTED WINS

A team's projected number of wins is then assigned a number value as follows:

CHART 6: PROJECTED WINS NUMBER VALUE	
0 or 1 win:	4
2 wins:	8
3 wins:	10.5
4 wins:	13
5 wins:	15.5
6 wins:	18
7 wins:	19.5
8 wins:	21 (the league average)
9 wins:	22.5
10 wins:	24
11 wins:	26.5
12 wins:	29
13 wins:	31.5
14 wins:	34
15 or 16 wins:	38

I then average this projected-win number value with a value (again, derived from my own research) for a team's letter power rating. (See Chart 7 below.)

CHART 7: LETTER POWER RATING VALUES	
E-	4
E	8
E+	10.5
D-	13
D	15.5
D+	18
C-	19.5
C	21 (league average)
C+	22.5
B-	24
B	26.5
B+	29
A-	31.5
A	34
A+	38

The average of these two numbers, rounded, becomes a team's starting number power rating. So, for the 2004 Packers I projected 9.28 wins for a number value of 22.5+. The Packers' letter power rating was B- (number value 24). The average of the two numbers was 23.25+, which I rounded up to a starting number power rating of 24 because I felt that the Packers would be better than most thought.

ADJUSTED POWER NUMBERS

During the season, I make adjustments to my number power ratings after each game as follows (see Chart 8 below). First, I return to the projected point spreads I used above to mathematically play out the season (the ones in which every home club got an additional 2 1/2 points). Then, based on what happens in the actual games, I create an **adjusted number**. If a team wins or loses to its projected spread by 4 1/2 points or less, I make no adjustments. When a team covers this projected spread by between five and 9 1/2 points, I move its adjusted number power rating up by one (down by one if they lose to the projected spread by between five and 9 1/2 points).

When a team covers its projected spread by between ten and 14 1/2 points, I move their adjusted number power rating up by two (down by two if they lose to the projected spread by between ten and 14 1/2 points). When a team covers the projected spread by 15 points or more, I move their adjusted number power rating up by three (down by three if they lose to the projected spread by 15 points or more). I also try to factor in injuries before the game has been played.

CHART 8: NUMBER POWER RATING ADJUSTMENTS	
Win/Loss Margin	**Number Power Rating Adjustment**
4 1/2 pts.	0
5-9 1/2 pts.	+/- 1
10-14 1/2 pts.	+/- 2
15 pts.	+/- 3

Then, to compute a team's *present* overall number power rating, I take its starting number power rating and average it with the continually adjusted number. The idea is to allow for adjustments without making the public's mistake of overreacting to any one game.

By game seven of 2004, the Packers had dropped to an adjusted number power rating of 19. Averaging 19 with their starting number of 24 gave them a number power rating at that point of 21.5. In game seven, the Packers played the Cowboys. The Cowboys' starting number power rating in 2004 was 21, but it had dropped to an adjusted number of 17 by that point. That made the Cowboys' number power rating 19 (the average of 21 and 17). The Packers thus were 2 1/2 points better than the Cowboys in the number power rating.

Also, the Packers' home advantage was just 1/2 point at that point in the season, while the Cowboys' road disadvantage was 2 1/2 points. The average of 1/2 and 2 1/2 gave the Packers a home edge of 1 1/2 points in this game. Adding the 1 1/2 point home advantage to their 2 1/2 point number power rating edge made the Packers a four point home favorite in this game on my number power ratings.

The Packers won the game, 41-20, and thus covered my number power rating by 17 points. The Packers' adjusted number power rating thus jumped to 22, with 23 1/2 being the new actual number power rating. At the same time, the Cowboys' adjusted number power rating dropped three points to 14, with 17 1/2 being the new actual number power rating. I make a maximum three-point adjustment when the game lands 15 points or more from my number power rating edge, as happened in this game.

The other adjustment I may make in team number power ratings comes after the fourth game, if I feel that my starting number was off by five or more points. What I do then is play over each team's season to this point using my new starting numbers. In 2002, for example, it became clear that I had made a big error in my starting number power rating for the Bengals—an error that cost me three bets early in the season. I had started them at 22. After their fourth game I changed their starting number power rating to 10 and then replayed their season in my number power ratings to that point.

Playoffs and Perfect Number Power Ratings

When the regular season ends, I take another hard look at my number power ratings to make any necessary adjustments for the playoffs. I base these new adjusted number power ratings largely on a team's actual regular-season performance, and call them my perfect number power ratings. The way I come up with the "perfect number" for each team is as follows.

A) First, I assign a number based on how many games a team has actually won during the season. The number to be assigned is derived from the table below.

CHART 9: TEAM WINS NUMBER

0 or 1 win(s): 4

2 wins: 8

3 wins: 10.5

4 wins: 13

5 wins: 15.5

6 wins: 18

7 wins: 19.5

8 wins: 21 (the league average)

9 wins: 22.5

10 wins: 24

11 wins: 26.5

12 wins: 29

13 wins: 31.5

14 wins: 34

15 or 16 wins: 38

B) I then calculate the average number of points per game by which a club outscored its opponents (or the average number by which they were outscored). Each point by which a team on average has outscored its opponents (or was outscored) is worth one point in this adjustment. These points are added to or subtracted from 21, the league average. I then compute the average of the numbers derived from Paragraphs A and B of this section. If the average falls directly between two numbers, I round to the one closer to 21.

C) Lastly, I factor in the difficulty of each team's schedule, taking a close look at the record of each opponent with other clubs while ignoring the opponents' games with the team I'm rating. For example, in 2002, the 49ers defeated the Arizona Cardinals twice. The Cards were 5-11 for the season. However, in games that the Cardinals did *not* play the 49ers, they went 5-9. Thus, the games against the Cards counted as two 10-18 games for the 49ers. For every 16 games that a team's set of opponents are over .500, I add a point to their perfect power rating. For every 16 games that a team's opponents played under .500, I subtract a point from their perfect power rating.

To illustrate, here is how I came up with my perfect power rating for the Raiders after the 2002 season. They had won 11 games, which corresponds to 26.5 on the number power ratings. They had outscored their opponents by 158 points, which is roughly 10 points a game over the league average of 21 (see paragraph B), for a number of 31. Rounded off, the average of 31 and 26.5 is 29. However, Raider opponents were 128-105-1 in non-Raider games. This is 23 games over .500. Because of the difficulty of their schedule, I added another point to the Raider perfect power rating, for a total of 30.

Now, this may seem like a lot of work for some awfully fine adjustments in a power rating. But the margin for error is so tight when fighting those 11 to 10 odds that I have found the work pays off.

HOME ADVANTAGE AND ROAD DISADVANTAGE

Over the long run in the NFL, the home field advantage has been shown to be worth about 2 1/2 points. Thus, in the first four games of a season, I give every home team a 2 1/2 point advantage and every road team a 2 1/2 point disadvantage, unless there's a *very* compelling reason not to. To start the 2002 season, for example, I gave the Chicago Bears just a 1 1/2 point edge at home. That was because they were playing their home games 150 miles away at Champaign, Illinois, and I felt that the constant travel from Chicago would hurt them. Also, the Bears were less familiar with this field than they were with their normal home at Soldier Field.

After the fourth week of the season, I look at how teams have actually fared at home and on the road and make adjustments in their home advantage or road disadvantage. The average between the home team's home advantage and the road team's road disadvantage becomes the home advantage for that game.

Starting in the fifth game, I adjust each team's home advantage or road disadvantage by a point every time they force their number power rating up or down two more times than they don't. For instance, in their twelfth game of 2002 at home against the Bears I gave the Packers a 4 1/2 point edge for being at home.

The Packers had pushed up their number power rating in home games against the Redskins, Dolphins, and Lions. In home games against the Falcons and Panthers, the Packers had no number power rating change because these games had fallen within 4 1/2 points of the number power rating spread. With a three game edge at home, I pushed the Packers home power rating edge up to 4 1/2 points. In that game, the Bears' road disadvantage was 3 1/2 points because their number power rating had fallen three times after road games and risen only once (it had also stayed the same once).

Since the Bears were a minus 2 on the road, their road disadvantage fell one point. Thus, in this game, the Bears had an overall four-point disadvantage on the road (the average of 3 1/2 and 4 1/2). The maximum advantage I give a team at home is 6 1/2 points and the most I take away from them on the road is also 6 1/2 points.

COMBINING THE LETTER AND NUMBER POWER RATINGS

Once I've arrived at both my letter and number power ratings, I combine them into a final power rating. I give 3/4 strength to the letter power rating because it is adjusted every week and better takes into account a team's current form. The number power ratings, though more objective, are totally dependent on scores, which at times can be deceptive.

Here is an example of how I make my final power rating. In Week Nine of the 2002 season, the Cowboys were scheduled to play the Lions at Detroit. The Cowboys were a D+ team and the Lions were a D club. Normally that would mean that my letter power rating would be pick, because the Lions would have a 2 1/2 point home advantage and the Cowboys would be 2 1/2 points the better club.

However, the Lions had moved up their number power rating twice at home while never losing ground on the number power rating at home, which gave them a 3 1/2 point home edge, while the Cowboys had a normal 2 1/2 point road disadvantage—they had moved their number power rating up once on the road, dropped ground twice, and stayed the same once. Take the average of 3 1/2 and 2 1/2, and the Lions got three points for being at home, making them a 1/2 point favorite in my letter power ratings.

In my number power ratings, the Cowboys were at 20 overall (present number 18 and starting number 22) while the Lions were at 14 1/2 overall (present number 14 and starting number 15). Thus the Cowboys were 5 1/2 points better than the Lions on the number power rating, and had a 2 1/2 point edge after figuring in the Lions' three point home edge. Giving 3/4 weight to the letter power rating (Lions by 1/2), made the final power rating Pick.

In the game, the Lions won by two points, 9-7. Since this result was 4 1/2 points away from the Lions' number power rating of plus 2 1/2, I made no adjustments for either team the next week.

In Appendix One of this book, I give a full season's game-by-game calculations for the 2004 Buffalo Bills' power ratings. This should help you later through the fine points of beginning to calculate your own.

THE FINE POINTS OF WINNING AGAINST THE POINT SPREAD
MAKING YOUR OWN NUMBERS

When you go to buy something, you have in mind a price that you are willing to pay. If the price in the store is higher than the price you had in mind, you shouldn't buy it.

It should be the same when you bet the NFL. Whenever you make a wager on the point spread, you are "buying" the team for a price in that game. If a team is a four-point underdog, you are "buying" the team plus four points. If a team is a five-point favorite, you are "buying" the team minus five points. The result of the game decides whether the purchase was a success.

Unfortunately, most bettors are willing to give or take just about any price on the team they favor. If football bettors would be as disciplined in wagering on games as they are in other purchases, they would be a happier and more successful crowd.

In the 2002-2003 Super Bowl, the Raiders were 3 1/2 point favorites over the Bucs. Most amateur bettors bet on the Raiders. Most professionals bet on the Bucs (as did I, in the last Super Bowl side I have bet to date). I had felt that the oddsmaker line should be Pick. My power rating on the game favored the Raiders by 1/2 a point. Thus, with the Raiders giving 3 1/2 points, the only way that I could bet the game would be to bet the Bucs.

Again, I felt the Raiders were priced far beyond what I considered to be the fair market price of the game, or **Pick**, and were also overpriced in terms of the relative talent of the two clubs (1/2 point for the Raiders). Thus the Raiders were simply too expensive to bet, no matter what the result of the game turned out to be.

How to Make a Price

You might now ask, "Why did you think that Pick was the right price on the Super Bowl? Why wasn't 3 1/2 the right price?"

I'll answer that by showing how I make my oddsmaker line.

The basic procedure is to think like one of best sports books' oddsmakers. A good starting point is to look at the teams' other recent lines. The week before the Super Bowl, the Bucs were four point underdogs in Philadelphia. I had made them five point underdogs in that game and my power rating on that game was seven. I felt that the Eagles were a better club than the Bucs. With a line of only four and the Eagles' strong home field advantage (remember it was a cold weather game, in which the Tampa Bay Bucs figured to struggle), I felt that the teams were being rated virtually even in strength by the oddsmakers.

Before the Conference Final games I had rated the Eagles and Raiders about equal. Thus, if they were to meet in the Super Bowl a week later, I figured the game would be even (or Pick 'em).

The Bucs won impressively in Philadelphia after having everything go against them early. The Eagles returned the opening kickoff 72 yards and scored a touchdown two plays later. The Bucs seemed ready to collapse and looked ready to lose a playoff game in Philadelphia by a big score for the third year in a row. But this time, instead of collapsing in the cold, the Bucs answered right away with a field goal drive to make the score 7-3. They then drove 96 yards for a touchdown to go up 10-7.

Later in the half, the Bucs answered an Eagles' tying field goal with an 80 yard touchdown drive to take the lead for good. Eventually, the Bucs won 27-10.

The Raiders won also, defeating the Titans 41-24. But their win was much less impressive. The Raiders took advantage of two Titan turnovers near halftime to take a 24-17 lead. Later, with a 27-24 lead, the Raiders appeared to be stopped, but got a key penalty on third down to keep alive the clinching touchdown drive.

I moved the Bucs up in my power ratings after their win. I now considered them equal to the Raiders. The one key question that I'd had about the Bucs was their ability to win on the road against a good team. They had answered that question emphatically in the win at Philadelphia.

If the Bucs had played the Raiders the week before, a good oddsmaker might have considered them about a field goal underdog. But not now. They were as good—if not better than—the Raiders and I felt that Pick was the fair market price. I was pleasantly surprised to see plus 4 1/2 on them in a spot, and took it.

The Bucs won handily, 48-21, in a type of game that I hadn't expected. I had felt that the game would be low scoring and close, with the plus four being key. Still, this game is a good example of how to make a good price and stick by it.

Let's look at a couple more examples of how I made a price in the 2002 regular season. First, I will show you a game that I lost in. It was the Week 4 game of the Jets at the Jaguars.

I made the price the Jaguars by 1 1/2. How did I come up with that number? The week before, the Jets had played at Miami, with the Dolphins six point favorites in that game. The Dolphins were a team that I rated a touchdown better than the Jaguars. Since the Jets got beaten badly in Miami (30-3), I made a large adjustment (2 1/2 points) against the Jets. Part of this adjustment was also due to the fact that the Jaguars were coming off of a bye week.

In the game before their bye, the Jaguars had played at Kansas City. In that game they were 3 1/2 point underdogs. If that game had been played at home, the Jaguars would have been about a one point favorite. Since I now considered the Jets and Chiefs about even, the Jaguars, I felt, should be a similar price against the Jets.

The Jets, it was true, had lost two straight rout games. However, the competition that defeated them (Patriots and Dolphins) was much tougher than the opponent-to-be (Jaguars). The Jaguars were a C- team while the Patriots and Dolphins were B clubs. Thus a bounce back seemed very possible. And, thus, 1 1/2 seemed like more than a high enough price.

I was very surprised when the first line on the game favored the Jaguars by 3 1/2. I was getting two points more than the fair market price on the Jets. So I took the Jets in this contest. The line eventually went down to and closed at 3 for the Jaguars.

The Jaguars won the game 28-3. This loss was part of a four game slide for the Jets. Eventually the Jets righted themselves and made the playoffs. The Jaguars finished way out of the playoff money at 6-10. But on this day they won. It happens.

There was another game in Week 4 that I wagered on that had a very different result. In that game I went against the public and the pros in betting the hometown Lions against the Saints. I took eight points early in the week, but should have waited since the line went as high as nine on game-day. The Lions won the game outright, 26-21. They led the whole game.

My oddsmaker (as well as my power rating) price on the game was six for the Saints. How did I make that price? The week before the Packers were 7 1/2 point favorites at the Lions. The week before that the Packers played at the Saints and went off as two point favorites. That meant that if the Packers played the Saints on a neutral field, the Packers would be about 4 1/2 point favorites.

Using the Packers as a barometer, the Saints should have been only a field goal favorite at Detroit. However, this needed adjusting since the Saints had thoroughly outplayed the Packers and defeated them 35-20. My adjustment on this was three points, which is equal to two classes of power ratings—a large adjustment!

However, the oddsmakers made an even bigger adjustment, opening the game at 7 1/2. And even this adjustment wasn't enough to scare off both amateur and pro bettors who laid the game up to 8 1/2 and 9.

My correct way of making the price saved me from a losing bet and helped lead me to a winning bet.

To win in the NFL, it is imperative that one has a way of making his or her own lines. This should be done before any prices are seen. Without this anchor, one has no way of knowing which side of a game has value and which doesn't. Knowing the fair market price will save a bettor from a lot of overpaying and poor value.

11

The Pro Bettor's Toolkit: Games 1-4

As important as it is, value in a line, as determined by my power ratings and prices, doesn't automatically make a game a wager for me. I also track a variety of statistical and situational factors that bear on a team's motivation. Without an emotional edge in a game in addition to value in a line, I won't put my money on it.

When I bet the NFL I divide the season into four segments: the first four games, games five through eight, the last eight regular season games, and the playoffs.

Below are the wagering situations I look for in each segment. I will explain the rationale behind these situations as I progress. In addition, for many of these wagering situations I adjust my power ratings. I mention how much of an adjustment I make in each situation.

OVERVIEW

Before I list the situations or pointers I look for in the first four games, let me explain why I bet all underdogs or "picks" in the early part of the season, and *almost* all underdogs the rest of the season as well. A **pick** game is a game in which no points are given or taken on either team. The bettor must simply pick the winner.

First, in over twenty years of handicapping and betting the NFL, I have yet to come across a long-term winning handicapper who does not bet mostly or solely under-dogs. I myself did not start to win with any consistency until I started betting mostly underdogs, too.

Second, NFL teams do their best to win a game. If you bet an underdog, this gives you two chances to win your bet. If the team wins the game outright, of course, the bet is won. But even if the team loses, there is still a chance you'll cover the point spread.

Also, in the last few minutes of a game, a team that is leading seldom tries to score more points. Instead, it tries merely to keep its current lead. The team that is losing, on the other hand, usually tries to score points until the very end. If a bettor has taken a favorite that is ahead but not covering with five minutes or less to go, that bettor is in big trouble. These bets become, in essence, wagers on games with several minutes "cut off." Giving points and losing time is a dangerous wagering combination.

Lastly, in the first part of the season, I find it much easier to locate false favorites to wager against and live underdogs to bet on than live favorites to bet. Therefore, in the first four games of the season, I *never* lay points.

Now let's discuss the emotional situations that play a role in the early part of the season. Since all of these mod-els are also used later in the season, I've included some examples from after the fourth game of the season.

POINTER ONE:
UNDERRATED DOG

Bet on an underdog when it is underrated in the point spread by four points or more.

This pointer is tied directly to power ratings. You are most likely to find games like these the first week or two of the season when the oddsmakers are relying most on teams' previous year's performances. Keeping close track of transactions (trades, etc.) from the previous year is the key to finding early season value in the point spread.

One such wager I made early in the 2002 season was on the road Dolphins plus 3 over the home Colts in Week 2. My letter power ratings had the Dolphins at B and the Colts at C+. That made the Dolphins a 1 1/2 point favorite in my letter power ratings after allowing for the Colts home field advantage. In my number power ratings, the Dolphins were at 27 and the Colts at 22. Again, given the Colts 2 1/2 point edge playing at home, the Dolphins had a 2 1/2 point edge in the number power ratings. With the letter power rating getting 3/4 weight, the Dolphins were 1 1/2 point favorites in my overall power ratings. Since they were getting three points, they were a bet. The Dolphins won the game, 21-13.

POINTER TWO:
HOME DOG AFTER
HOME LOSS AS FAVORITE

When a team loses as a favorite at home and is a home underdog the next week, look to bet on the underdog.

When a team is favored, the public *expects* it to win. While teams don't necessarily keep close track of the point spread, they are certainly aware when they are favored to win. Such a team is embarrassed when it fails to win a game it was expected to win. The next week, practices will be hard. The team will be looking to redeem itself. As an underdog at home, the team will really want to show that the fans' lost confidence is a mistake. Teams in this situation—egged on by the home crowd—will try hard to get back what was taken from them the week before.

This is a very strong wagering situation. I adjust my power rating by up to one point in favor of the home team when this situation comes up. If I don't feel that the underdog is competitive, I will adjust less or not at all.

POINTER THREE: MONDAY NIGHT WINNERS

If a team wins and covers on Monday night against a divisional rival and then plays against a non-divisional foe, bet against the Monday night winner in the non-divisional game. Warning: do not use this model if a bye week falls between the Monday night game and the next game.

Monday night games have a huge influence on the betting public's behavior. The game is in its own exclusive time slot and has a larger viewing audience than any other game. The media also tend to pump up and trumpet teams that play well on Monday night. When a team also covers the spread in the Monday night game, this means that it performed over public expectations. As a result, oddsmakers often have to make an overadjustment for a team that does well on Monday night.

In addition, teams get especially fired up for Monday night encounters. This is a great chance to show the nation—and the thirty-one other teams watching—that they are a good team. When they play a divisional rival, the emotional fires are even more stoked since divisional games are worth so much more than non-divisional games. Plus, since division rivalries occur twice a year, anger over recent games is easier to remember.

But after a team wins a divisional game, the win is often followed by an emotional letdown. Also, after defeating an opponent on a Monday night, the next game is now six—instead of the usual seven—days away. This makes a letdown even more likely, especially when the next week's game is against a non-divisional foe.

These emotional factors and oddsmakers' overadjustment will often make the team playing against the Monday night winner a betting value. Once again, the correct use of power ratings shows if and how much the oddsmakers are overadjusting against a team that beats and covers against a divisional rival on a Monday night. This is a huge situational edge. I penalize a team one point when they win and cover in a divisional Monday night game and play a non-divisional team the next week.

One example of this model came up in Week 4 of the 2003 season when the Lions—11 1/2 point underdogs—visited the Broncos. The Broncos had defeated the Raiders (a team they lost twice to in 2002) 31-10 the previous Monday night. Against the Lions, who were to go 0-8 outright on the road in 2003, the Broncos went through the motions. The Broncos won, 20-16, but never came close to covering.

POINTER FOUR:
BIG SPREAD RANGE UNDERDOG

Bet on the underdog when it is ten points or more lower than its opponent on the spread range.

The **spread range** is a measure I've developed to track how teams are doing against the point spread. The rationale behind it is that oddsmakers are so closely in tune with how teams are doing against the spread. When teams are performing well against the spread, the oddsmakers usually look to make those teams more expensive to bet the next week. On the other hand, when a team is doing poorly against the point spread, oddsmakers try to make those teams more attractive to bettors by giving them extra points. I am looking to go against more expensive teams and bet the teams being given value by the oddsmakers. I count on my power ratings to provide an independent gauge of how much—if at all—the oddsmakers are over-compensating.

Here's how to keep track of how teams are doing on the spread range. If teams cover the closing point spread by 1/2 to three points, they receive one point. Covering by 3 1/2 to six points earns two points; covering by 6 1/2 to nine points gives a team three points; while covering by 9 1/2 to 12 points gives a team four points. Covering by 12 1/2 to 15 points gives a team five points; and covering by 15 1/2 or more points gives a team six points. (See Chart 10 below.) Losing to the point spread by the above margins gives a team a negative point score by the same amounts. I keep a running tabulation of this for each team throughout the season.

I look for games the first four weeks of the season where there is a ten-point or more difference between the teams. I look to wager on the lower team if it is an underdog.

CHART 10: SPREAD RANGE	
Cover Margin	**Spread Range Score**
1/2 to 3 pts.	1
3 1/2 to 6 pts.	2
6 1/2 to 9 pts.	3
9 1/2 to 12 pts.	4
12 1/2 to 15 pts.	5
15 1/2 + pts.	6

In Week 3 of the 2002 season, the Chiefs played at the Patriots. In their first game, the Chiefs defeated the Browns by one point as two point underdogs (plus 1). In their second game, the Chiefs lost by seven points to the Jaguars as 3 1/2 point favorites (minus 4). Thus the Chiefs' spread range total after two games was minus 3.

In their first game, the Patriots defeated the Steelers by 16 points as 2 1/2 point underdogs (plus 6). In their second game, the Patriots defeated the Jets by 37 as one point underdogs (plus 6). Thus the Patriots' spread range total after two games was plus 12, or 15 points higher than the Chiefs'. The Patriots went off against the Chiefs as 8 1/2 point home favorites but won in overtime by only three. The Chiefs, the team behind on the spread range and undervalued, had covered.

POINTER FIVE: FIFTY-POINT SWING

Bet on the seemingly worse team.

Let's say that Team A is playing Team B. Team A won its game the week before and Team B lost. If Team A's winning margin plus Team B's losing margin equals 50 points or more, we have what I call a **fifty-point swing game**, and I am looking to wager on Team B in the game the next week.

For example, in Week 4 of the 2002 season, the Houston Texans played the Philadelphia Eagles. The week before, the Eagles had defeated the Cowboys by 31 points (44-13) while the Texans had lost to the Colts by 20 points (23-3). This represented a 51-point swing (31 + 20 = 51). In this game, the Eagles went off as 19 point favorites (I took 20 1/2 on the game), but won by only 18, 35-17.

The rationale behind the fifty-point swing bet is that the team that won big will tend to have a letdown, while the team that was beaten badly will be looking to bounce back. The team that won big is likely to be overconfident and less well prepared since its opponent looked bad the week before. The team that looked poor the week before will go all-out to compete against and defeat the team that looked so strong the week before.

This is another situation for which I make a one point edge in favor of the seemingly inferior team.

POINTER SIX:
MONDAY OR SUNDAY NIGHT HOME UNDERDOGS

Bet any home team Monday or Sunday night underdogs. This has done better for Monday night underdogs over the years, but I think that Sunday night home underdogs will eventually catch up.

Home underdogs in these nationally telecast games tend to have very high intensity. The players badly want to protect their home field. As the underdog, a team feels slighted by the public and has something to prove.

In recent years there have been some adjustments made by the oddsmakers against Monday night home underdogs. Again, this is why the use of power ratings is so important. If your power rating indicates that the home underdog is not a good bet, pass the game. If the power rating indicates that the home team is underrated, you have a good bet since the oddsmakers have not made the needed adjustments.

POINTER SEVEN:
ROUT LOSSES AND ROUT WINS

When a team is an underdog after a rout loss on national television, bet on this team in the next game. When a team is a favorite after a rout win on national television, bet against this team in the next game.

THE PRO BETTOR'S TOOLKIT: GAMES 1-4

I define a **rout loss** as a loss by 21 points or more. Go with a team that has just lost a rout on Sunday or Monday night. Go against a team that has just won a rout game on Sunday or Monday night.

When a team wins a blowout on Sunday or Monday night, a letdown is natural. The team has just proven to itself, the thirty-one other teams watching, and the nation that it is a good team. The next week, both players and coaches will tend to be a bit more lax at practice. As a favorite, the team is being built up even more by the media and the public. It's hard for a team not to get swayed by all this praise. This makes a letdown even more likely. In addition, the rout win on national television might give the winning team some extra respect by the oddsmakers the following week. These extra points could well make them a poor value.

On the other hand, when a team gets blown out on a Sunday or Monday night, it is truly embarrassed. The next week's practices are dedicated to proving that the team isn't as bad as it just looked. The media's downgrading of the team often adds to the intensity of the week's game preparation. Meanwhile, the upcoming opponent might be lulled into a false sense of security by the team's poor previous game.

This is another strong wagering situation where I adjust my power ratings 1/2 point in favor of the team coming off of the rout loss or 1/2 point against the team coming from a national TV blowout win.

The Lion-Bronco game mentioned above in Pointer Three, the model about teams that win a Monday night divisional game and then play a non-divisional game, also fits this model since the Broncos won the Monday night game by 21 points over the Raiders.

POINTER EIGHT:
FAVORITE AFTER BIG SCORE WINS

Look to bet against a team that has scored 30 points or more in wins for each of two consecutive weeks and is a favorite in their next game, unless a bye week comes before it or between the high scoring games.

Scoring 30 points or more in wins is a decent accomplishment in the NFL. But doing it for two straight weeks often seems to lead to a feeling of complacency the following week. Suddenly the quarterback's timing is off a fraction of a second and linemen don't block quite as well as they did the two weeks the team won so handily. This often leads to an outright loss and even more often a loss to the point spread as favorites. Meanwhile, the opponent's defense will have spirited practices to get ready to face what seems to be a superb offense. I adjust my number 1/2 point against a team that has scored 30 points or more in two or more straight wins.

POINTER NINE:
FAVORITE COMING OFF
DIVISIONAL GAMES

Look to bet against a team that is coming off two or more consecutive divisional games if the next opponent is a non-divisional team and the team is favored by seven or more points. Do not bet against the team if a bye week interrupts this pattern. Teams often have a letdown playing a nondivisional game after at least two divisional games. If the team is also a significant favorite (by a touchdown or more), the players tend to consider the upcoming game an easy win and get less emotionally charged for it.

POINTER TEN:
DUE-UPS AND DUE-DOWNS

Due-ups and **due-downs** are among the most powerful handicapping tools I've ever developed. They are tied in with the number power ratings I give teams.

Here is how the "due-up" and "due-down" model works. When a team first gets five points or more above its starting number power rating, it becomes due-down. I look to bet against such a team. When a team first gets five points or more *below* its starting number power rating, it becomes a team that is due-up, and one I look to bet.

Throughout the season, I look to bet on teams that are due-up if the due numbers they have hit are **fresh** dues— numbers they had not yet reached in the season. It is the same with betting against teams that are due-downs and are hitting fresh dues. Teams that are due-up or due-down on numbers that have been reached before are much less bettable than those reaching fresh dues. Let's look at an example of a due game from the early part of the 2002 season.

In Week 3 the Broncos hosted the Bills, and went off as 7 1/2 point home favorites. The Broncos had started the season at 22 in my number power ratings. In their first game, as 3 1/2 point underdogs in my number power rating, the Broncos covered their number power rating by 10 1/2 points in a 23-16 win over the Rams. This pushed their number to 24. In Week 2, the Broncos won by ten (24-14) at San Francisco and covered the number power rating (plus 5) by 15 points, making for a three point adjustment in their number power rating. Since their number power rating had moved to 27, five points above their starting rating, they were now due down.

The 7 1/2 point underdog Bills covered against the Broncos in this game in a 28-23 loss.

Sometimes a team that is due-up or due-down doesn't bounce back as expected. If the team goes farther in the up or down direction immediately after reaching the due-down or due-up point, it becomes **star due-down** or **star due-up**. If a team immediately moves its number power rating farther up in a due-down situation or farther down in a due-up situation, I look *strongly* to bet against such a team.

Here is an example of a star due from the 2002 season:

In 2002 I started the Saints at 19 for their number power rating. By Week 3 they had gone up to 24 and were due down against the Bears. The Saints were 2 1/2 point underdogs on my number power rating spread, but won the game by 6 points, 29-23, a game I lost. Since they had covered their number power rating spread by 8 1/2 points, their power rating number went up to 25 and made the Saints star due down in their next game at Detroit. The public bet the Saints in this game from a seven point favorite to an 8 1/2 point favorite. The Saints lost the game outright, 26-21.

In 2002, I started the Titans at 24 in their number power rating. By their fifth game they had gone down to 19. The Titans were now due up. In that game, the Titans lost to the Redskins, 31-14. Since my number power rating had favored the Titans by 7 in that game, their number power rating went down to 16 in their next game against the Jaguars. The Titans were now star due up. They were 2 1/2 point home underdogs against the Jaguars.

What made this game an especially good bet was that the Jaguars were also due down. In addition, the Titans were not only star due, but had the combination of coverage (they had beaten the Jaguars outright at home the last three times), number (my overall power rating favored the Titans by 1/2 point in this game) and fatigue (Jaguars had

had two fairly strong emotional efforts in their last two games) working for them. More on these other factors in coming pages. The Titans won the game outright, 23-14.

When a team continues to go up or down in star due situations they become **double star due-up** or **double star due-down**. This very seldom happens. One team that was triple star due-up in the 2002 season was the Rams against the Raiders in Week 6. The Rams, eight point home underdogs, won outright easily, 28-13.

When a team gets four points off of its starting number power rating for the first time, it becomes a team that is **may-due-up** or **may-due-down**. When a team repeats (for the first time) a number that is five or more points away from its starting number, it is also may-due-up or may-due-down. Another way in which a team can be may-due up or down is by repeating its number power rating of the previous week when it was already due-up or due-down. If a team moves towards its starting number power rating but is still five or more points above or below it after being due-up or due-down or any type of star due the previous week, the team becomes may-due-up or may-due-down. However, if a team repeats for the third time a number that is five or more points above or below its starting power rating, it is no longer may-due-up or may-due-down. Here are a few examples of teams that were may-due-up and may-due-down.

In Week 3 of the 2002 season, the Patriots were due down against the Chiefs. Their starting number power had been 24 and they were now at 29. Their number power rating in this game was 8 1/2. The Pats won by three. Since the result fell 5 1/2 points away from the number power rating, this pushed their number power rating down to 28, or 4 points above their starting number power rating. The next week the Patriots were may due down against the Chargers. Their number power rating was 1 1/2 in this game. The Patriots lost by seven, which pushed their number power rating down to 27. Now they were no longer any kind of due.

The Chargers started their 2002 season with a number power rating of 20. In their first game, the Chargers covered their number power rating by 20 1/2 points over the Bengals, pushing them to 23. In Week 2, the Chargers covered their 11 1/2 point number power rating against the Texans by 9 1/2 points in a 24-3 win. This win pushed their number power rating to 24 and made them may due down in their next game against the Cards. In that game, the Chargers won by eight and covered the number power rating by nine points, which took them from may due down to due down the next game against the Patriots.

What to Look for in Conjunction With Dues

Dues are a powerful handicapping tool. They become more powerful when the team due-up has the following advantages (or the team due-down has the following disadvantages):

Coverage

The main point of coverage is how the team has done or would have done at the given point spread at the same game site in the last year or two.

In Week 5 of the 2002 season in the Chiefs-Jets game, the Jets were a star due up. In addition, they had beaten the Chiefs by 20 the previous year at New York. Thus the Jets had coverage working for them in this due situation. This was a due that lost as the Chiefs won and covered the three point spread, 29-25, with a very late touchdown.

Number

Number means power rating—in this case, the combined letter and number power rating. When the team that is due-up has the power rating in its favor, it has the number favoring them. When the team that is due-down has the power rating working against them, the number is instead working for their opponent.

In Week 6 of 2002, the Vikings hosted the Lions. They were 4 1/2 point favorites in this game. My own power rating on the game favored the Vikings by 8 1/2. Thus the number favored them. The Vikings won and covered, 31-24.

Revenge

A team is said to want **revenge** if it has lost to its opponent within the last year (that is, within the same season or the previous one).

Fatigue

There are two ways in which **fatigue** can be a factor for a team. One is when a team is playing in a short work week against a more rested club. Usually this involves a team playing on Sunday that played the previous Monday night.

Another way a team can have a fatigue disadvantage is if it has played two or more consecutive games with a high (1 or 2) emotional rating. (See Pointer Fifteen below.) A team can also have a fatigue disadvantage when it has had a number-one emotional rating in its last game if that game was played no more than a week before.

Thus, there are four factors to look for in conjunction with dues: coverage, number, revenge, and fatigue. When the team due-up, or the team facing a club that is due-down, has two of these factors working for it, the game is very likely to become a wager for me. When three or all four of the factors are working for the team due-up, or against the team that is due-down, the game is an almost automatic wager.

There is one exception, and that occurs when the number I made the team as an oddsmaker is less than the spread on the underdog or more than the spread on the favorite. In this case I will pass the game since I never wager against my own line. But this seldom happens in due games since teams that are due-up tend to be teams that have performed poorly recently and thus are unpopular with the public.

The oddsmakers are trying to give these teams more value in order to get the betting public to wager on them. Teams that are due-down tend to be popular teams since they have recently done well. The oddsmakers are trying to divert money from those teams and give points to make the other team more attractive.

When multiple factors favor the due team, they often are a very strong play.

For example, in Week 3 of 2002 the Lions hosted the Packers, who were 7 1/2 point road favorites. The Lions were due up. They wanted revenge for a loss in their last game to the Packers, and they had coverage favoring them (no loss at home by over two points to the Packers since 1996). Thus the Lions had the combination of due, revenge and coverage working for them. They covered in a 37-31 home loss.

POINTER ELEVEN: SANDWICH GAMES

I look to wager against a team in a divisional series sandwich game. A **sandwich game** is a non-divisional game that take place when a team has just played at least two straight divisional games and has at least two more straight divisional games coming up after the non-divisional contest. The games must take place in consecutive weeks; if a bye week pops up somewhere in this stretch, the game is not a divisional sandwich game. In this situation, a team figures to let down since there are more important games on both sides of the non-divisional affair.

With the league now using four team divisions, each team plays just six divisional games a season. Thus these sandwich games are almost obsolete. One that took place in the 2002 season was the Packers' Week 12 game at Tampa. The Packers were coming from divisional games against the Lions and Vikings and had divisional games against the Bears and Vikings upcoming. The Bucs won and covered this game, 21-7, as three point favorites.

I take away 1/2 point on the power ratings from a team in a divisional series sandwich game.

POINTER TWELVE: PHONY WINS AND PHONY LOSSES

I look to bet on a team coming off of a phony loss. I look to bet against a team coming off of a phony win. After a lot of research, I started using this model in 1997.

What do I mean by a phony win or phony loss? In the vast majority of games, the team with the higher average-gain-per-pass wins. If a team wins a game having the lower average and the losing team committed more turnovers, the team that won has gained a **phony win**. The team that lost has suffered a **phony loss**. Average-gain-per-pass-play is computed in the following way (*USA Today* box scores carry the statistic).

1) Pass attempts are considered each pass attempt plus each time sacked when attempting to pass.
2) Passing yards are considered the yards gained on passing plays minus the yards lost on sacks.
3) Dividing the total passing yards by pass attempts provides the average yardage per pass play.

For example, let's say a team completes 27 of 40 passes for 280 yards. Let's say the team also suffers two sacks in the same game for a total of ten yards in losses. The total number of pass attempts would be 42 (40 pass attempts plus two sacks), while the total passing yardage would be 270 yards (280 yards gained on passes minus ten yards lost on sacks). Dividing 270 by 42 shows that the team averaged 6.4 yards per pass attempt.

When a team wins a game with the lower pass-yards-per-attempt average while the losing team committed more turnovers, I feel that the winning team has won a lucky game. They are likely to cut corners in practice the next week and play poorly the following week. I will be looking to take advantage. Meanwhile, the team that lost will be more fired up for the next game and determined to win. Their performance in the last game shows that they are very close to winning.

In Week 3 of the 2002 season, the Cards lost to the Chargers, 23-15. In that game, the Cards gained 200 net yards passing on 39 attempts, including sacks, for 5.13 average yards per attempt. The Chargers had 164 yards on 33 attempts for an average of five yards per attempt. The Cards had three turnovers in the game and the Chargers committed one. The Cards were thus coming from a phony loss. They defeated the Giants the next week as three point underdogs, 21-7.

I deduct 1/2 point from teams coming from a phony win and add 1/2 point to teams coming from a phony loss.

POINTER THIRTEEN:
SLOPPY WINS

I look to bet against a team coming off of what I call a **sloppy win**. What is a sloppy win? It is a win where the winning team committed at least three turnovers and had more turnovers than the losing team. Such a team has developed the bad habit of turning over the ball and is less likely to get rid of that habit since they are coming off a win.

In Week 1 of the 2002 season, the Titans committed four turnovers in a 27-24 win over the Eagles. The Eagles committed three. Thus the Titans were coming from a sloppy win. They lost their next game in Dallas, 21-13, as 3 1/2 point favorites.

Betting against sloppy win teams is a powerful handicapping tool not really known to the betting public. I take 1/2 point away from a team coming from a sloppy win.

POINTER FOURTEEN:
BET AGAINST HOME FAVORITES
AFTER A POOR DEFENSIVE EFFORT

When a team gives up 35 or more points in regulation and loses and is a home favorite the next week, I look to bet against them. Usually such a team is too poor a defensive team to be giving points.

One such game took place in Week 3 of the 2003 season. In Week 2, the Chargers gave up 37 points in a 13-37 loss to the Broncos. Next week, money came in late on the Chargers (The Computer Betting Group leading the way) and pushed them to a two point favorite over the Ravens. The Ravens won outright, 24-10.

POINTER FIFTEEN:
HUGE EMOTIONAL EFFORT
FOLLOWED BY A LETDOWN

I used this model for years starting in Game 5. I have seen that it works early in the season as well.

I rate each team's emotional effort in each game on a scale of 1 (highest emotional effort) to 4 (a very flat emotional effort). An emotional effort of 2 is an above average effort and 3 is an average emotional effort. When a team has a number 1 emotional effort, I look to go against them the next week. Again, a bye between games ruins this model. Also, if a team has two or more straight number 2 efforts, I look to go against them in their next game.

In Week 2 of the 2003 season, I bet—and lost—on the Jaguars over the Bills. The Bills had put out what I considered a number 1.5 emotional effort (between 1 and 2, but still huge) the week before in their 31-0 rout win over the Patriots. After the Jaguars, the Bills would be playing divisional rival Miami in a nationally televised Sunday night game. I felt that the Bills would let down against the Jaguars: a non-divisional opponent in this classic sandwich game. I lost this bet as the Bills won and covered as three point favorites, 38-17.

Still, this is a strong model. I take one point away from a team that had a huge emotional effort the week before. I take away 1/2 point if the team had a 2 emotional effort and it was their second straight week with an effort at least that strong.

POINTER SIXTEEN: LOOKAHEAD

When a team has a key game the next week and might not be that emotionally up for the present week, I consider it a **lookahead** situation. I often look to bet against a team that might be looking ahead.

In Week 1 of the 2003 season, the Cowboys were hosting the Falcons. In their next game, the Cowboys were going to New York to play the Giants (one of their new head coach Bill Parcell's former teams) in a Monday night game. I took the Falcons in this game and the Falcons won, 27-13, as two point underdogs. In retrospect, this game was an aberration and probably a lucky win for me. The Cowboys won their next five games and ended up in the playoffs while the Falcons lost their next seven and collapsed without Michael Vick. I had felt that Vick's absence was being overrated in the Week 1 price.

I take away 1/2 point from a team in a lookahead spot.

POINTER SEVENTEEN: REVENGE

This is a complicated model. Not all teams that want revenge for a loss earlier in the season or want to avenge a loss from the previous season get it. A team has to be playing decently or have shown that they are a good revenge team for me to consider using this model to make a bet.

In Week 4 of the 2003 season, the Bengals traveled to Cleveland to meet the Browns who had beaten them twice in 2002. The Bengals had played very well in losing at Oakland as 11 1/2 point underdogs two weeks previous to this game. I felt this showed coping ability, though the Raiders ended up being a much worse team than I had thought they were at this point in the season. Many bettors agreed with the Bengals on this game, as the line went from 6 for the Browns down to 4 1/2. The Bengals won straight up, 21-14.

I use revenge much more as a model in the later parts of the season. In revenge games I add between zero and one point to the team desiring the revenge. This depends, as I wrote above, on coping and how well teams do in revenge spots. In the above example, I gave the Bengals 1/2 point.

One item that I've added to games in the first four weeks: a team must have value in the price for me to bet them. In the past I made this stipulation only after the first four weeks but now I include the early season games as well.

POINTER EIGHTEEN: VALUE

Value means that I must have a two point edge either in my power rating or in my oddsmaking line. Where a key number (4, 6, 7, 10, 11, 13, 14) is involved I need a 1 1/2 point edge. Where 3 is involved (the most important number), I need just a one point edge. Value can also mean that a team has good coverage (against the present spread) against a team at the location where the game is being played.

And remember—it can't be said too often—in *all* bets, the power rating must favor the team I want to bet. Also once again, the teams I bet in the first four weeks are underdogs or pick teams exclusively.

12

The Pro Bettor's Toolkit: Games 5-8

As in games one through four, a team must have emotional motivation as well as value favoring them. Again, any teams I bet must have my power ratings showing they have the edge. Very occasionally I might go against my power ratings if there is a compelling reason to do so. However, this is very infrequent. As always, I never go against what I made the game as an oddsmaker.

I also am willing to wager on favorites at this point in the season. However, I am much tighter on favorites than on underdogs. I very seldom give more than three points in a game.

In games 5 through 8, I seek the same emotional edges that I seek in games 1 through 4. I also look for some other situations.

POINTER ONE:
REVENGE GAMES

As in Games 1 through 4 I look to bet a team wanting revenge. Again, in revenge games, a team is trying to avenge a loss to an opponent. This loss must have taken place within the last year.

Revenge can be a surprisingly strong motivating force in the NFL and I look to wager on the team that wants it. To get a better feel for the revenge situation I often look to see how the team wanting it has performed in revenge situations the last year. The better a team has performed in other revenge situations, the more likely I am to bet it.

Also important, as noted before, a team does better in revenge spots if they have shown they can cope and are playing well.

If a team has done well in revenge situations recently and is coping well, I add up to a point to the power rating for them.

POINTER TWO:
EMBARRASSING PERFORMANCES

I look to wager on a team that has just suffered a humiliating loss—either losing by a big score or to a bad club. I also look to bet a team that has had very poor offensive or defensive numbers in their last game, or to wager against a team that has just put up outstanding offensive or defensive numbers.

Teams that put up big numbers are likely to let down in their next game. Teams that put up especially poor numbers or were humiliated tend to have hard practices and to be up for the next week's game. As in revenge games, I make sure to research how teams have done coming off other big losses in recent times.

If a team has done well in this situation, I add 1/2 a point to their power rating.

POINTER THREE: HOME DOGS

As in the first four weeks of the season, I look to wager on a home underdog if the team lost the week before as a home favorite.

POINTER FOUR: EMOTIONAL FOLLOW-UP

As in games one through four, I look to wager against a team if it has just had a particularly emotional game, with an emotional rating of one, against another team. I also look to wager against a team if they have had two or more consecutive slightly less emotional, with emotional ratings of two, games.

POINTER FIVE: SANDWICH GAMES

As in games one through four, I look to wager against a team in a divisional series sandwich game.

POINTER SIX: OUT-OF-DIVISION FAVORITES

As in games one through four, if a team has played two or more consecutive divisional games and is now playing a nondivisional game (again no bye week involved), I look to wager against the team if they are favored by seven points or more.

POINTER SEVEN:
FOLLOW-UP PERFORMANCES

If a team is strong against the spread after an outright loss—I check back one year on this—I will look to bet them after a loss. If a team plays poorly after a win, I will look to bet against them after a win. Getting to know each team's personality is important in using this model.

I am willing to make up to a one point adjustment for a team that does well off of a loss or against a team that does poorly after winning.

In the 2004 season in their fifth game, the Ravens played at the Redskins after a loss the week before. Going back to the 2002 season, the Ravens were 13-1-1 to the spread after losses. I rewarded the Ravens one point in my power ratings for this. Since my power rating favored the Ravens by 1 1/2 points, taking a point on them was a good bet. The Ravens won the game, 17-10.

POINTER EIGHT:
MONDAY NIGHT FOLLOW-UP

As in the first four games, I look to bet against a team that has won and covered a Monday night game against a divisional opponent, and who is now playing a nondivisional team.

POINTER NINE:
LARGE POINT SWINGS

As in the first four games, I use the 50-point swing model. In other words, if Team A's margin of win and Team B's margin of loss the previous week add up to 50 points or more, I am looking to bet Team B this week.

POINTER TEN:
SUNDAY OR MONDAY NIGHT HOME UNDERDOGS

As in the first four games, I look to bet Sunday or Monday night home underdogs when the power rating favors them and they have value in the price.

POINTER ELEVEN:
UNDER-THE-LIGHTS FOLLOW-UP

As in the first four games, I look to wager on teams that lost a rout on Sunday or Monday night and look to wager against teams that won a rout under the night lights of national television.

POINTER TWELVE:
BIG SCORING TEAMS

As in the first four games, I look to bet against a favorite that scored a total of 30 points or more in each of the last two weeks in winning efforts.

POINTER THIRTEEN:
PLAYOFF POTENTIAL

I look to wager on must-win underdogs if they are usually in-contention teams. What I mean by a **must-win underdog** is a team that would be virtually out of the playoff picture or placed in a very disadvantageous spot concerning the playoff race with a loss. And, again, the team must be one that usually makes the playoffs and thus one for which a playoff absence would be a huge failure for the franchise.

In Week 6 of 2004, I made what ended up being my biggest bet of the season. I took the Packers as 3 1/2 point underdogs at Detroit. At 1-4, the Packers were three games behind in the NFC North. The Packers were perennial playoff contenders. A loss in this game would put them in a terrible situation as far as making the playoffs was concerned. The Packers were also coming off of a rout Monday night home loss to the Titans.

Of course, the betting public—including many so-called pros—loaded up on the overpriced Lions. They were bet from plus 1 to as high as 3 1/2 point favorites. The Packers came through in this must-win game, 38-10.

POINTER FOURTEEN:
SPECIAL RIVALRIES

I look to wager on an out-of-contention underdog in a nationally telecast game if it is one in which they are playing a long-time rival. These are games in which out-of-contention teams look to get very fired up.

POINTER FIFTEEN:
BIG GAME AHEAD

If a team has a big game coming up the next week and might be overlooking the present game, I will be considering a bet against them.

POINTER SIXTEEN:
GOAL MIND SET

When a team has a goal it is trying to reach, I sometimes will wager on this team. In the last game of 2002, the Bills hosted the Bengals. The Bills were 7 1/2 point home favorites. Though the Bills were out of contention, they had the incentive of being a .500 team for the season if they won this game. Having been 3-13 in 2001, this represented a major accomplishment.

The Bills also wanted to win at home to create more fan support for 2003. At 2-13, the Bengals just wanted to end the season. Whatever they could salvage from the wreckage of the 2002 season had been done in their home upset win of the Saints the week before. The Bills won and covered handily in this game, 27-9.

I give the team with a goal mind-set 1/2 point in my power ratings.

POINTER SEVENTEEN: PHONY WIN FOLLOW-UPS

As in games one through four, when a team is a favorite after a phony win I look to wager against them. If a team is an underdog after a phony loss, I look to wager on them.

POINTER EIGHTEEN: DUE-UPS, DUE-DOWNS, MAY-DUES, AND STAR-DUES

I continue to use these pointers from the first four games of the season.

POINTER NINETEEN: SLOPPY WINS

As in games one through four, I look to bet against teams coming off sloppy wins.

SUMMARY

The pointers discussed for games five through eight of the season are powerful indicators of team emotion. But having an emotional edge alone is not enough reason for me to wager on a team after its fourth game of the season. The teams I wager on must also have a value edge at this point. In other words, an underdog must be getting more points than I think they should be getting. If I am willing to wager on a favorite, the team must be giving fewer points than I think they should be giving. There are five ways in which a team can get enough value.

Price Value

First, a team can be getting at least two points over the line I have set for a game—or 1 1/2 points if a key number like four, six, seven, ten, eleven, or fourteen is involved. If the key number three is involved, I need just a one-point edge.

Power Rating Value

Second, a team can be getting two extra points over my power rating—again, 1 1/2 if a key number is involved other than three, or one point if three is involved.

Conditions Value

Third, a team might play especially well or poorly on grass or turf (using just the last year's results) or at home or away. This might make the team a good value as an underdog (in a spot where they play well) or a bad value as a favorite (in a spot where they play poorly). In addition, value might exist if a team plays especially well or poorly as favorites or underdogs.

Spread Comparison Value

Fourth, a team can be getting two extra points (1 1/2 points if a key number other than three is involved, or one point if three is involved) over recent spread comparisons. Here is an example of what I mean by spread comparisons.

In Week 12 of 2002, the Bills hosted the Dolphins. Over the previous three weeks, both teams had been three point road underdogs against the Jets. According to those spreads, the Bills should have been 2 1/2 or 3 point home favorites. However the betting public was so turned off by the Bills' loss the week before at the Jets, and so turned on by the Dolphins' 30-3 home win over the Chargers the previous week, that the Dolphins were bet up to 2 1/2 point road favorites. The Bills won, 38-21.

Spread Range Value

The fifth and last way teams can have value is if they are ten points or more lower than their opponents on the spread range.

Let's take a look at a game that was a wager for me in the second segment of the 2002 season.

In the eighth game for each club, the Eagles played at the Bears. They went off as seven and 7 1/2 point favorites in this game.

The emotional factors strongly favored the Bears. They wanted revenge for a playoff loss to the Eagles a year ago. The Eagles were coming from a Monday night win over a divisional rival, the New York Giants. The week before that the Eagles had won a key game against the Bucs and thus were coming from 2 and 1 1/2 emotional efforts. The Eagles also were coming from a phony win over the Giants. Lastly, the Bears were a fresh double star due up. The one emotional factor working against the Bears was that they were 0-4 to the number after a loss. Still I deducted 1 1/2 from the Eagles' power rating overall.

The Bears also had value in this game at plus 7 1/2 since my oddsmaking and power rating line on the game was 6.

Thus the Bears had emotion and value working for them in this game. The game fell right on my number as the Eagles won, 19-13.

13

The Pro Bettor's Toolkit: Games 9-16

In this segment of the season I continue to look for teams with both emotional and value edges. However, now a team has to have something else going for it as well. By this point in the season, a team must either have shown that they can cope with the class of opponent they are facing, or the opponent must have shown that they have problems coping.

At this time of the year, I look much more closely at scrimmage match-ups than I do earlier in the year. I don't look at them nearly as closely as most in the media, but I do give scrimmage match-ups a consideration in the last segment of the season.

When evaluating coping, I look to see how teams have played at home, on the road, on grass, and on turf.

But, as I have mentioned, I give my hardest look at how they have played teams of the ranking of the coming opponent.

I use all of the emotional and value pointers that I did in games five through eight and I also add two more.

Spread Range

On the spread range, teams must now be at least 20 points apart for me to consider wagering on the lower-ranked team. At this point in the season, a ten-point spread range difference is not that unusual or significant.

Undefeated Home Dog

If a team is undefeated at home and a home underdog, it tends to have an emotional edge. When a team is an underdog at home and has defeated all previous comers that season, it tends to feel insulted about being made an underdog at home. The home underdog is looking for respect and will be emotionally charged for the game.

Example

Let's look at an example of a wager I made in the last segment of the season in 2002.

The Ravens were three point road favorites against the expansion Texans. At 6-7, the Ravens were pretty much out of playoff contention, but could reach 8-8 or even 9-7. To do so in a year they had conceded would be primarily a rebuilding year would be a great accomplishment.

The Ravens in 2002 were 5-1 to the number after a loss. The Texans, who had won at the Steelers the week before, were 0-3 to the number after wins. They had played their worst ball in such games (including a 35 point home loss to the horrible Bengals). The Ravens also were coming from a phony loss while the Texans were coming from a phony win. The one minus for the Ravens was that they had divisional games against the Browns and Steelers next to finish the season. Overall the Ravens got 1 1/2 extra points in my power ratings due to their emotional edges.

In terms of value, my power ratings favored the Ravens by four. Thus they had value giving three or less.

In terms of coping, the Ravens had won at the Bengals—a team in the Texans class. The Texans had lost to the Bengals at home, which showed that they could play poorly in this game against a team much better.

The game itself was close but the Ravens won and covered, 23-19, as the game fell right on my power rating.

14

The Pro Bettor's Toolkit: Betting the Playoffs

In this part of the season, my wagering formula changes. Here I don't look for emotional edges since both teams are usually equally up for playoff encounters, though there are a few exceptions. What I look for is a team with a value edge in the price, as well as enough of an edge at the line of scrimmage to justify selecting them at the price that exists.

Specifically, I look for a three point or better edge in my power ratings, and I never go against my own odds-maker line.

One playoff game that I wagered on after the 2002 season was the Giants taking four against the 49ers. My letter power rating on the game favored the 49ers by 1 1/2. I rated both clubs as C+ teams but gave the 49ers just a

1 1/2 point edge at home and the Giants a 1 1/2 point dis-advantage on the road. In my number power ratings, the 49ers were 21 (remember these are perfect power ratings done for the playoffs) and the Giants were 23 1/2. Thus the Giants had a one point edge in the number power ratings. Giving 3/4 weight to the letter power ratings made the 49ers a one point favorite. In the playoffs I look for three point edges. Getting plus 4 on the Giants provided that edge for me.

With the 49er defense being banged up the Giants figured to move the ball well on them, especially through the air. The Giant offense had played much better ever since their coach, Jim Fassel, had taken over the play-calling in their eighth game. The Giants also had the physical type defense that figured to bother the 49er offense.

In the game, the 49ers made the second biggest play-off comeback in history to win 39-38. However, the Giants covered the spread.

In the last part of this book, I'll go through every game I wagered on in the 2004 season. There, you'll learn more about how I apply the emotional, value, coping, and scrimmage pointers.

15

Other Types of Bets

EXHIBITION GAMES

There are some handicappers who claim to do very well wagering on the exhibition games. I am not one of them.

I don't wager on these games because it seems a bad idea to me to wager real money on games that don't count in the standings. I don't like being in a position where I care more about the team's winning than the team does.

There are some bettors who claim that they find out by research—reading newspapers from around the league—which teams care about the exhibition games and which teams don't. This might be true, but the linesmakers have access to the same facts. Thus, that edge is limited.

However, by watching the exhibition games I have noticed that most teams tend to substitute at the same time. Trying to gauge which second- and third-team players will be trying harder seems like a rough task to me.

I don't even know how these games could be power rated. I have enough trouble power rating each team's first string during the regular season. Trying to power rate a team's third-string players going against another team's second-string players seems impossible—at least for me.

PROPOSITION WAGERS

In contrast to exhibition games, I believe proposition wagers are beatable. The main characteristic that a proposition player needs is the ability to do research. I have taken part in several types of proposition bets over the last few years, particularly pre-season Super Bowl futures and over/under bets on the number of team wins for a season. I continue to look at Super Bowl futures during the season and especially at the beginning of the playoffs.

On over/unders for the season, I first power rate each team. Then I mathematically play out each team's schedule using my letter power ratings, which I have converted into projected point spreads using my Letter Rating Point Differences chart (Chart 3). In addition, on my projected point spreads, every home club gets 2 1/2 points. I then translate each result into a decimal equivalent and add up the decimals to forecast a final win total for each team.

For example, let's take the Baltimore Ravens of 1997. Their first game at home was against Jacksonville. I rated the Jaguars (without Mark Brunell at the time) as a C team. The Ravens were rated a D. At home a D team is a three-point underdog against a C team. That translates to plus .40 on the decimals equivalent chart. In their second game the Ravens would play the Cincinnati Bengals at home. Before the 1997 season began I had rated the Bengals a C+ team. A D team at home against a C+ team is a 4 1/2-point underdog. In decimals, that translates to .357—or .36 rounded off.

OTHER TYPES OF BETS

The Ravens' 16-game total was 6.19 games won. Since I found no sports books offering a totals line on them of under 8 1/2 wins or over four wins, I did not wager on the Ravens in the season over/under totals.

In wagering on team season over/unders, I look for at least a two-game difference between my total and what is posted. I found and won two such propositions in 1996. I won two of three in 1997. From 1996 through 2001, I went 11 and 3 on season over/unders.

Unfortunately, 2002 was a bad season for me on these bets, with a horrid 0 and 3 record on them. In 2003, I went 2-0 on season over/under plays. In 2004, I decided to include season wagers where there was a 1 1/2 game difference between my number and what was posted. This caused me to make two extra season bets: under 5 1/2 wins on the Cards (my projected number was 3.98) and over 8 1/2 on the Vikings (I had projected 10.37 wins for them).

Since I lost each of those bets by 1/2 game in the last game of the season (the Cards won six games and the Vikings—after a 5-1 start—won eight games), I felt that some larger force was punishing me for deviating from my usual stance of needing a two game edge. I went 2-1 on my two-game edge bets in 2004, winning with the Texans over six wins and the Titans under ten wins and losing on the Eagles under 11 wins. In the future, I will stick with teams where I have a two game edge!

Super Bowl propositions are many and varied. By doing diligent research, a handicapper can usually find a few that can be beaten. I found one in 1996 involving field goals. A couple of Vegas books put up the proposition that both field-goal kickers in the Patriots-Packers Super Bowl would kick at least 30-yard field goals. If you wanted to wager that they would, you had to give 1.15 to 1. To bet that they wouldn't, you had to give 1.05 to 1 odds.

That Super Bowl was played in the New Orleans Superdome. Thus the "weather conditions" would be perfect. In 1996 dome games, I saw that in 60 percent of them both field-goal kickers did *not* kick field goals of 30 yards or more. Thus the real odds against both field-goal kickers making at least one 30-yard field goal each were actually 1.5 to 1. Giving only 1.05 to 1 gave me a significant edge, which paid off in a winning bet.

In the 2005 Super Bowl I bet Brian Westbrook of the Eagles to get under 67 1/2 (and went further going under 69 1/2) yards rushing. He had gone under this total in nine of the 15 games he played. I felt I had a bigger edge than this since I felt that the Eagles would lose the game. When teams are losing, they rush less. Westbrook ended up with 44 yards rushing in the game, despite a fluke 22-yard run on the last play before halftime.

The linesmaker does not set proposition lines via research. Rather he comes up with a number by feel that he thinks will generate equal money on both sides. That is why proposition bets are bettable and beatable. Again, research and patience (passing most of them as bets) are what is needed to come out ahead.

Again, 2002 was a bad one for me in Super Bowl propositions. I went a terrible 1 and 4 on them. An early interception in the game cost me two of these bets. In 2003, I again struggled with Super Bowl proposition bets. However, as shown in the 2004 season diary later in this book, I bounced back somewhat in the 2004 Super Bowl.

MONEY LINES

Many years ago, before point spreads were invented, football was bet via odds. You would give odds on the favored team or take them on the underdog. As I wrote earlier in this book, the problem with this type of wager was that mismatch games were difficult to put odds on that would generate business for the bookies.

A few bookies and Las Vegas sports books still allow bettors to wager odds on NFL games. Another term for wagering odds is "betting the money line." In the money line, there is always a difference between what an underdog gets and a favorite gives. This difference represents the bookmakers' edge on the game. For example, a seven-point favorite might be plus 2.40 on the underdog and minus 3.00 on the favorite. In this situation, if you want to bet the underdog to win the game outright you must put up one dollar for every 2.4 dollars you wish to win. If you want to bet the favorite to win outright you must put up three dollars for every dollar you wish to win.

I have done a careful study of money lines and have found that most of the time there is no real value in wagering them. For the most part, the true money line price on a game is a number between what the favorite must give and what the underdog takes. In the example just given, the true odds of a seven-point favorite winning a game in the NFL are 2.60-1. Odds of 2.60 are between 2.4 and 3.0.

However, there are occasionally times when a money line wagerer does have an edge. This is when the money line has been adjusted because of betting action. At the new price, a bettor might have an edge or be able to wager on a number that is different from what the true money line is.

Before I give some examples, let me show what the correct money lines are on different point spreads. I have computed these lines from nearly twenty years' research. Please see the chart on the next page.

The place where a money line bettor often has the biggest edge is on games in the two and 2 1/2 point-spread area. Often you will see 1.25 to 1 on a 2 1/2-point underdog. The real line should be just 1.10 to 1 as the underdog wins the game outright about 10/21 of the time. On two-point underdogs, a bettor can often get 1.10 or 1.15 to 1. The real odds there are just 1.08 to 1. I bet several of these underdogs on the money line in 1996. I found just one in 1997.

Unfortunately, bookmakers have become smarter since 1997 as they have greatly lowered their money lines in these games. Some don't offer them at all on less than three point favorites. I have bet on just two since the 1997 season. However, you should still be aware of the money line value of under three point underdogs.

For other point spreads, if value is to be found in the money line it is usually on the underdog. This is true for two reasons.

First, sports books often jack up the price on money line favorites since they know that most bettors will give rather than take the odds. They try to stay a step ahead of the bettors by doing this.

Second, the money that comes in on money lines usually is on the favorite. You should look at underdogs on the money line, especially if you are in Vegas, where a number of sports books put up money lines on games. To see if the underdog has value, use this chart to compare equivalents with what is available. If you like the underdog in such a game, it might be wiser to wager the money line than the point spread.

CHART 11:
CORRECT MONEY LINES
FOR EACH POINT SPREAD

Point Spread	Correct Money Line
1	1.03
1 1/2	1.05
2	1.08
2 1/2	1.10
3	1.50
3 1/2	1.60
4	1.70
4 1/2	1.80
5	1.90
5 1/2	2.00
6	2.20
6 1/2	2.40
7	2.60
7 1/2	2.80
8	3.00
8 1/2	3.20
9	3.40
9 1/2	3.60
10	3.80
10 1/2	4.00
11	4.25
11 1/2	4.50
12	5.00
12 1/2	5.50
13	6.00
13 1/2	7.00
14	8.00
14 1/2	9.00
15	11.00
15 1/2	14.00
16	17.00
16 1/2	20.00
17	25.00
17 1/2+	30.00

16

Keeping Records

RECORDS

When handicapping and wagering on the NFL, it is essential to keep records. You will need them to calculate spread ranges and power ratings, to make lines and track motivational factors, and, later in the season, to research propositions.

Fortunately, if you're just beginning to keep records, it is the recent ones that are the most important for handicapping. In fact, for the majority of your work, the most you need to go back is two years. In these days of free agency, the majority of starters on teams will not have been together any longer than that.

I keep the following records on every team:

1) WEEK-TO-WEEK RECORDS

Since I need to know whether a team is covering the point spread, each week I record the final score and closing point spread of each game. I note this information in both an overall point spread record and a team point spread chart.

KEEPING RECORDS

Each team's point spread chart is broken into six categories: three for home games and three for away games. Specifically, I note when teams are small home favorites (1-3 points), medium home favorites (3 1/2 to 6 1/2 points), or large home favorites (seven points or more). I also keep the same breakdown of away favorites, and home and away underdogs. I list the rare games that are "pick" (even or no point spread) in a separate spot on the same page.

An example follows of the chart for the Jacksonville Jaguars. On November 3, 2002, the Jaguars visited the Giants. Chart 11 is the entry for that game:

| | | Road Team's | Home | Home Team's | Closing Point | Jaguar Spread |
Date	Road Team	Score	Home Team	Score	Spread	Record
11/3	Jack	17	at NYG	24	+3	4-4

CHART 11: WEEKLY GAME RECORDS

The entry indicates that the Jaguars lost this game, 24-17 and closed as three point road underdogs. The 4-4 after the point spread shows the Jaguars' record against the point spread after this game.

You can see from the following chart that the Jaguars' main strength was as underdogs where they went 5-2 to the number (3-1 home and 2-1 road). As road favorites, the Jaguars did poorly going 1-4 to the number. The Jaguars' main weakness as road favorites was in the small (1-3 points) road favorite category where they went 1-3 against the spread. They also went 1-3 outright in this category.

Chart 12 below is the Jaguars' point spread chart at the end of the 2002 season:

CHART 12: TEAM POINT SPREAD RECORD

Pts.	Home Favorites				Road Favorites			
	W	L	O	T	W	L	O	T
1-3	2	1	1	0	1	3	3	0
3 1/2-6 1/2	0	0	0	0	0	1	0	0
7+	0	1	1	0	0	0	0	0
TOTALS	2	2	2	0	1	4	3	0

Pts.	Home Underdogs				Road Underdogs			
	W	O	L	T	W	O	L	T
1-3	2	1	1	0	0	0	1	0
3 1/2-6 1/2	1	0	0	0	1	1	0	0
7+	0	0	0	0	1	0	0	0
TOTALS	3	1	1	0	2	1	1	0

W=Won, L=Lost, O=Outright (for favorites means lost outright, for underdogs means won outright), T=Tied

2) NUMBER POWER RATING SPREAD

On the same page as a team's schedule and spread I note in red the team's number power rating spread for a given game. On the other side I note the number power rating that the team had going into the game. When that number becomes five or more above or below the team's starting number power rating, it is easy to note that the team is due-up or due-down. This fact is duly recorded in my handicapping sheets.

3) SPREAD RANGE

Near the bottom of each page where a team's scores and spreads are noted, I keep an up-to-date spread range beneath the other data. Here is the spread range record for the New York Giants in 2002:

+1, +7, +6, 0, +1, -3, -6, -4, -2, -3, -6, -8, -5, +1, +7, +8

You can see from this record that the Giants started strongly, slumped in the middle of the season and then finished strongly.

4) EMOTIONAL RATING

Below the spread range I list a team's emotional rating after each game. I pay particular attention to situations where a team has had a 1 or 1 1/2 emotional rating the last game, or two or more consecutive games with a two or higher emotional rating. In these situations, remember, I am looking to go against a team that might now be flat. If a team had a four (flat) emotional rating, I look for a possible bounce-back.

5) CHARACTER RATING

Below the emotional rating, I give each team a character rating after each game as follows:

1: This highest rating is given to a team that has battled to the end, often in a lost situation. The "1" is also sometimes used for a team that made a great comeback. One team in the 2004 season that got a "1" character rating was the Ravens in their Game 7 10-15 loss to the Eagles. Despite missing star running back Jamal Lewis who was suspended for this game, the Eagles never gave up despite trailing 15-3 at one point. They then had a long drive to cut the deficit to 10-15 and were driving late for a potential winning score when the Eagles stopped them.

1a: This second highest rating is used for a team that has won by consistently making the big plays. A game in which I used this rating was in 2002 in the Giants' Week 2 win over the Rams. The Giants nearly blew a 17-0 lead in this game, but made big plays offensively and defensively (they held the Rams twice with the score at 26-21) to win this game.

2: The rating for an average game. I use this character rating more than any other.

3: I rate a team at "3" when it seems to quit in a game. But I use this rating only seldom over the course of a season. If a team quits in a game, I almost never wager on that team again until they have proven to me that they have an improved attitude. One team that got this character rating in 2002 was the Rams in their Week 14 49-10 loss to the Chiefs. It was noted by several writers—as well as by Chiefs players—that the Rams gave up after falling more than two touchdowns behind.

3a: This is given when a team loses a game because the key plays went against them. The Raiders got a "3a" rating in their Week Eight 2002 20-10 loss to the Chiefs. A couple of special team errors as well as two key turnovers (one when they were down 13-10 but had the ball with a chance to go ahead late in the game) contributed to the Raider loss.

Character ratings can come in handy. When you find a team that has won a close game after accumulating a bunch of 3a ratings, this often means the team has turned the corner and might need to be raised in their letter power rating. These ratings also show which teams know how to win (those that get 1a's) and which know best how to lose (those that get mostly 3a's).

During their eight-game losing slide in 2002, the Carolina Panthers earned three 3a grades. They finally won in their twelfth game at Cleveland: a game where the key plays, especially defensively, were made by the Panthers. The Panthers then won three of their last four games—including one the last week of the season that knocked the Saints out of the playoffs.

6) OFFENSIVE/DEFENSIVE RATINGS

Below the character ratings I keep a team's offensive and defensive ratings. In running, passing, and special teams, I give each team game ratings between 1 and 5, with 1 as the best rating, 5 the worst, and 3 at exactly average.

Here is a typical newspaper box score from the 1997 season and how I rated both teams in each category. The game was the Week 1 Monday night affair between the Chicago Bears and the Green Bay Packers.

	1ST	2ND	3RD	4TH	FINAL
CHICAGO	0	11	0	3	24
GREEN BAY	3	15	6	14	38

SCORING SUMMARY:

1ST QUARTER:

GNB - FG, RYAN LONGWELL 38 YD, 4:23.

Drive: 7 plays, 19 yards in 2:43.

Key plays: Schroeder 46-yard punt return to Chicago 39; Favre 9-yard pass to Brooks on 3rd-and-3 to Chicago 22.
GREEN BAY 3-0

2ND QUARTER:
CHI - TD, RAYMONT HARRIS 1 YD RUN (TODD SAUERBRUN PASS TO JIM FLANIGAN FOR TWO-POINT CONVERSION), 4:57.
Drive: 14 plays, 87 yards in 8:37.
Key plays: Kramer 22-yard pass to Jennings to Chicago 35; Kramer 8-yard pass to Proehl on 3rd-and-1 to Green Bay 48; Kramer 15-yard pass to Wetnight on 3rd-and-8 to Green Bay 19; 3-yard pass interference on Packers' Evans on 3rd-and-3 to Green Bay 9. CHICAGO 8-3

GNB - TD, JEFF THOMASON 1 YD PASS FROM BRETT FAVRE (BRETT FAVRE PASS TO DORSEY LEVENS FOR TWO-POINT CONVERSION), 9:09.
Drive: 1 play, 1 yard in 0:05.
Key plays: Evans 27-yard interception return to Chicago 1. GREEN BAY 11-8

CHI - FG, JEFF JAEGER 42 YD, 13:04.
Drive: 4 plays, 7 yards in 2:04.
Key plays: Carter 14-yard interception return to Green Bay 31. CHICAGO 11, GREEN BAY 11

GNB - TD, ROBERT BROOKS 18 YD PASS FROM BRETT FAVRE (RYAN LONGWELL KICK), 14:12.
Drive: 5 plays, 80 yards in 1:08.
Key plays: Favre 10-yard pass to Henderson to Green Bay 30; Favre 44-yard pass to Brooks on 3rd-and-2 to Chicago 18; Favre 5-for-5 for 80 yards. GREEN BAY 18-11

3RD QUARTER:
GNB - FG, RYAN LONGWELL 36 YD, 6:36.
Drive: 7 plays, 40 yards in 4:11.
Key plays: Levens 10-yard run to Chicago 40; Favre 18-yard pass to Thomason to Chicago 22.

GREEN BAY 21-11
GNB - FG, RYAN LONGWELL 29 YD, 10:45.
Drive: 4 plays, 16 yards in 2:48.
Key plays: Schroeder 27-yard punt return to Chicago 27; Levens 16-yard run to Chicago 11. GREEN BAY 24-11

4TH QUARTER:

GNB - TD, DORSEY LEVENS 1 YD RUN (RYAN LONGWELL KICK), 6:48.
Drive: 11 plays, 85 yards in 5:56.
Key plays: Favre 19-yard pass to Mayes to Chicago 43; Favre 20-yard pass to Mayes to Chicago 24; Favre 10-yard pass to Mayes to Chicago 14; Levens 11-yard run to Chicago 3. GREEN BAY 31-11

CHI - TD, RICKY PROEHL 22 YD PASS FROM ERIK KRAMER (TWO-POINT CONVERSION FAILED), 11:32.
Drive: 14 plays, 80 yards in 4:39.
Key plays: Kramer 12-yard pass to Engram to Green Bay 38; Kramer 11-yard pass to Penn to Green Bay 34; Kramer 12-yard pass to Wetnight to Green Bay 22. GREEN BAY 31-17

GNB - TD, GABE WILKINS 1 YD FUMBLE RETURN (RYAN LONGWELL KICK), 12:24. GREEN BAY 38-17
CHI - TD, RAYMONT HARRIS 68 YD RUN (JEFF JAEGER KICK), 12:52.
Drive: 2 plays, 68 yards in 0:28. GREEN BAY 38-24

TEAM STATISTICS	CHI	GNB
FIRST DOWNS	19	18
Rushing	6	7
Passing	11	10
Penalty	2	1
3RD-DOWN EFFICIENCY	5-16	2-9
4TH-DOWN EFFICIENCY	1-2	0-0
TOTAL NET YARDS	336	315
Total plays	74	55
Average gain	4.5	5
NET YARDS RUSHING	164	107
Rushes	30	31
Average per rush	5.5	3.5
NET YARDS PASSING	172	208
Completed-attempted	17-41	15-22
Yards per pass	3.9	8.7
Sacked-yards lost	3-20	2-18
Had intercepted	2	1
PUNTS-AVERAGE	6-48.0	4-40.0
RETURN YARDAGE	166	204
Punts-returns	1-4	5-107
Kickoffs-returns	7-148	2-53
Interceptions-returns	1-14	2-44
PENALTIES-YARDS	13-91	6-28
FUMBLES-LOST	1-1	1-1
TIME OF POSSESSION	32:47	27:13

PLAYER STATISTICS

Missed field goals:
None.

Chicago rushing:
Raymont Harris 13-122
Rashaan Salaam 16-41
Erik Kramer 1-1

Green Bay rushing:
Dorsey Levens 22-80
Brett Favre 7-18
William Henderson 2-9

Chicago passing:
Erik Kramer 17-41 for 192 yards, 2 INT, 1 TD

Green Bay passing:
Brett Favre 15-22 for 226 yards, 1 INT, 2 TD

Chicago receiving:
Raymont Harris 4-36
Bobby Engram 3-24
Chris Penn 2-28
Keith Jennings 1-22
Ryan Wetnight 3-32
Ricky Proehl 2-30
Rashaan Salaam 2-20

Green Bay receiving:
Jeff Thomason 5-58
Robert Brooks 3-71
Mark Chmura 1-30
Derrick Mayes 4-54
William Henderson 2-13

Chicago tackles-assists-sacks (unofficial):

Bryan Cox 5-3-0
Tom Carter 5-2-0
Ron Cox 4-3-1
John Thierry 2-1-0
Carl Simpson 0-3-0.5
Team 2-0-0
Jim Flanigan 1-0-0
Michael Lowery 3-0-0,
Anthony Marshall 1-1-0
Corey Dowden 1-0-0
Erik Kramer 1-0-0
Anthony Peterson 0-0-0

Marty Carter 5-2-0
John Mangum 5-2-0
Barry Minter 0-4-0
Alonzo Spellman 1-2-0.5
Walt Harris 2-0-0
James Burton 1-1-0
Marlon Forbes 2-0-0
Paul Grasmanis 0-1-0
Fabien Bownes 0-1-0
Van Hiles 1-0-0
Chris Penn 1-0-0
Todd Sauerbrun 1-0-0

Green Bay tackles-assists-sacks (unofficial):

Bernardo Harris 4-5-0
Eugene Robinson 4-3-0
Brian Williams 1-5-0
Gabe Wilkins 1-4-0.5
Santana Dotson 1-3-1
Tyrone Williams 4-0-0
Mike Prior 2-2-0, Darius
Robert Brooks 0-0-0
Terry Mickens 1-0-0
Darren Sharper 1-0-0

Leroy Butler 3-6-0
Reggie White 3-3-0.5
Wayne Simmons 3-2-0
Gilbert Brown 3-1-1
Doug Evans 3-0-0
Roderick Mullen 2-0-0
Holland 0-2-0
Lamont Hollinquest 1-0-0
Bill Schroeder 1-0-0
Jeff Thomason 2-0-0

Interceptions:

Chicago (Marty Carter 1 for 14 yards)
Green Bay (Doug Evans 1 for 27 yards, Roderick Mullen 1 for 17 yards)

Fumbles lost:

Chicago (Erik Kramer)
Green Bay (Jeff Thomason)

KEEPING RECORDS

Opponent's fumbles recovered:
Chicago (Barry Minter)
Green Bay (Gabe Wilkins)

Officials:
Referee-Dick Hantak
Umpire-Carl Madsen
Head linesman-Dale Williams,
Line judge-Dave Anderson
Back judge-Lloyd Peters
Side judge-Tom Fincken
Field judge-Mike Carey

Looking first at the Packers' stats, I gave the Packers a 3 1/2 (with, again, 1 as the best rating and 5 the worst) in the running game. They got minus two yards rushing in the first half and while they did much better after halftime, ending up with 107 yards on 31 carries, the Packers averaged just 3.5 yards a rush. They got seven first downs rushing, which is good for 31 rushes.

In passing I gave the Packers a 2. Brett Favre had averaged 8.7 yards per attempt: a great number since the league average is about six. He also completed better than 2/3 of his passes. However, his interception and the fact that he was sacked twice in just 24 attempts stopped the grade from being a 1 or 1 1/2.

On offensive special teams, I gave the Packers a 2. They got 107 yards on five punt returns and as you can see from the scoring summary, two of the punt returns (46 and 27 yards) set up short field goal drives. The Packers also made all three field goal attempts plus managed a 26.5 -yard average on kickoff returns—a good deal better than the league average.

On defense I gave the Packers a 3 in run defense. Although the Bears had gained 164 yards on 30 attempts, a

68-yard Raymont Harris touchdown run happened only after the game had been decided. Without this run the Bears' totals would have been 29-96 or 3.3 yards a rush. The Bears also had just five first downs rushing without the Harris run. Without that late long run I would have given the Packers a 2 or a 2 1/2 in run defense.

In pass defense, I gave the Packers a 2 since they had stopped the Bears from completing even half of their passes. In addition, the Packers yielded just 3.9 yards a pass attempt—a good number. In fact, the only reason the Packer pass defense grade wasn't higher was that the Bears had two early long drives that were fueled by Erik Kramer passes. One of them was a 14-play, 87-yard drive that ended in a touchdown. The other was a drive of over 45 yards that ended in a failed fourth down play.

Since these drives took place when the game was close, I couldn't give the Packers a higher grade. On special team defense, I gave the Packers a 2 1/2 since the Bears' punt return average was just four yards on one punt (other three were not returned) and the kickoff return average against them was okay (about 21 yards).

Despite the Packers' better-than-average ratings, after the game I lowered their letter power rating from A- to B+ for several reasons. First, they lost tight end Mark Chmura in the game, and as 1996 showed, the Packer offense needed him. Second, though the Packers had scored 38 points, two of the four touchdowns (a fumble recovery in the endzone and an interception return to the Bears' one-yard line) were basically scored by the defense. One other touchdown came in the two-minute drill before halftime against a prevent defense.

Thus the Packers' offense had managed just one really legitimate touchdown drive in the game. Two of the three Packers' field goals were off 16- and 19-yard drives set up by special teams, so the Packers' offense was not as impressive as I'd expected against a vulnerable Bears' defense.

The Bears earned a grade of 3 on rushing offense and a 4 on passing offense. Though Erik Kramer was sacked just three times, he was under pressure most of the game. Because of their poor punt return average, I gave the Bears just a 3 1/2 on offensive special teams.

On their rushing defense, I gave the Bears a grade of 2 1/2 since they'd held the Packers to just under 3 1/2 yards a rush. In pass defense, I gave the Bears a four since their defense yielded 8.7 yards a pass attempt. And because of their poor punt coverage, I gave the Bears a 4 on special teams' defense.

Overall, the Bears had put up a better fight than I had expected. However, I attributed that mostly to the heated rivalry between the teams—which can often produce closer games than expected. Thus after this game I did not change the Bears' letter power rating of D.

7) COPING ABILITY

Coping ability, as mentioned earlier, is basically a team's record against teams of the same class as their current opponent. In my records, with each team's wins and losses, I note the letter power rating of the foe to whom they just lost or won. I also note whether the game was at home or on the road. These ratings show a team's coping ability.

Coping ability is particularly important in handicapping games nine through sixteen. I also look for coping ability before betting a team whose opponent is a B or better letter-power-rated club, or when I consider backing a D or worse letter-power-rated club.

Chart 13 shows how the regular season coping record for the 2002 New York Jets looked:

185

CHART 13: COPING RECORDS

Teams Beaten:
D+(A), D+(H), B-(A), C(H), D(A), C-(H), C+(H), C+(A), B-(H),

Teams Lost To:
B)H), B+(A), C(A), C(H), C-(H), B-(A), D(A),
Key: H= Home   A=Away

A key game in the Jets season was their third win of the season where they defeated the Chargers (a B- team) on the road. This game showed coping ability, especially for a key late road game at New England (a C+ team), which the Jets won.

8) TEAM ROSTER BOOK

I also keep a team roster book in which I list every player on each team's roster and whether he is a starter or not. In addition, I list the player's position, height, weight, overall experience, and experience with the team. Lastly, I list how many games the player participated in the year before.

I use my roster book as a strong guide in setting each team's power ratings at the start of the season. This book shows how each unit of the team stacks up in terms of playing together and overall experience. The example below is a page from my 1997 team roster book. It shows the Carolina Panthers' offensive line.

CHART 14: TEAM ROSTER BOOK

No	Name	Pos*	Ht/Wt	Exp	W/Car	Games In 96
CENTERS						**Games**
52	Elliot	C-G	6/3 295	5	2	16 st g
65	Garcia	C	6/1 295	3	2	14 st c
63	Rodenhauser	C	6/5 280	10	2	16
60	Greeley	C	6/2 270	2	0	0
GUARDS						
75	Skrepenak	G	6/7 325	6	1	16 st g
TACKLES						
78	Brockermeyer	T	6/4 300	3	2	12
66	Campbell	T-TE	6/4 270	3	2	9 st t
76	Davidds-Garrido	T	6/6 313	2	1	12 st t
73	Wilson	T	6/7 283	1	0	0

Key: **bold st**= starters, c= center, g= guard, t= tackle

   * Pos=position

From my roster charts I could see that the Panthers' offensive line was one that had been together longer than most in the NFL. Three of its starters (Campbell, Garcia, and Elliot) were in their third year together on the line. The other two starters (Skrepenak and Davidds-Garrido) had played with the Panthers in 1996. In addition, none of the starters were past their sixth year in the NFL, which meant that this line could be together for years to come.

Now, it happens that the Panthers' offensive line at times struggled to get the job done in 1996. With no real changes made in the roster, I knew that the unit did not figure to get much better and would continue to be mediocre in 1997.

9) BOX SCORES

I also have a notebook in which I paste box scores—two sets of box scores for each game. One is for each team; the other is the *USA Today* scoring summary of each game. If I wish later to see how a team has done in a particular game, it is just a flick of a notebook page away. If, for example, in a possible revenge situation I want to know if the previous winner piled on points late in the game, my box score notebook answers that question, along with many others.

In addition, box scores pay off as key sources of information for researching proposition bets, especially on the Super Bowl.

10) OTHER STATISTICAL RECORDS

I also keep an eye on other stats during the season. I note, for example, how well each team plays on grass and turf. I sometimes consider this factor as part of my determination of a team's coping ability. This is especially important in the second half of the season.

The two most important stats I track, however, are how teams do after wins and losses—especially how teams perform after rout wins and losses of 21 points or more. I keep these records for two years, and consider the most recent performances to be the most critical.

I also note how teams do after they have a good offensive game, scoring 30 points or more; a good defensive game, giving up fewer than 14 points in a win; or a poor defensive game, giving up 30 or more points in a defeat.

As mentioned earlier, emotional edges are stronger in games after rout wins or losses. If my power ratings favor the side with the emotional edge, I'll probably bet it.

KEEPING RECORDS

Another stat I keep is team touchdowns for and against. In 2003, the Panthers gave up two touchdowns more than they scored. This led me to believe for much of the season that the Panthers weren't as good as their record (11-5). I did well going against the Panthers during the season but lost two playoff games—one with the service—going against them in the playoffs where they played better than I thought they would.

I also keep track of team sacks for and against and turnovers for and against.

Lastly, I write up small game summaries for each regular season game played. In these summaries I try to tell the real story of the game—one that might be hidden by the stats.

Here is an example of a game summary I wrote in the 2004 season. It was the Bills' game eight against the Jets—a game they won, 22-17.

"Bills used two takeaways to set up ten points (21 yard touchdown 'drive' and 12 yard field goal 'drive'). Bills broke 10-all halftime tie with a 77-yard touchdown drive that put them ahead for good. Bills defense contained the Jets running game (two first downs) but gave up a number of big passing plays (10.2 yards per pass attempt versus). After Bills fell behind 7-10, they went 72 yards for a field goal right before halftime. Bills had 19-12 first down edge and 37 1/2-22 1/2 clock edge."

17

More Winning Tips

USING THE MEDIA

When you read the paper or listen to the radio or watch television coverage of the NFL, you should filter out opinions and hone in on facts.

Local columnists tend to report more like fans than objective viewers. If the local team wins a game or two, the columnist often thinks the team is a serious contender. If the team loses badly, the columnist gets pessimistic about the upcoming game. The columnist—as opposed to the beat writers—is asked to come up with an angle or view on the team that no one else has written about. These angles usually stress how the team has been playing recently.

At many newspapers, the beat writer—the reporter who follows the team—is told by his editors to play down the negative aspects of the team and emphasize the positive aspects. Sometimes the team itself insists on this approach. When the positive approach is followed, the beat reporter gets more access to players and team personnel. But this cheerleader approach can be very expensive for a bettor. A handicapper has to have an objective view of the team in his area, as well as all others.

Reading mid-week quotes from players is not likely to help your handicapping, either. Most NFL players are extreme optimists when it comes to predicting their team's fortunes.

When watching television or reading game reports, ignore all this and pay attention instead to how a team reacted to a tough situation in the game. How did they respond when the other team scored to go up by four points? How did they handle the important third down plays? How did the back-up guard play? Did the team run to his side? Was the quarterback sacked right after he came in? This is the information you need in ranking a team for next week. And, most importantly, in adjusting a team's letter power rating, keep in close perspective the other games it has played. Whatever you do, don't make the amateur's mistake of overreacting to the last game!

The only way to get an edge out of what players and coaches say is to listen to statements they make *immediately* after a game. For example, I have found that when players and coaches fill their post-game talks with "should haves" and "could haves," it tends to be a signal that the team will continue to find a way to lose. These teams get a lot of 3a's in my character ratings. The players and coaches who can look objectively at even the toughest losses are those who will play hard in most circumstances and be great bets in bounce-back situations. These teams often get character ratings in the 1's and 1a's.

In the section where I dissected a box score, I covered a little about how to read stats. Here's some additional information that can be helpful.

The NFL insists on ranking teams according to total yards. This can be very misleading. For instance, when a team has a significant lead in a game, they will often play a soft prevent defense and give up lots of passing yards. The team that's behind will get lots of passing yards, which is often garbage yardage. Yet these yards can make the losing team leader in the passing stats and give the winning team one of the worst pass defense records.

The most significant passing stat by far—and the one you should be watching most closely—is yards gained per pass attempt. Sacks—and yards lost in sacks—are considered pass attempts and yards lost on passing. The team that wins the pass per attempt battle wins the game over 3/4 of the time. Meanwhile, teams that get totals of 350 yards or more passing will lose the game far more than 1/4 of the time.

It is also considered good when a team has a lot of rushing attempts. Too many people confuse a lot of rushing attempts with winning. However, it is often only *after* a team gets the lead that they start to run the ball, so they can eat up the clock.

I think a better indicator of a team that truly runs the ball well is the ratio between rushing first downs and rushing attempts. When the ratio is smaller than 1:4, the team has rushed the ball well. And getting first downs means that the team was really able to use the rush to work on the clock.

In summary, don't get confused by stats—although some are useful objective measures, many others are just a bunch of numbers. You will be better able to discern important stats by looking at box scores closely than by listening to a bunch of statistics on television.

INJURIES

During the week, a topic to read about is injuries. Here it is crucial to have a team roster that can help you see who the possible backup is and—more importantly—how much experience he has and how long he has played with the team. Still, overall I feel that injuries are very much overrated. The Patriots have won the 2004 and 2005 Super Bowls despite being hit very hard by injuries both seasons. In 2003, the Patriots went 14-2 against the point spread, despite all their injuries. In the 2004 season, the Pats held the very explosive Colts to three points in their playoff win despite being without their starting cornerbacks.

The NFL sends out injury lists a couple of times a week. Teams rate players as **probable**, which supposedly means that there is a 75 percent chance the player so listed will play; **questionable**, which supposedly means that there is a 50 percent chance the player so listed will play; **doubtful**, which supposedly means that there is a 25 percent chance the player so listed will play; and **out**, meaning the player is out and definitely won't play. Over the years I have found these lists to be very misleading. Probable players play much more often than 75 percent of the time. Questionable players play much more than 50 percent of the time. The only time that questionable players tend to miss games is when they were also out the previous week.

It is for doubtful players and those who are definitely out that you should consult your roster book.

Something else to look at in reading papers is whether the injured player is practicing. When he is, it is just about a sure bet that he will play in the coming game. The information on whether a player is practicing is usually in the Friday or Saturday paper.

The betting public tends to overreact to injuries. The only time when I make a serious adjustment in my power ratings is when an extremely important player is out. In 2004 when Marc Bulger, Rams starting quarterback, was out, I docked the Rams three points, lowering their letter power rating to D+ from C.

As it turned out, it probably wasn't enough since backup Chris Chandler showed that he was no longer an NFL caliber quarterback in big losses to the Panthers and Cards.

It's important not to overadjust for injuries—often backups do a good job and the team overcomes injuries, especially if it is just for a game or two. As I wrote earlier, there is not much difference between the best and worst NFL players. In addition, injuries are generally already factored into the oddsmakers' line. In fact, they are most often overpriced in it!

NFL SUNDAY TICKET

Though getting NFL games on satellite obviously costs money, the expense is well worth it for the coverage of additional games. The networks telecast only about 41 games per season. The NFL Sunday Ticket allows you to view possibly 215 of the 256 regular-season games.

As I wrote earlier, if I could view every game I would do it because I can get much more information actually watching a game than I can by reading highlights of it or viewing highlights on television. Watching a game can help a handicapper make more accurate grades in a team's offensive and defensive performances. If a team has poor passing statistics, you can see whether the cause was strong defensive pressure, good secondary coverage, or the quarterback just missing open receivers. If a team had excellent running stats you can judge for yourself whether they were due more to good running or good blocking.

Other factors too become clear when you watch rather than read about a game—third- down conversions, for example. If a team has done well in that department, you can see if it was because the team often had just a yard or two to go or because they converted lots of dramatic third-and-longs. Often one or two big plays totally turn a game around. Sometimes the play is in the box score, but sometimes it is not. Sometimes after a key play the team that was victimized plays with less spirit. This can be gauged much better by watching the game on television.

When you watch games you should try not to overreact the way that announcers do. Announcers often try to make every drive and every play the key one. Whenever something important happens, the announcers are quick to come up with a statistic that underscores the importance of what happened or how it ties in with other game events that the announcers now consider important.

Try not to get swept up by that hoopla. The announcer is trying to make the game more interesting and exciting. He is not trying to give you information that will help you win a wager.

A problem with reading about games is that reporters are limited in the amount of time they have to report a story and how much room they have to say it. Reporters all work on deadlines, which can be as early as two hours after a game is finished. A good part of that time is spent interviewing players and getting to the interview itself. Reporters, by virtue of the scarcity of time, must cut corners in reporting a game.

There is no way that every drive can be covered, so they concentrate on the scoring and highlight drives. But sometimes non-scoring drives can show keys to a game—especially non-scoring drives after a score. How was the team trying to retaliate stopped? Were they stopped cold or did they advance the ball and get hurt by penalties? This is often left out of the game story.

So, I highly recommend the NFL Sunday Ticket. The knowledge you get about the games can pay for the cost many times over.

HAVING ACCESS TO GOOD PLACES TO BET

Nothing in this book can be turned into financial gain unless you have places to bet. For many, this might be the hardest part about overcoming the NFL point spread. The Internet is providing a number of reliable sports book options that give access to early betting numbers (Olympic, CRIS, and Canbet are currently among the best), but in some states wagering via the Internet is illegal. Not having access to Las Vegas and early betting numbers makes beating the odds much more difficult.

If you are used to dealing with neighborhood ("outlaw") bookies, you are often dealing with someone who will throw out a long-term winner. Many even throw out bettors merely for shopping for the best price. I know one bookmaker who will get rid of a bettor if (s)he bets early and gets a better price than the later price three times in a row! He'll get rid of this bettor even if (s)he loses!

If your neighborhood book doesn't give you access to early—Sunday night and Monday morning—lines, he is costing you money. In addition, if you are relying on one book and don't have access to a variety of late closing lines, it is also costing you money. Most amateur bettors put up with this nonsense. If you are serious about betting and want to win, don't.

For myself, I use reputable and carefully selected Internet and offshore books, as well as a number of money movers who have access to both early and late lines. Some people give me access to great numbers in return for me helping them get winners. I no longer deal with outlaw offices.

In the 2004 season, there were 14 games in which shopping around made a difference in the outcome for a bettor. With 14 games representing 5.24 percent of the

267 total games, just having good access to numbers and using it to shop wisely can make the difference in whether or not you overcome the 11 to 10 odds.

Assuming now that you have access to good early and late numbers, you should approach weekly betting in two sessions.

The first session takes place very early in the week (Sunday night and mostly Monday). In this session, you should wager on games that meet one or both of two criteria: first, if you think the line will move in an unfavorable direction, and second, if you think the oddsmakers have made a mistake in the line. Then you want to capitalize before the whole betting world gets in on the bargain.

The second betting session takes place late in the week—usually on Sunday morning. You usually wait until late on those bets on which you are going against public opinion, when you think public opinion will move the line and make the side you like a better value. In these later bets it shouldn't make any difference to you who has made the line move, whether it is the "smart money" or "the public" (AKA the suckers). You should still step up if you are confident through your handicapping that you have the edge.

Let's look at some examples of early and late betting from the 2002 season.

In Week 8, the Lions visited the Bills. With the Bills coming from a big win at Miami and with a key game against the Patriots (the Drew Bledsoe Revenge Game) up next, a Bills letdown seemed likely. Early in the week, there were 7 1/2's around on the Bills. With my power rating at six for the Bills, the Lions had value at plus 7 1/2. I took it and the line then went down to and closed at seven. The Bills won by exactly seven points, 24-17. Without early access I would have missed out on a winning bet.

In Week 3, the Redskins visited the 49ers. As an odd-smaker, I made the game 8 1/2 for the 49ers, which was also my power rating on the game. The first number had the 49ers favored by seven. One of my main models—the loser off a rout Monday night loss—favored the Redskins. However, I couldn't bet the early number since it went against both my power rating and oddsmaker lines.

A key reason to wait if one wanted to bet the Redskins in this game was that they had run up the score in a 38-7 exhibition win over the 49ers. Professional and wise guy bettors, knowing this, figured to push the line up on the 49ers. And they did. The line reached 10 shortly before game-time. I actually was able to get plus 10 1/2. The game fell ten as the 49ers won, 20-10. By having late access and not betting early, I was able to get a win instead of a loss.

Then there are the games you can win no matter which side you like—as long as you have good betting access. One such game was the 2002 49ers-Giants game in Week 1. The early line had the 49ers favored by 2 1/2 over the home Giants. Public and pro money poured in on the 49ers. The line quickly went to three and then to four and beyond that in places.

The 49ers won the game by three points, 16-13. Early bettors could have won on the 49ers giving 2 1/2 and late bettors could have gotten well over three on the Giants. Such a result is called a middle: a bettor's best friend and a bookie's worst nightmare. However, once again, having access to varied lines was key.

In general, I feel that the early-week line is more vulnerable than the late-week line because of the built-in vulnerability of linesmaking. Linesmakers have to try to feel the pulse of the betting public and anticipate what bettors are going to do. There is no way that linesmakers can be correct about this every time—just wait until you make your own lines! When the linesmakers are wrong in anticipating the public in the early line, it is time to bet and bet quickly. Later in the week, the line often reflects the changes made in it by professional bettors. The line then gets less action. Thus, I make and will probably continue to make the majority of my bets in the early part of the week.

Do I ever misread what a line is going to do? Do I sometimes bet early and later regret it because I could have gotten a better line?

Sure—but not often. You'll be surprised how quickly your expertise grows on predicting the movement of the line.

MONEY MANAGEMENT: UNDERSTANDING THE LONG HAUL

By now you should understand that you won't win every game you bet; you won't win every week; you won't make money every month; and you won't even be able to win money every season. Very few people understand what the long haul of betting the NFL means, so let's look at it from a statistical point of view.

A good NFL handicapper will win between 55 and 60 percent of his bets over a long period of time. Over a short span almost any results are possible. I learned that once again in the 2002 season where I personally ended up the season about 3 1/2 bets behind. I won in the next two seasons, though.

Before you seriously bet the NFL, you should make sure you understand standard deviation. There are excellent books on the mathematics of gambling available, so I am not going to go into any great detail here. Suffice it to say that, in NFL wagering, if it were a given that someone would win 60 percent of his bets, one standard deviation for one hundred wagers would be 4.9 games.

Thus, roughly speaking, he would win between 55 and 65 bets out of a hundred wagers 68.26 percent of the time. He would win between 50 and 70 bets (within two standard deviations) 95.44 percent of the time, and he would win better than 70 of a hundred bets 2.28 percent of the time and win fewer than 50 bets 2.28 percent of the time. Since a bettor needs to win approximately 53 bets out of a hundred to beat the 11 to 10, the sixty percent bettor can expect to fail in this goal 5.48 percent of the time.

And one hundred bets is actually *more* than a season's worth of betting for most good handicappers. As for people who don't have access to more vulnerable early numbers, 100 bets is more like two seasons' worth of NFL wagering. And 60 percent might be stretching what most handicappers can hit over the long haul.

Now let's look at the short run. Many times media outlets get excited when someone wins something like 15 of 20 bets. Assuming that the expected win rate for media people against the point spread is 50 percent—and that might be stretching it!—their "win streak" will happen about once every 55 trials. With all of the thousands of people who make selections in the media, this will happen several times a year. But over a short run—like twenty selections—it is virtually meaningless. There is no way of knowing that someone who has had a run like this won't "revert to form" and win ten or fewer bets out of his next twenty.

But even for the most competent handicappers, losing seasons are an inevitable fact of life in wagering on the NFL. The best handicapper in the universe will lose more than one season in twenty. An average winning NFL handicapper will probably lose one season in three or four.

As for myself, in a typical season I will wager on close to 100 NFL games. I can bet that many since I have excellent access to numbers—numbers the average winning bettor sometimes doesn't get. My lifetime win rate in pro football, including my early years, is approximately 57 percent; in 2003 and 2004 combined it was about 61 percent. At this point I feel I am more than justified in expecting a win rate of 57 percent. That still leaves me at roughly an 18 percent chance in any given season of losing money in a full season for all my work—due solely to standard deviation. Again, this sad fate befell me in 2002.

As for a beginning handicapper, let's say you work hard and within a few years are hitting a win rate of roughly 56 percent. Over the long haul, at 80 bets per season, that win rate will average out to 45 winners and 35 losers a year. I am assuming no ties for this example. If you win fewer than 42 of the 80 bets you will lose money against the 11 to 10. This will happen about 20 percent of the time (the number of times you can expect to fall 4/5 of a standard deviation or more south of expectations). That means you will have a losing season just about one of every five seasons—and this with a better than 56 percent chance of winning every bet! Once every 43 seasons you can expect to go 36 and 44 or worse, meaning that you will end up over 12 bets behind, assuming all bets are for the same amount.

But how do you even know in your early years what your skill level really is? Let's look at my own 1996 and 1997 seasons. In 1996, I went 50-30-4. In 1997, I ended up 55-45-2. Thus in 1996 I won over 62 percent of my wagers while in 1997 I won only 55 percent. If those were your first two years, would you consider yourself a 62 percent winner or a 55 percent winner or something in between? If your third year you hit only 50 percent, would that be due to standard deviation or a lower skill level than you'd hoped for?

To top it off, even the most talented handicappers will never be machines. There will be times when you are just off in evaluating teams. At times like this, your power ratings will be off and your record will suffer. Despite a winning past record, you may not really be a favorite on your current bets.

What is the long haul in NFL betting? How many games must be bet on before a skilled handicapper can count on being ahead even if he's had a pretty rotten run of luck (say, two standard deviations south of expectation)?

If you win 55 percent of the time, the magic number is about 1,500 bets. Or probably close to twenty years of betting the NFL (and you'd *still* have over a 2 percent chance of being in the red). If you can hit 57 percent, the time needed is 500 bets or about seven seasons. If you can hit the magic 60 percent, the time needed is about 180 bets or about two seasons.

Thus betting the NFL is a long-time project in terms of profit. You have to be heavily fortified in bankroll and perseverance. You cannot overreact to the short-term slumps that will inevitably occur.

18

Hard Work:
A Week in the Life
of a Professional
Sports Bettor

As you may have gathered by now, handicapping and betting the NFL are hard work. Let me describe a typical week during the football season.

During the afternoon on Sunday, I watch the NFL games on my satellite dish and regular television. I try to follow about six games closely, and read about the others later. Usually I try to watch games I have *not* bet, because I tend to have a more realistic and less emotional view of them than on ones where I have a financial interest. I switch to the games I wagered on in the last half hour, while keeping an eye on the other games I've been watching, especially if they are close.

Between seven and eight o'clock Eastern time, I have SportsCenter of ESPN on my television as I update scores and statistics in my records. I watch the highlights on SportsCenter to get a feel for the ebb and flow of the day's games, especially the ones I didn't watch.

At 8:30 p.m. (Eastern time) I tune into the Sunday night game. I miss the beginning as I get box score print-outs from my computer from the early games. At around ten o'clock (at halftime of the Sunday night game) I get box scores from the later games. I watch the Sunday night game as I examine the box scores and try to find out what the real story of each game was. I rate each team on how it did in terms of running and passing the ball, as well as how it defended in those areas.

After I finish that, I make any adjustments that seem called for on each team's power ratings. I also adjust each team's home and road point-rating at this time.

When I finish adjusting all my ratings, I then play odds-maker. Like the crew at Las Vegas Sports Consultants and the crews at the offshore books, I try to make numbers on each of the following week's games according to what I believe the fair market should be—in other words, what I think will equally divide the betting public. After doing this, I make power ratings for each game that are meant to reflect the *actual* differences in strength and skill between the teams. After coming up with these power ratings, I add or subtract points based on my various emotional models. My power ratings can turn out very similar to or very different from what I made the game as an oddsmaker.

By around 2:00 a.m. I have finished my numbers and ratings and am ready to check out the early Vegas lines. I compare these early lines with my own numbers and power ratings and review any differences. A significant difference between the early Vegas line on a game and my own ratings and numbers may mean there is value in the line and that the game is a possible bet for me.

HARD WORK

I then look for various conditions that I seek in games. These may be different at different times of the season. If a team falls into these parameters and the Vegas line has value, it means I will probably want to bet that game. By late Sunday or early Monday morning I have a rough idea how my next week's betting is shaping up. Occasionally by Sunday night I am making my first bets.

After a few hours' sleep I get the Monday morning papers. I read papers from around the country on my computer during the day to try to get a better feel for the ebb and flow of the previous day's games. I also try to find out about key injuries, though as time goes on I am less and less concerned about injuries except to the top superstars. Occasionally I find something that makes me alter my Sunday night power ratings.

By midday I am ready to bet on some more games. I get prices from my money movers and sports books and bet the games where I think the current price will soon disappear. On other games I wait for a better price as the week goes on.

By the time I am finished with Monday's research, it is just about time for the Monday night game. Most of the time I have passed on this game as a betting proposition, as I pass on the majority of games on the card. Other times I have bet this game earlier in the week. Sometimes I am waiting until the last moment to bet this game if I think the price may move more in my direction.

Before watching the Monday night game I also get updated lines for next week. The lines on late Monday are what I consider "settled lines," and they are lines that I *never* go against. For instance, if the Steelers are 9 1/2 point favorites over the Bengals on late Monday, I will never give more than 9 1/2 on the Steelers or take less than 9 1/2 on the Bengals.

As I watch the Monday night game I clip box scores and *USA Today's* scoring summaries from the previous day's games into a notebook. These can be helpful later when I'm looking for information about past games, which I sometimes do when handicapping.

At the end of the game I update my power ratings of the two teams that played and handicap their games for the upcoming week. Monday night results can be very important in my handicapping. Often these games give the betting public an inaccurate view of the teams since the extra exposure of a Monday night game may make teams perform better or worse than they really are. Since oddsmakers must adjust the week's lines to allow for this public perception, a smart handicapper can often get more points or give fewer than what the teams really merit.

On Tuesday morning, I get another line update—especially on the teams that played on Monday night. Sometimes I will bet a game then, particularly the next game of one of the teams that played on Monday night. During the rest of the week, I continue to get line updates every day. I keep in tune with any games I still want to bet and stay aware of any moves in the line on those games. If I think a price will disappear because of some money coming in on the side I like, I make my bet as soon as possible. Otherwise, I wait.

I also continue to read what I can about injuries. I give *Pro Football Weekly* (PFW) a good read to keep up with roster changes and team depth charts. These charts tell me how important injuries really are.

All during the week I keep in touch with my clients, keeping them apprised of current news and lines and advising them when and where to bet.

Usually lines don't move much between Monday night and Sunday. But sometimes big betting action suddenly does come in on Sunday. Occasionally this pushes a game out of line enough that I will want to bet the *other* side. I am in touch with my movers on Sunday morning and make any final bets before the games.

Virtually all of the successful sports bettors I know have similar work habits. We don't just roll out of bed and make bets. We don't go by information on "fixed" games or other "inside information." The information I use is available to anyone who makes the effort to get it. If you want to profit from handicapping the NFL, you will have to make a similar effort.

How do you beat the sports books betting the NFL? By perfecting your handicapping until you have achieved a solid win rate, managing your bankroll so that you don't go broke on bad luck before you have a chance to get to your winning bets, and building your bankroll by betting for maximum return.

What is a good money management plan for betting pro football? Some suggest using the Kelly Criterion. In using Kelly, a bettor bets the same percentage of his bankroll as what he perceives his percentage edge to be in every game. For example, if a bettor felt that he could expect to win 60 percent of his bets, he would bet 16 percent of his bankroll on a game.

This percentage is gotten by subtracting 40 percent from 60 percent and then subtracting an additional four percent due to the cost of the vig. The resulting percentage is a 16 percent edge.

I personally don't agree with full Kelly betting because, unlike in a game like blackjack where one can gauge close to an exact edge or disadvantage, I don't feel a sports handicapper can accurately gauge a consistent edge in wagering on NFL games. Sometimes a handicapper will be in a slump and simply be off in his evaluations of teams. Then he may actually be betting at a disadvantage. The emotional pressure of even a brief slump with huge full Kelly bets can cause huge anguish for a bettor, which, in turn, because of its added distraction, will probably have negative effects on his handicapping.

I feel that a much sounder approach is to make a basic bet of 2 percent of your bankroll on NFL wagers. Games that you feel are strong plays can be bet up to 2 1/2 percent of your bankroll; games that are less certain deserve a backing of 1 1/2 percent of your bankroll. As a handicapper's bankroll goes up or down, he should make adjustments in the amounts bet. A bettor can also bet a little bit more on a game if the line goes the other way and a key number is hit. This amount should be about 10 percent of the original bet. For example, in the 2003 season in Week 9, I took 3 on the Jets against the Giants. On Sunday morning right before the game, there were some 3 1/2's around. I bet a little more on the Jets taking 3 1/2. Too bad I didn't make my whole bet at plus 3 1/2 since the Giants won by 3 (31-28) in overtime.

Let's say a bettor has a $10,000 starting bankroll for betting the NFL. I'd recommend a basic bet of $200—2 percent of his bankroll—a game. Large bets could be $250 a game and small bets $150 a game. If his bankroll grows to $11,000, the basic bet should be increased to $220 a game. If his bankroll goes down to $9,000, the basic bet should be cut back to $180 a game.

My approach may sound conservative, but it will keep a bettor around for the long run. I still well remember going broke in my early NFL betting days when I sometimes bet as much as 10 percent of my bankroll on games. In the 1979 NFL season I went broke with such foolhardy betting. I'll never forget one week where I went 0-5 on my bets and 9-0 in the games I didn't bet! I want my readers to avoid that sad fate.

In a good season, using the above methods, a winning handicapper can increase his bankroll by 25 percent in a typical five-month NFL season. That is the equivalent of an over 50 percent annual return on investment. That is a better return than you'll get in a bank, money market account, or even, historically, in the stock market.

To win betting pro football, start by perfecting your handicapping. If you follow the advice I have given in this book, the odds are that you, too, will be a long-term winner betting the NFL. I would give *over* 11 to 10 odds on that!

19

Following a Team Through the Year

In this chapter I follow the Buffalo Bills through the 2004 season to show how I made and changed their number and letter power ratings from week to week.

The Bills ended the 2003 season with a C- letter power rating. I felt that they were an underrated team going into 2004. Their defense was strong since it had given up just thirty touchdowns in 2003, despite getting just eighteen takeaways. On offense, the additions of a healthy Willis McGahee, a running back injured just about all of 2003, and rookie wide receiver Lee Evans would make their offense much more powerful. I thus started the Bills with a letter power rating of C+. I projected the Bills to win 8.68 games when I played out the season mathematically, so I started them with a number power rating of 22.

GAME 1
VERSUS JACKSONVILLE
JAGUARS (C+)

I saw this as an equal matchup. The Jaguars letter power rating was also C+ and their number power rating was—like the Bills—22. Since the Bills were at home and since home edge—and road disadvantage—is 2 1/2 points for the first four games, the Bills were 2 1/2 point favorites in both letter and number power rating. Since the line was 3 for the Bills all week, there was really no power rating edge for either club.

The Bills lost, 13-10, on a Jaguar touchdown pass on the last play of the game. However, I noted that the two Bill scores were set up on interception returns to the Jaguar 18 and 3 yard lines. The Jaguars outplayed the Bills by more than the score indicated. I thus moved the Bills letter power rating down to C from C+. Since the Bills lost on the number power rating by 5 1/2 points, I moved their number power rating down to 21—actually 21 1/2, since 21 1/2 is the average of 22, the starting number power rating, and 21.

GAME 2
AT OAKLAND RAIDERS (C)

The Bills and Raiders were both at C in my letter power ratings. The Bills were at 21 1/2 in my number power ratings, while the Raiders were at 19. There were two emotional situations with the Raiders that cancelled each other out. They were coming off of a phony loss (plus 1/2 point), but also had a big Sunday night revenge game with Tampa Bay, the team to which they'd lost the Super Bowl after the 2002 season, coming up next (minus 1/2 point). The Raiders were favored by 2 1/2 points in my letter power rating, while the number power rating came up Pick. The Bills had a 2 1/2 point edge that was negated by the Raiders' 2 1/2 point home edge. Combining the two power ratings, with the letter power rating getting 3/4 weight, made the Raiders two point favorites in my final power ratings. The Raiders closed as three point favorites, which meant that there was an edge for the Bills in my power ratings.

The Bills lost, 13-10. Their offense continued to struggle, scoring their one touchdown late versus a prevent defense. The Bills' defense continued to play well, but their offense was still performing below my expectations.

The Bills letter (C) and number power rating (21.5) stayed the same, since they lost to the number power rating by just three points.

GAME 3
VERSUS NEW ENGLAND
PATRIOTS (B)

With a line of plus 5 1/2 and 6 around early, I felt that the Bills were being underpriced in this game. Eventually the game closed at 4 1/2. However, there were no major models of mine that favored them so I passed the bet.

With the Patriots (B) on the road, they were three point favorites over the Bills in the letter power rating (remember the jump from B- to B is 2 1/2 points). The Patriots number power rating was 29 (versus the Bills 21 1/2) and with the 7 1/2 point edge minus the Bills 2 1/2 point home field edge, the Patriots had a five point number power rating edge. There were no changes in the power ratings due to emotional edges or disadvantages. The total power rating was 3 1/2 for the Patriots.

The Bills offense did better in this game, scoring 17 points, though one touchdown was on a kickoff return. The Bills were in the game right until the end. Very late, the Bills were trailing 24-17 and were about to tie the Patriots from inside their 20. Then quarterback Drew Bledsoe was sacked and lost a fumble that was returned for a touchdown, making the final score 31-17.

Since the final score was misleading and because the Bills played the defending champions tough, I kept their letter power rating at C. Because the Bills lost to the number power rating by 8 1/2 points, I lowered their number power rating down to 20—actually 21 after averaging the adjusted number with the starting number.

GAME 4
AT NEW YORK JETS (C)

Since the Jets were 3-0 and the Bills were 0-3, the early line on this game was 7. However, I saw this as an even game and bet the Bills since I had a four point plus power rating edge. The emotional situations evened themselves out with the Jets coming off a phony win (minus 1/2 point), while the Bills were poor recently (2-6-3 to the number) off losses (minus 1/2 point).

The Jets were 2 1/2 point favorites in my letter power ratings. Both teams were C clubs and the Jets had a 2 1/2 point edge being at home. The Jets had a 3 1/2 point edge in my number power ratings, with a number power rating of 22 plus a 2 1/2 point home edge versus the Bills' 21. The total power rating favored the Jets by 2 1/2. Though the line went down to 6 1/2, the Bills still had a significant edge in the power ratings in this game.

The Jets won the game, 16-14. I won my bet, but I wasn't at all convinced I had bet the right side in the Bills. The Jets got off to a 13-0 lead but twice lost turnovers deep in Bills' territory and also missed a 29-yard field goal. The Jets thus could have been ahead by much more. The Bills then scored two quick touchdowns to go up, 14-13. The Jets answered with a 60-yard field goal drive that won the game. The Jets had the following stat edges: 1) 24-17 in first downs, 2) 383-252 in yards, 3) 6.8-5.2 yards per pass attempt, 4) 33 1/2-26 1/2 in time of possession. The Jets also converted eight of 14 third downs.

Because of the Jets' control of the game, I moved the Bills down to C- in my letter power ratings. The Bills' number power rating stayed the same since they actually covered the number power rating (plus 3 1/2) by 1 1/2 points.

GAME 5
VERSUS MIAMI DOLPHINS (D+)

The Bills' home field edge now was just 1 1/2 points, since they had lost points on their number power rating at home for two straight games. Combined with the Dolphins' road disadvantage (2 1/2 points), the Bills' home edge in this game was two points. Both teams were coming off two straight fairly strong emotional efforts (minus 1/2 point for both) and the Dolphins were coming off a phony loss (plus 1/2 point). This gave the Dolphins a half-point emotional edge. The Bills' letter power rating was three over the Dolphins (1 1/2 point edge, plus two points at home, minus 1/2 point Dolphin emotional edge). The Bills had a number power rating of 21, while the Dolphins' was 18. The Bills' number power rating edge in this game was 4 1/2 points. The total power rating favored the Bills by 3 1/2 points. Being able to take plus 7 on the Dolphins in this game made it a bet for me. The game featured heavy betting on the Dolphins and the game closed at 4 1/2.

The Bills won their first game of the year, 20-13. The offense gained 341 yards against a good Dolphin defense. Very late, the Bills could have added to their lead but instead ran out the clock inside the Dolphin 10. The game really wasn't as close as the score indicated.

Off this win, I moved the Bills up to C in my letter power ratings. Since the Bills covered the number power rating by just 2 1/2 points, it stayed the same at 21. Their home field edge also stayed at 1 1/2 points.

GAME 6
AT BALTIMORE RAVENS (C+)

The Bills lost one point in the power ratings this week since they were coming off three straight fairly strong emotional efforts (minus 1/2 point) and the Ravens were coming off a bye (plus 1/2 point for the Ravens).

The Ravens had a 2 1/2 point home edge in this game. With a point added to the power rating for the Ravens, they had a five point edge in the letter power ratings. With a number power rating of 23, the Ravens were two points better than the Bills, who were at 21. The letter power rating for the Ravens was 5 1/2 and the total power rating was 5. This game opened at 5 1/2 for the Ravens and closed at 4 1/2. There was little edge in the power ratings in this game.

The Bills had five turnovers in the game, which cost them dearly in a 20-6 loss. Two turnovers led to 10 Raven points and another was an interception in the Raven endzone as the Bills were about to score a touchdown. The Bills had a 270-160 yardage edge in the game and had a 4.6-2.6 yards per pass attempt edge. Thus the Bills were much better in this game than the final score indicated.

Since the Bills' offense continued to struggle, I kept them at C in my letter power ratings. Since they lost on the number power rating by 8 1/2 points, the Bills dropped to 20 1/2 in the number power ratings.

GAME 7
VERSUS ARIZONA CARDINALS (D+)

I thought that the line on this game would favor the Bills by 5. I almost gave the early 2 1/2 since my odds-maker line and power ratings (see below) strongly favored the Bills. However, since the Bills seemed out of contention, I passed the game. The game eventually closed 4 1/2 for the Bills.

Since the Bills had just a 1 1/2 point edge at home and the Cards had a 2 1/2 point road disadvantage, the Bills had a two point home edge. The Bills had a one point edge in my emotional models. The Cards were coming off a monster emotional effort in a win over the rival Seahawks (minus 1 point). The Bills were coming off a phony loss (plus 1/2 point), though they also had a big game against divisional rival New York next week (minus 1/2 point).

Overall, the Bills had a six point edge in the letter power ratings (three points better than Cards, plus two points at home, plus one point emotional edge), and with the Cards being at 15 1/2 in the number power ratings (versus Bills 20 1/2), the Bills had an eight point edge in the number power ratings. Their overall power rating edge was 6 1/2—a big power rating edge against the point spread.

The Bills won in a rout, 38-14. However, they won mostly because of good field position and because punt returns consistently gave them a short field to work on. The Bills gained just 209 yards in the game and were out-first-downed, 19-11.

I thus kept the Bills at C in the letter power ratings. Since the Bills covered the number power rating by 16 points, they moved up the maximum of three points in them, and actually went from 20 1/2 to 22.

GAME 8
VERSUS NEW YORK JETS (C+)

The Bills now had a 2 1/2 point home edge, but the Jets had just 1/2 point disadvantage on the road; thus the Bills' home edge in this game was just 1 1/2 points.

The Bills had significant emotional edges in this game. First, the Jets were coming off a Monday night rout win (minus 1/2 point). Second, the Jets had been emotionally up for two straight weeks (minus 1/2 point). Third, the Jets were 0-2-1 to the number after their last three wins (minus 1/2 point).

The Bills were 1 1/2 point favorites in the letter power rating (Jets 1 1/2 points better, minus 1 1/2 points Bills' home edge, minus 1 1/2 points Bills' emotional edges). The Jets were 24 in the number power ratings, while the Bills were at 22. That gave the Bills a one point edge in the number power ratings and a 1 1/2 point edge in the total power ratings. Most bettors were able to get three points on the home Bills, which gave them huge value considering the power ratings. I was able to take 3 1/2 on the Bills in my bet on the game.

The Bills were impressive, winning with a score of 22-17. They overcame a 7-10 deficit with a 72-yard field goal drive. They then took the lead for good with a 77-yard touchdown drive. The defense knocked Jets quarterback Chad Pennington from the game with a shoulder injury.

I still kept the Bills at C in my letter power ratings. I wasn't really sold on their offense. Since the Bills covered the number power rating by just four points, their number power rating stayed the same at 22.

GAME 9
AT NEW ENGLAND PATRIOTS (B)

There were no emotional edges in this game. Both teams were coming off phony wins. While the Bills wanted revenge, I wasn't at all sure they could get it against a team in the Patriots' class.

With the Patriots having a 2 1/2 point edge at home and the Bills having a 2 1/2 point road disadvantage, the Pats' overall home edge was 2 1/2 points. The letter power rating favored the Patriots by 8 (5 1/2 points the better team plus 2 1/2 points at home). In number power ratings, the Patriots were at 29 while the Bills were at 22, which gave the Patriots a 9 1/2 point edge in number power rating. The overall power rating edge for the Patriots was 8 1/2 points. The game opened at 8 1/2 for the Patriots and a flood of Bills money pushed the line down to 7. The Patriots had some value on the closing point spread.

The Patriots dominated the Bills, winning 29-6. The score would have been much worse if the Patriots didn't have to settle for five field goals. The Bills' only score came on a punt return. The Patriots had the following stat edges: 1) 25-8 in first downs, 2) 428-125 in yards, 3) 82-41 in plays run, 4) 41 1/2-18 1/2 in possession. This game showed that the Bills were not ready to challenge an elite team, especially on the road.

Since it was an elite team the Bills lost to and since the rout wasn't at all unexpected by me, I kept the Bills at C in my letter power ratings. In number power ratings, the Bills lost by 14 1/2 points and sank to 20 (actually 21).

GAME 10
VERSUS ST. LOUIS RAMS (C+)

The Bills had an overall 2 1/2 point edge for being at home. They had a 2 1/2 point home edge while the Rams had a 2 1/2 point road disadvantage. The Bills had a one point emotional edge in the power ratings. They had lost a rout game last week to the Patriots and were 2-0-1 to the number after their last three rout losses. The Rams were coming off a huge emotional effort last week in their win over the Seahawks in a battle for first in the NFC West (minus 1 point), though the Bills had been emotionally up the last two weeks (minus 1/2 point). The Bills had a two point edge in the letter power ratings (minus 1 1/2 points, plus 2 1/2 for being at home, plus 1 point emotional edge).

In number power ratings, the Bills were at 21 while the Rams were at 20, giving the Bills a 4 1/2 point edge in them. The overall power rating edge favored the Bills by 2 1/2. Someone gave me the Rams minus 3 on an outlaw line and I bet the Bills at plus 3 right away. At plus anything, the Bills had value (there was plus 1 and plus 1 1/2 around for most bettors). The Bills were bet heavily late and closed as two point favorites, giving them a very slight edge in the power ratings on the closing line.

The Bills overcame an early 0-10 deficit and won going away, 37-17. In the third quarter, which opened with the game tied at 17, the Bills used two long punt returns to break the game open. One was returned for a touchdown and the other to the Ram 5, from which the Bills scored another touchdown. The Bills' offense averaged seven yards per pass attempt. Still doubtful, I kept the Bills at C in my letter power ratings, probably in error, as the offense was now finally starting to click. In the number power rating, the Bills rose up to 23 (actually 22 1/2), having covered the number power rating by 15 1/2 points.

GAME 11
AT SEATTLE SEAHAWKS (C+)

With the Bills' road disadvantage now at 3 1/2 points and the Seahawks' home edge at 2 1/2 points, the Bills lost three points for being on the road. There were no emotional edges in this game. The Seahawks were 4 1/2 point favorites in the letter power rating. In number power ratings, the Seahawks were two points ahead of the Bills (24 1/2 to 22 1/2), which gave them a five point number power rating edge. The Seahawks' overall power rating edge was 4 1/2 points. The Seahawks went off as four point favorites in this game, which I thought was a very cheap price. My oddsmaker line was seven for the Seahawks. I was tempted to bet them but had no emotional edges—plus, I hate betting favorites.

I would have lost badly if I had bet the Seahawks. The Bills had their first road win of the year in a 38-9 rout win. They won easily despite having three interceptions. The Bills punted just once in the game, and gained 434 yards. They averaged 7.3 yards per pass attempt. The game was never close after the Bills led 17-3 at halftime.

Probably one week too late, I pushed the Bills up to C+ in my letter power ratings. Covering the number power rating by an astounding 34 points pushed the Bills up to 26 (actually 24) in number power rating. They would now be may due down in their next game.

GAME 12
AT MIAMI DOLPHINS (D+)

The Bills had just a 1 1/2 point disadvantage on the road since the Dolphins' home edge was a mere 1/2 point, while the Bills' road disadvantage was 2 1/2 points. The Bills had a point disadvantage in emotional factors in this game. They were coming off a sloppy win (three turnovers in win last week—minus 1/2 point), plus had scored 30 plus points in two straight wins (minus 1/2 point).

The Bills were two point favorites in my letter power ratings (4 1/2 points better, minus 1 1/2 being on road, minus 1 point emotion versus). In number power ratings, the Bills were at 24 while the Dolphins were at 17 1/2. This gave the Bills a four point edge in number power ratings. In overall power ratings, the Bills had a 2 1/2 point edge. With the line closing as high as six (consensus closing line was five for the Bills), I strongly considered betting the Dolphins because of their strong value. However, the Dolphins were without their leading tackler, Zach Thomas. I remembered the Dolphins being routed without him in Tennessee last year, 31-7, in a game I lost. I decided to pass the game.

The Bills won and covered in a wild game, 42-32. They trailed 14-24 in the second quarter and came back to win and cover. Seven takeaways, three of which resulted in touchdowns, including a spread-clinching interception return for a touchdown, plus a kickoff return for a touchdown, greatly helped the Bills. The Bills again did well passing, getting 7.8 yards per pass attempt.

I kept the Bills at C+ in my letter power ratings. Since they covered the number power rating by six points, they moved up to 27 (24 1/2) there. Next week, the Bills would be a fresh due down.

GAME 13
VERSUS CLEVELAND BROWNS (D)

The Bills had an overall 3 1/2 point edge at home since they had a 2 1/2 point home edge, while the Browns—very poor on the road—had a 4 1/2 point road disadvantage. The emotional edges evened out. The Bills lost 1/2 point since they had scored 30 plus points in three straight wins while the Browns lost 1/2 point since they were 2-6 against the spread after their last eight out-right losses.

The Bills had a 10 1/2 point edge in the letter power ratings (seven points better—remember, the jump from D+ down to D is 2 1/2 points—plus a 3 1/2 point home edge). In number power ratings, the Bills were at 24 1/2, while the Browns were at 18. The Bills had a ten point edge there and the total power rating favored the Bills by 10 1/2. With the line moving late as high as 12 1/2 (the closing line was 11 1/2), I favored the Browns. However, their team seemed in total chaos and their rookie quarter-back, McKown, was incompetent. I am hesitant to bet D or worse teams, so I passed the game.

Good thing I passed as the Bills romped, 37-7. The Bills' defense held the Browns to 17 total yards and they won easily despite three turnovers.

Since I felt that the game said more bad things about the Browns than good things about the Bills, I kept them at C+ in my letter power ratings. Having covered the number power rating by 20 points, the Bills went up to 30 (actually 26) in number power ratings. The next week, the Bills would be a fresh star due down.

GAME 14
AT CINCINNATI BENGALS (C+)

This seemed to be the week to go against the Bills. The Bengals—despite using Jon Kitna at quarterback for an injured Carson Palmer—seemed a decent opponent that could exploit the Bills' weaknesses. I was able to take plus 3 and later plus 3 1/2 on the Bengals, who were the favorites in my power ratings.

The Bengals gained a point in emotional edges. The Bills had scored 30 or more points in wins four straight times (minus 1/2 point), plus the Bengals wanted revenge for last year's loss to the Bills. The Bengals had beaten the

Broncos at home and the Ravens on the road in revenge games this year, two teams at least as good as the Bills, plus the Bengals had gone 8-4 to the number in their last 12 revenge games, so plus 1/2 point for revenge.

The Bengals had a 2 1/2 point edge for being at home (2 1/2 point advantage and 2 1/2 point Bills' road disadvantage). So their letter power rating edge was 3 1/2 points. In number power ratings, the Bills had the edge, 26-21 1/2. The Bills were one point road favorites in number power ratings. In overall power ratings, the Bengals had a 2 1/2 point edge, giving me great value in my bets on them at +3 and +3 1/2. The line closed with the Bills favored by three.

The Bills struggled on offense in this game getting just 212 yards. However, their defense and special teams won the game. Two interceptions set up Bill field goals. Another interception was returned for a touchdown. A blocked punt by the Bills was returned for another touchdown. These 20 points were more than the difference in a 33-17 Bills' win.

I kept the Bills at C+ in my letter power ratings, since I considered their win over the Bengals to be a little bit lucky. In number power ratings, the Bills went up to 33 (27 1/2) since they covered the number power rating by 15 points. The Bills were now a fresh double star due down. At 8-6, the Bills suddenly had slight playoff hopes, though potential tiebreakers hurt their chances. The Bills had seemed totally out of the playoffs when they were 0-4 and later 3-6.

GAME 15
AT SAN FRANCISCO 49ERS (E+)

The Bills were lucky that they would be playing probably the worst team in football this week in the 49ers. Also, the Bills had just a 1 1/2 point road disadvantage

(2 1/2 point road disadvantage combined with 49er 1/2 point home edge) in this game.

The Bills had a 1/2 point edge in emotional models this week. Though they had scored 30 or more points in five straight wins (minus 1/2 point), the Bills were 5-2 against the spread after outright wins this year (plus 1/2 point) and the 49ers were 4-7 to the number after outright losses this year (minus 1/2 point).

The Bills had an 11 point edge in letter power ratings (12 points better, plus 1/2 point emotional edge, minus 1 1/2 road disadvantage). In number power ratings, the Bills had a huge 27 1/2-11 edge over the 49ers, which gave them a 15 1/2 point edge in the number power rating on the game. The Bills' overall power rating edge in this game was 12 points. With the line going between 10 and 11 during the week, the Bills had the value in this game.

The Bills won a laugher over the inept 49ers, 41-7. They scored on seven straight possessions starting in the second quarter. The Bills had a 27-12 edge in first downs, a 441-189 yardage edge, with most of the 49er yards coming in garbage time, and a 35-25 minute edge in possession. The Bills converted nine of 14 third downs.

Because of their great play for several weeks, I now moved the Bills up to B- in my letter power ratings. Since the Bills again easily covered the number power rating (by 18 1/2 points), they moved up three points again, now to 36 (actually 29). The Bills were now a fresh triple star due down. With some teams ahead of them losing, the Bills now actually had a shot at the playoffs. At 9-6, they needed a win in their last game plus a Jets' loss in St. Louis.

GAME 16
VERSUS PITTSBURGH STEELERS
(B, HOLDING OUT SEVERAL STARTERS)

At 14-1, the Steelers had clinched home field advantage in the AFC playoffs. The Bills were fighting for their playoff lives. Even with this huge edge, I made the Bills just 6 1/2 point favorites as an oddsmaker. The Steelers had a history of playing well in last-week games when they had little to play for and were assured of the playoffs.

I gave the Bills a huge six point edge in emotional points. The Steelers had no incentive (minus 3 points) and their great rookie quarterback, Ben Roethisberger, wouldn't play (minus 2 1/2 points). The Bills also were in a must-win game (plus 1 point). The Bills had scored 30 or more points in six straight wins (minus 1/2 point), the Steelers were 9-4 to the number after wins this year (plus 1/2 point), though the Bills were 6-2 to the number after outright wins this year (plus 1/2 point). The Bills overall home edge was 2 1/2 points (2 1/2 point home advantage and Steelers 2 1/2 point road disadvantage).

The Bills had a six point edge in letter power ratings (an even plus six points due to emotional edges). In number power ratings, the Steelers were at 26 1/2, while the Bills were at 29. Overall, the Bills had an 11 point edge in number power ratings. The total power rating edge for the Bills was seven points.

The line opened at nine for the Bills, went as high as ten, and closed at 9 1/2. I felt that I had given the Bills every benefit of the doubt in terms of emotional edges, and that they were way overpriced in this game. I strongly considered betting the Steelers, but passed since this game was truly nothing but an exhibition game for them, though I was aware that the Steelers never mailed in games the last game of the season.

I regretted not betting the Steelers. They defeated the Bills, 29-24 and knocked them out of the playoffs. The Bills would have made the playoffs had they won, since the Jets lost in St. Louis, 32-29. The Steeler defense played well and let the Bills convert just two of 12 third downs.

I made the Bills' final letter power rating B-. Since they lost to the number power rating by 16 points, the Bills went down to 33 (actually 27 1/2) in number power rating to end the season.

The Bills were underrated the first part of the season by the linesmakers. Their strong defense made them better than the public realized. Later in the season, the Bills improved, going from C- to B- in my letter power ratings. However, like most teams that seem great on offense, the Bills became overrated the last few games of the season, though maybe not against the pathetic 49ers, and this overpricing led to a spread loss to the Steelers, a team considerably better than the Bills.

With a new quarterback in J.P. Losman, the Bills may not be as overpriced as they might have been if Drew Bledsoe had stayed on. The Bills defense figures to be strong. This is the kind of situation that makes a team a good bet early the next season.

In summary, with power ratings, it's important to try to be objective in observing each game result and comparing that result to other games the team has played. It is almost always a mistake to overreact to one game.

20

A Full Season of NFL Bets

This chapter is a complete account of my betting decisions over an entire NFL season. It includes my pre-season evaluations of each team and my starting power ratings on them.

It is not meant to be a section of the book you plow straight through on your first reading. Instead, it is the kind of material you may want to return to later, as you work through making lines and adjustments in your power ratings.

In each week, I show my betting models at work. The account covers each game I bet and why; any errors I made in betting and timing (since this is an honest account); and other games I passed as betting propositions, as well as my reasons for passing.

2004 PRE-SEASON EVALUATIONS

I start by examining each team one week before the season begins, listing every starter lost and gained, as well as promising rookies drafted. I also list each player's position. After assigning every team a letter power rating, I use these letter power ratings to play out the season mathematically. I list each result as a money line and decimal number, and after adding up the results for each team, I have projected won-lost records for the whole league. Then, averaging the letter power rating with the won-lost record, I end up with a starting number power rating for each team. The average number power rating for the league is 21.

NFC East

DALLAS COWBOYS

Gained: Rookies: Julius Jones (RB), Jacob Rogers (OT)
Vets: Keyshawn Johnson (WR), Marcelius Wiley (DE), Eddie George (RB)
Lost: Mario Edwards (CB), Quincy Carter (QB)
Outlook: Cowboys took a step down on offense with Vinny Testaverde replacing Carter at quarterback. Offensive line is a good unit. Defense—with Darren Woodson out early in the year—is missing two starters from last year in the secondary. Front seven on defense is strong. Last year the Cowboys were just plus three (scored three more than they gave up) in touchdowns. Coach Parcells usually does well with teams in his second year, but I doubt he'll have the Cowboys in the playoffs again this season.
Letter Power rating: C
Number power rating: 21
Projected record: 8-8

A FULL SEASON OF NFL BETS

NEW YORK GIANTS

Gained: Rookies: Eli Manning (QB), Chris Snee (G)

Vets: Jeremy Shockey (TE, healthy), Carlos Emmons (LB), Brent Alexander (S), Will Peterson (CB, healthy), Shawn Williams (S, healthy)

Lost: Kerry Collins (QB), Keith Hamilton (DT), Kenny Holmes (DE)

Outlook: Giants not only lost last eight last year, they lost seven of them by double digits. Offensive line is in flux, which won't help new quarterback Kurt Warner, who isn't mobile. Front seven on defense has six new starters. Team will improve as season progresses but will struggle early. Manning should be quarterback later in the year.

Letter Power rating:

D first eight games, D+ second eight games.

Number Power rating: 16

Projected Record: 6-10

PHILADELPHIA EAGLES

Gained: Rookies: Shawn Andrews (G-OT), Matt Ware (S-CB)

Vets: Jermaine Mayberry (G, healthy), Terrell Owens (WR), Jevon Kearse (DE), Brian Dawkins (S, healthy), Derrick Burgess (DE, healthy), Jeremiah Trotter (LB)

Lost: Duce Staley (RB), John Welbourn (G), Bobbie Williams (G), James Thrash (WR), Brandon Whiting (DE), Carlos Emmons (LB), Bobby Taylor (CB), Troy Vincent (CB)

Outlook: Eagles have five new starters on defense, including two new cornerbacks. Defense looks very suspect versus the run as they were last year. Running game on offense also is suspect. Good offensive line, but little depth. Owens is a game-breaking receiver and Donovan McNabb is an elite quarterback who knows how to win. However, losses, especially on defense, make me doubt that the Eagles will again reach Conference Title Game.

Letter Power rating: C+
Number Power rating: 22
Projected Record: 9-7

WASHINGTON REDSKINS

Gained: Rookies: Sean Taylor (S)
Vets: Mark Brunell (QB), Clinton Portis (RB), Cory Raymer (C), James Thrash (WR), Marcus Washington (LB), Shawn Springs (CB)
Lost: Bryan Johnson (RB), Jeremiah Trotter (LB), Champ Bailey (CB), Jon Jansen (OT, injury)
Outlook: Redskins collapsed at end of last year losing ten of last twelve. Coach Joe Gibbs should bring in new and better mentality. Portis is a great running back and will greatly help. Brunell, however, is on last legs at quarterback. The defense has seven new starters and is very suspect against the run. Redskins will improve later in the year as Gibbs' teams tend to do. In 1981, in Gibbs' first year, the Redskins started out 0-5 and went 8-3 the rest of the way.
Letter Power rating: C- first eight games, C second eight games.
Number Power rating: 20.
Projected Record: 8-8.

NFC North

CHICAGO BEARS

Gained: Rookies: Tommie Harris (DT), Terry Johnson (DT), Nathan Vasher (CB)
Vets: Bryan Johnson (RB), Ruben Brown (G), John Tait (OT), Adwade Ogunleye (DE)
Lost: Chris Villarrial (G), Marty Booker (WR)
Outlook: Team has new coach and new defensive system. The offense looks very suspect and lacks playmakers. I

don't really believe in Rex Grossman at quarterback. In-juries in the secondary to start the year hurt the defense. The front seven looks stronger than last year. Defense will have to keep the Bears in the game. Will be a bad bet as favorites. Bears another team that will get better as the year goes on.

Letter Power Rating:
D+ first eight games, C- second eight games.
Number Power Rating: 18
Projected Record: 7-9

DETROIT LIONS

Gained: Rookies: Roy Williams (WR), Kevin Jones (RB), Teddy Lehman (LB)
Vets: Damien Woody (G), Stephen Alexander (TE), Charlie Rigers (WR, healthy), Fernando Bryant (CB)
Lost: Bill Schroeder (WR), Ray Brown (G)
Outlook: Team went 5-3 outright and versus spread at home last year and 0-8 (4-4 versus spread) on the road. Have added promising rookies in Williams and Jones. However, neither showed that much in pre-season. Have new guards on the offensive line. The defensive line is the strength of the defense. Boss Bailey will be missed at linebacker early in the year and secondary has two new starters. Lions will struggle early, but offense will come on later in the year.

Letter Power Rating:
D+ first eight games, C- second eight games.
Number Power rating: 18
Projected Record: 7-9

GREEN BAY PACKERS

Gained: Rookies: Ahmad Carroll (CB), Joey Thomas (CB)
Vets: None significant
Lost: Gilbert Brown (DT), Antwan Edwards (S), Mike McKenzie (CB, holdout)
Outlook: Packers were an excellent plus 22 in touchdowns last year. Brett Favre shows no signs of slowing up at quarterback. Offense looks very strong, though receivers are average. McKenzie's holdout badly hurts secondary. Front seven on defense looks decent.
Letter Power Rating: B-
Number Power Rating: 24
Projected Record: 9-7

MINNESOTA VIKINGS

Gained: Rookies: Kenechi Udeze (DE), Dontarrius Thomas (LB), Darrion Scott (DE), Nat Dorsey (OT)
Vets: Antoine Winfield (CB)
Lost: Greg Biekert (LB)
Outlook: Vikings collapsed at end of last year going 3-7 after a 6-0 start and losing three game lead in division. Team seems eager to make amends. Defense has added three good rookies and seems much stronger than last year. Offense looks very powerful though there is little quality depth on the offensive line. Vikings should win division.
Letter Power Rating: B
Number Power Rating: 26
Projected Record: 10-6

NFC South

ATLANTA FALCONS

Gained: Rookies: DeAngelo Hall (CB), Michael Jenkins (WR)
Vets: Rod Coleman (DT)
Lost: Juran Bolden (CB)
Outlook: Having Michael Vick healthy is the main change from last year. However, the defense is still suspect and will give up a lot of points. In addition, the offense is now going to the West Coast offense, which usually takes a season to learn. Falcons will be overrated all season due to Vick.
Letter Power Rating: C-
Number Power Rating: 20
Projected Record: 8-8

CAROLINA PANTHERS

Gained: Rookies: Chris Gamble (CB), Kerry Colbert (WR)
Vets: Mark Fields (LB, healthy)
Lost: Kevin Donnally (G), Jeno James (G), Greg Favors (LB), Deon Grant (S), Reggie Howard (CB)
Outlook: Panthers' 11-5 record last season was very misleading. They were minus two in touchdowns. Panthers lost lead in fourth quarter seven times last year, which shows that the defense was very overrated. Seven of the eleven wins were by three points or less. Offensive line has been revamped, which will hinder the offense. I am not sold on Jake Delhomme at quarterback. Defense has three new starters in the secondary. Panthers will take a step back this season and probably miss the playoffs. Look to bet against.
Letter Power Rating: C-
Number Power Rating: 20
Projected Record: 8-8

NEW ORLEANS SAINTS

Gained: Rookies: Will Smith (DE), Devery Henderson (WR), Courtney Watson (LB)
Vets: Ernie Conwell (TE, healthy), Brian Young (DT)
Lost: Terrelle Smith (RB), Jerry Fontenot (C)
Outlook: Aaron Brooks' quad injury is the main concern on offense. Outside of that, the offense is very strong. The defense is where the Saints have question marks, especially in the secondary where two starters are in eleventh-plus year. Saints will probably be best as underdogs and bad bets as favorites.
Letter Power Rating: C
Number Power Rating: 21
Projected Record: 9-7

TAMPA BAY BUCCANEERS

Gained: Rookies: Michael Clayton (WR)
Vets: Mike Alstott (RB, healthy), Charlie Garner (RB), Derrick Deese (OT), Ian Gold (LB), Mario Edwards (CB), Brian Kelly (CB, healthy), Tim Brown (WR)
Lost: Keyshawn Johnson (WR), Keenan McCardell (WR, holdout), Warren Sapp (DT), Nate Webster (LB), John Lynch (S), Joe Jurievicus (WR, injured)
Outlook: Bucs were 7-9 last year, but were plus nine in touchdowns. Difficulty of repeating as Super Bowl champs dragged down the Bucs last season. Bucs made a large number of changes. There are three new starters on the offensive line. The wide receivers and running back are also new. The defense lost Sapp and Lynch, but have capable replacements in Ellis Wyms and Jermaine Phillips. The Bucs should be the class of a fairly weak division.
Letter Power Rating: C+
Number Power Rating: 23
Projected Record: 9-7

NFC West

ARIZONA CARDINALS

Gained: Rookies: Larry Fitzgerald (WR), Karlos Dansby (LB), Darnell Dockett (DT-DE), Alex Stepanovich (C)
Vets: Bertrand Berry (DE), Kyle Vanden Bosch (DE, healthy), Duane Starks (CB, healthy)
Lost: Pete Kendell (C), Marcel Shipp (RB, injury), James Hodgins (RB, injury), Dexter Jackson (S, injury)
Outlook: Cards were two different teams last year. At home they were 4-4 (6-2 to the spread) and just minus five touchdowns. On the road they went 0-8 (0-8 to the spread) and were minus 25 in touchdowns. On offense, the Cards have already been crippled with injuries, losing RBs Shipp and Hodgins to injuries for the year and WR Anquan Boldin for half the season. Coach Green is remaking the offensive line. The defense seems in better shape. Berry is a good pass rusher and Starks and Vanden Bosch return from injuries. Like last season, Cards will play better at home.
Letter Power Rating:
E+ first eight games, D- second eight games.
Number Power Rating: 12
Projected Record: 4-12

ST. LOUIS RAMS

Gained: Rookies: Steven Jackson (RB)
Vets: No one significant
Lost: Grant Wistrom (DE), Brian Young (DT), Dave Wohlabaugh (C), Kyle Turley (OT, injury)
Outlook: Rams are a team on the way down. Offensive line is in chaos having lost Wohlabaugh and Turley. The defense gave up under 17 points just once in the last 11 games last season and now have lost two key defensive linemen. Run defense is very suspect. Marc Bulger showed late last year that he was very vulnerable to pressure.
Letter Power Rating: C.
Number Power Rating: 21
Projected Record: 9-7

SAN FRANCISCO 49ERS

Gained: Rookies: Rashaun Woods (WR), Justin Smiley (G), Isaac Sopoaga (DT)
Vets: Brandon Whiting (DE), Eric Johnson (TE, healthy), Jamie Winborn (LB, healthy)
Lost: Jeff Garcia (QB), Garrison Hearst (RB), Derrick Deese (OT), Ron Stone (G), Terrell Owens (WR)
Outlook: 49ers have seven new starters on offense. 49ers lack playmakers among receivers. The defense should be so-so, but they did give up 41 touchdowns last season. 49ers should get better on offense as the year progresses.
Letter Power Rating:
D- first eight games, D second eight games.
Number Power Rating: 14
Projected Record: 5-11

SEATTLE SEAHAWKS

Gained: Rookies: Marcus Tubbs (DT), Michael Boulware (S), Sean Locklear (G)
Vets: Grant Wistrom (DE), Bobby Taylor (CB)

Lost: Randall Godfrey (LB), Shawn Springs (CB)
Outlook: Seahawks won just two of eight on the road last year, but one win was must-win at San Francisco in finale. Offense looks explosive and almost unstoppable. The defense looks a little suspect at linebacker, especially with Chad Brown out early in the year. Seahawks may actually be overpriced early in the season. Still should win division rather easily.
Letter Power Rating: B-
Number Power Rating: 24
Projected Record: 10-6

AFC East

BUFFALO BILLS

Gained: Rookies: Lee Evans (WR), JP Losman (QB)
Vets: Willis McGahee (RB, healthy), Daimon Shelton (RB), Chris Villarrial (G), Troy Vincent (CB)
Lost: Ruben Brown (G), Antoine Winfield (CB)
Outlook: Despite 6-10 mark last year, Bills were just minus three in touchdowns. Offense really struggled, but defense gave up just 30 touchdowns despite just 18 takeaways. Problem this year is that the offensive line looks really weak and Drew Bledsoe is an immobile quarterback. If Bledsoe has time he has good receivers to throw to (Eric Moulds, Josh Reed, and rookie Evans). The defense continues to be very strong. Bills should definitely improve on last year's record.
Letter Power Rating: C+
Number Power Rating: 22
Projected Record: 9-7

MIAMI DOLPHINS

Gained: Rookies: Vernon Casey
Vets: Jeno James (G), Antwan Edwards (S), Reggie Howard (CB), Marty Booker (WR)
Lost: Ricky Williams (RB), Tim Ruddy (C), Todd Perry (G), Todd Wade (OT), Adewale Ogunleye (DE)
Outlook: Dolphins will really struggle on offense this season due to: 1) Losses of Ricky Williams and David Boston (injured), 2) Very questionable quarterback play, 3) Offensive line having four new starters. The defense, despite the loss of Ogunleye, is still very strong versus both the run and pass. Dolphins will be best as underdogs.
Letter Power Rating: C
Number Power Rating: 21
Projected Record: 8-8

NEW ENGLAND PATRIOTS

Gained: Rookies: Vince Wolfolk (DT), Marquise Hill (DE)
Vets: Corey Dillon (RB), Adrian Klemm (OT, healthy), David Patten (WR, healthy), Roosevelt Colvin (LB, healthy)
Lost: Antwan Smith (RB), Damien Woody (G), Ted Washington (DT), Bobby Hamilton (DE)
Outlook: Pats gave up just four touchdowns at home last year in the regular season. Offense should improve with Dillon at running back. Tom Brady is a great quarterback and the offensive line is very underrated. The defensive line lost two quality players. The secondary, though strong, has three players in tenth-plus year. However, most important is that head coach Bill Belichick is a defensive genius who can stop any offense. Team could well repeat as champs.
Letter Power Rating: B+
Number Power Rating: 29
Projected Record: 12-4

NEW YORK JETS

Gained: Rookies: Jonathan Vilma (LB), Derrick Strait (CB)
Vets: Justin McCareins (WR), Wayne Chrebet (WR, healthy), John Abraham (DE, healthy), Eric Barton (LB), Pete Kendall (C), Quincy Carter (QB)
Lost: Marvin Jones (LB), Mo Lewis (LB), Sam Garnes (S)
Outlook: Main concern on offense is that this is Curtis Martin's tenth year. Chad Pennington is a solid quarterback and the offensive line is a solid unit. The defense looks somewhat suspect, especially against the run.
Letter Power Rating: C
Number Power Rating: 21
Projected Record: 8-8

AFC North

BALTIMORE RAVENS

Gained: Rookies: Devard Darling (WR)
Vets: Kevin Johnson (WR)
Lost: No one significant
Outlook: Unless Kyle Boller improves at quarterback, Ravens will be about where they were last season—a great defensive team with an offense that has to run to win. Ravens gave up 17 or fewer points in ten games last year.
Letter Power Rating: C+
Number Power Rating: 22
Projected Record: 8-8

CINCINNATI BENGALS

Gained: Rookies: Chris Perry (RB)

Vets: Bobbie Williams (G), Daryl Gardener (DT), Nate Webster (LB)

Lost: Corey Dillon (RB), Mike Goff (G)

Outlook: Bengals are rolling the dice starting Carson Palmer at quarterback. The rest of the offense looks very good. The defense is porous both versus the run and the pass. Bengals should be involved in a lot of high-scoring games. I don't like poor defensive teams.

Letter Power Rating:

C- first eight games, C second eight games.

Number Power Rating: 19

Projected Record: 7-9

CLEVELAND BROWNS

Gained: Rookies: Kellen Winslow Jr. (TE)

Vets: Jeff Garcia (QB), Terrelle Smith (RB), William Green (RB, healthy), Jeff Faine (C, healthy), Kelvin Garmon (G), Steve Heiden (TE, healthy)

Lost: Tim Couch (QB), Brant Boyer (LB, injury)

Outlook: Browns were just minus four in touchdowns despite 5-11 record. Browns have made many improvements on offense. However, the offensive line still looks suspect. The defense has had few changes. Browns still look weak against the run while the pass defense looks decent.

Letter Power Rating: C-

Number Power Rating: 19

Projected Record: 7-9

PITTSBURGH STEELERS

Gained: Rookies: Ben Roethlisberger (QB), Ricardo Coldough (CB)

Vets: Duce Staley (RB), Marvel Smith (OT, healthy)

Lost: Jason Gilden (LB), Rodney Bailey (DE), Brent Alexander (S), Kendall Simmons (G, injury)

Outlook: With Staley starting at running back, Steelers should greatly improve their running game. Steelers have good receivers, but I don't trust Tommy Maddox that much at quarterback. Defense is good versus the run and will improve versus the pass. Bill Cowher is a coach I highly respect.

Letter Power Rating: C
Number Power Rating: 21
Projected Record: 8-8

AFC South

HOUSTON TEXANS

Gained: Rookies: Duanta Robinson (CB), Jason Babin (LB-DE), Glenn Earl (S)

Vets: Jarrod Baxter (RB, healthy), Todd Wade (OT), Seth Payne (NT, healthy), Robaire Smith (DE), Gary Walker (DE, healthy)

Lost: No one significant.

Outlook: Texans made big strides last year. In last six games they lost by three points at home to the Patriots, Colts, and Titans. They could make a big jump in record this season. The pieces are in place on offense and the defense—with Payne and Walker back on the defensive line and adding Smith there as well—should be much better as well. Texans have outside shot at the playoffs. A tough division stands in their way.

Letter Power Rating: C+
Number Power Rating: 22
Projected Record: 8-8

INDIANAPOLIS COLTS

Gained: Rookies: No one significant.
Vets: No one significant.
Lost: Adam Meadows (OT), Marcus Washington (LB)
Outlook: Colts probably have the best offense in the NFL. Defense still suspect, but figures to improve under coach Tony Dungy's care, despite not adding anyone of note. Defense is young but gaining experience.
Letter Power Rating: B
Number Power Rating: 26
Projected Record: 10-6

JACKSONVILLE JAGUARS

Gained: Rookies: Reggie Williams (WR), Daryl Smith (LB), Greg Jones (RB)
Vets: Ephraim Salaam (OT), Greg Favors (LB), Deon Grant (S), Juran Bolden (CB)
Lost: Mark Brunell (QB), Kevin Johnson (WR), Fernando Bryant (CB), Tony Brackens (LB)
Outlook: Bryan Leftwich's play at quarterback probably the key to the Jaguar season. The Jaguars won their last four at home last year, but never won on the road (3-5 versus the spread). I still am not really sold on Leftwich. Defense extremely strong versus the run, but still suspect versus the pass. However, Grant and Bolden should help the secondary. Like the Texans, the Jaguars' playoff chances are hurt by a tough division.
Letter Power Rating: C+
Number Power Rating: 22
Projected Record: 8-8

TENNESSEE TITANS

Gained: Rookies: Ben Troupe (TE), Antwan Odom (DE), Rich Gardner (CB)

Vets: Antwan Smith (RB)

Lost: Eddie George (RB), Frank Wycheck (TE), Justin McCareins (WR), Jevon Kearse (DE), Robaire Smith (DT), Pete Simon (LB, injury)

Outlook: Titan losses on defense figure to hurt more than losses on offense. Chris Brown seems an improvement over George at running back. Drew Bennett and Erron Kinney should be able to replace McCareins and Wycheck. Losses of Kearse, Smith, and Simon on front seven on defense won't be easily replaced. Titan defense gave up 17 or less just once in last six games last season. Defensive decline figures to continue.

Letter Power Rating: C
Number Power Rating: 21
Projected Record: 7-9

AFC West

DENVER BRONCOS

Gained: Rookies: DJ Williams (LB), Tatum Bell (RB)

Vets: Garrison Hearst (RB), Raylee Johnson (DE), John Lynch (S), Champ Bailey (CB)

Lost: Clinton Portis (RB), Ephraim Salaam (OT), Shannon Sharpe (TE), Ed McCaffrey (WR), Bertrand Berry (LB), Ian Gold (LB), John Mobley (LB), Mike Anderson (RB, injury)

Outlook: Though many say Broncos have good running system, running game will suffer without Portis. Broncos hurting at second receiver with McCaffrey retiring. Defense has six new starters, though two in the secondary (Bailey and Lynch) are elite players. Defense should be the stronger unit. If Jake Plummer is consistent at quarterback and a running back does well, Broncos will be an elite team. I have some doubts about that.

Letter Power Rating: B-
Number Power Rating: 24
Projected Record: 10-6

KANSAS CITY CHIEFS

Gained: Rookies: No one significant
Vets: John Welbourn (G)
Lost: John Tait (OT)
Outlook: Chief offense (63 touchdowns) best in the NFL last season. However, the receivers are not that great and the offensive line (two starters in twelfth season) is showing age. Priest Holmes still one of the best running backs. Gunther Cunningham's return to coach the defense should help. The defense collapsed late last season, holding just one opponent in last eight under 17 points.
Letter Power Rating: B-
Number Power Rating: 24
Projected Record: 9-7

OAKLAND RAIDERS

Gained: Rookies: Robert Gallery (OT)
Vets: Kerry Collins (QB), Rich Gannon (QB, healthy), Ted Washington (DT), Warren Sapp (DT), John Parrella (DT, healthy), Bobby Hamilton (DE)
Lost: Charlie Garner (RB), Lincoln Kennedy (OT), Dana Stubblefield (DT), Rod Coleman (DT), Eric Barton (LB), Tim Brown (WR), Barrett Robbins (C), Rod Woodson (S)

Outlook: Raiders had biggest fall of a Super Bowl team of any team in history. Team largely remade for this season. They have a new coach (Norv Turner) and a new vertical offense. However, four new starters on the offensive line and Rich Gannon being better at the short passing game may hurt new offense. Running game looks weak. Sapp and Washington new on the defensive line but all defensive line starters are in tenth-plus season. The defense also has a new system. Raiders are hardest team for me to read going into the season.
Letter Power Rating: C-
Number Power Rating: 19
Projected Record: 7-9

SAN DIEGO CHARGERS
Gained: Rookies: Philip Rivers (QB), Igor Olshansky (DT), Dave Ball (DE)
Vets: Mike Goff (G), Randall Godfrey (LB), Jason Ball (C, healthy), Tim Dwight (WR, healthy),
Lost: Cory Raymer (C), Kelvin Garmon (G), Vaughn Parker (OT), Stephen Alexander (TE), David Boston (WR), Raylee Johnson (DE), Marcellus Wiley (DE), Kwamie Lassiter (S)
Outlook: Chargers have superb running back (LaDanian Tomlinson) but little else. Whoever is quarterback figures to struggle behind a porous and revamped offensive line and without good receivers. The defense is not very good against either the run or the pass. Probable ninth straight season out of the playoffs coming up.
Letter Power Rating: D-
Number Power Rating: 13
Projected Record: 4-12

2004 BETTING SUMMARY

Before the season began, I made five season over/under win bets. On normal plays I look for two plus game differences between my projected wins for the team and the number available. Where there are 2 1/2 or more game differences, I make a large bet. I am willing to make a small bet where there is a 1 1/2-2 game difference.

I made small bets on the Cards under 5 1/2 wins (laying 1.30) and the Vikings over 8 1/2 wins (laying 1.90). My projections had the Cards winning 3.98 games and the Vikings 10.37 games. I made a large bet on the Titans under 10 games (laying 1.60). My projections had the Titans winning 7.42 games. My normal plays were on the Eagles under 11 wins (laying 1.50) and the Texans over six wins (laying 1.75). My projections had the Eagles winning 8.85 games and the Texans winning 8.33 games.

I got off to a so-so start for the season splitting my two wagers.

Week One
Bucs plus 3 over Redskins: Normal Play

My power ratings favored the Bucs by one in this game, which gave me a four point edge—something I often seek in Week One. The Redskins were playing the Giants next week. They had lost eight of their last ten to the number before playing the Giants. I took 1/2 point away from the Redskins due to this stat.

I could have gotten away with a push in this game. The Redskins kicked a field goal with 16 seconds left that pushed their lead from three to six (16-10). The announcers felt that the Redskins would run the ball rather than risk having a kick blocked and possibly returned for a touchdown. However, I would have been lucky with a push. The Bucs scored their touchdown on a fumble return and looked very old on offense. They were thoroughly outplayed in this game and I lowered their rating from C+ to C-.

Packers plus 3 1/2 (even money) over Panthers: Normal Play

My power ratings had the Packers favored by 2. Thus I had a huge numbers edge. I was shocked that money poured in on the Panthers in this game—even on the night of the contest (the game was a Monday night game). I personally could have gotten plus four on the game, though plus 3 1/2 at even money is a better percentage play than plus four laying 11-10.

The Packers controlled most of the game in their 24-14 win. Two straight turnovers by the Panthers on their first two second-half possessions that the Packers turned into touchdowns turned a 10-7 squeaker into a very comfortable 24-7 lead. I was never in any danger after that.

Other Games I Looked At

Browns plus 4 over Ravens

If I could have gotten plus 4 1/2, I would have played the Browns since I would have had a four point edge in my power ratings. But the best I could get was plus 4. This game was heavily bet by the betting public on the Ravens who went from 2 1/2 point favorites to as high as four (a huge move since the key number of 3 was passed). This game was a huge win for the books since the Browns easily won outright, 20-3.

Saints plus 3 1/2 over Seahawks

If I had gotten plus four on the Saints I would have bet them for sure since I would have had a four point edge in my power ratings (which were Pick on this game). I strongly considered taking less since the Saints--who lost to the Seahawks in their opening game last season—were

10-4 to the number in revenge games since 2000. However, the Saints' quarterback, Aaron Brooks, had physical problems—a quad injury—in the pre-season, which stopped me from taking less than plus four. Good thing as the Seahawks rolled, 21-7.

Week One and Season Record: 1-1

Week Two

This week I had five bets. I did okay, going 3-2. I was both lucky in two of the games I won and a little unlucky in one of my losses.

Colts plus 3 over Titans: Normal Play

With my service I stated that if I were a wise man instead of a wise-guy, this would have been the only game that I bet. The Colts had a lot going for them this week.

First, the price itself was very attractive. This was the same price (plus 3) that the Colts were against the Pats last week. I consider the Pats about eight points better than the Titans. The Colts also had two more days of rest than the Titans. My power rating favored the Colts by 2 1/2 in this game and my oddsmaker line favored them by 1 1/2. Later in the week, the game closed at 2 1/2 for the Colts, so in terms of line value, I did the right thing betting early.

In terms of emotional edges, the Colts were coming off a phony loss while the Titans came off a phony win. This was worth a point to the Colts. In addition, though this wasn't one of my models, the Colts needed a win in this game to avoid falling into a two game hole in the division.

The Colts won, 31-17, and I covered my bet by 17 points. Most touts and handicappers would be gloating over a win like that. However, I considered myself somewhat lucky to win. The Titans led for most of the game and had a few chances to bury the Colts. The Titans failed on fourth and inches at the Colt 3. Before the Titans kicked a short field goal (when up 7-3), they dropped two passes in the endzone. Later in the game when the score was tied at 17, the Titans looked like they had completed a touchdown pass. However, before the receiver came down with the ball, the Colt defender stole it for an interception. Like I said, I had breaks in this game.

Texans plus 4 over Lions: Small Play

I wasn't really crazy about this bet. The Texans' loss last week to a poor Charger team turned me off. A loss like that can kill the confidence of a young team like the Texans. And in this game, the Texans were going into a dome to play a strong home team in the Lions.

However, I go with my numbers. My power rating on this game (even after downgrading the Texans after last week's loss), favored the Texans by one. That gave them a five point edge in my numbers. Plus the Texans were coming from a phony loss (plus 1/2 point).

Just as in last week's game, turnovers killed the Texans—they committed three and had one takeaway. The Lions won, 28-16. Despite outgaining the Lions in this game, the Texans were the wrong side. In the second half, the Lions twice scored touchdowns right after the Texans drew within a touchdown.

Bears plus 10 over Packers: Normal Play

The price drew me to this game. My oddsmaking line was 7 1/2 and my power rating was eight. Thus the Bears had value. Also, the Packers were coming from a phony win over the Panthers, which gave the Bears 1/2 point in my numbers.

One play turned this game around. The Packers were down 3-7, but were about to take the lead when the Bears returned a fumble 95 yards for a touchdown. This 14 point swing was the difference in the game as the Bears won outright, 21-10. This game, along with the Panthers' outright win over the Chiefs as seven point underdogs destroyed virtually every teaser bettor. Once again it was shown that just because a team is a big favorite doesn't mean that they'll even win the game. Spiro the Greek of Olympic Sports was speaking in chuckles after these two big underdog outright winners destroyed all of the "wise guy" teaser bettors.

Vikings plus 4 over Eagles: Normal Play

For the second straight week, I was taking a road underdog in the Monday night game. And for the second straight week, it was strictly a numbers play. My power ratings favored the Vikings by 1 1/2 in this game, which gave them a 5 1/2 point edge in my power ratings—an almost automatic bet.

Though the Eagles looked great on offense (they punted just once in this game), I was a little bit unlucky. The Vikings twice got to the Eagle one yard line. Once their quarterback, Duante Culpepper, lost a fumble. Another time the Vikings settled for a field goal. On another drive, a Viking touchdown run by Culpepper was called back on a holding penalty. The Vikings again settled for a field goal. The first Eagle touchdown was set up on a phantom holding call on the Vikings on a third down play. The Eagles would have punted if not for that call. Another Eagle touchdown to Terrell Owens should not have counted since Owens was fumbling the ball when he went out of bounds in the endzone. The Vikings, stupidly, didn't challenge the call. With any breaks I would have won this bet.

Jaguars plus 3 1/2 (minus 1.05) over Broncos: Small Play

My models and parity work best when I am betting teams in the D+ to B- range. With the Broncos being a B team, I was a little bit scared and made a smaller play. The Broncos' sloppy win of last week was my emotional model in this game. That cost the Broncos 1/2 a point in my numbers. With my power rating favoring the Broncos by just 1/2 a point, the Jaguars had value taking 3 1/2.

The Jaguars won outright 7-6. They were outgained by the Broncos, 376-176. Thus I considered myself lucky to win. The Jaguar touchdown was set up by a 55-yard punt return—something you can't count on before a game is played.

Another Game I Looked At
Rams plus 3 over Falcons

For a fair part of the week, I thought I'd take plus 3 on the Rams over the Falcons. I rated the Rams a C team and the Falcons a D+ team. At plus 3, the linesmaker was making these teams about equal, which I thought was incorrect. In addition, the Falcons were coming off a phony win. With my power rating favoring the Falcons by 1/2 a point, the Rams had value.

Two factors kept me off this game. First, the Rams were coming from a sloppy win. Second, though less important, the Rams had beaten the Falcons in a Monday night game last year, 36-0. I don't like betting against a team that lost a rout—especially on national TV—within the last year to this week's opponent. The Falcons beat the Rams soundly, 34-17.

Week 2 record: 3-2
Season record: 4-3

Week Three

In the third week, I had my worst performance of the season thus far, going 1-2. The two losses were normal plays, while the win was a small bet.

Browns plus 4 over Giants: Normal Play

This was another numbers play for me. My power ratings favored the Browns by 1 1/2 points, giving me a 5 1/2 point edge in my numbers.

During the week the public and the wise guys all bet this game like it was over before it started. Very early, the money showed on the Browns, driving the line from 3 Giants to 1 1/2. Then money poured in the rest of the week on the Giants due mostly to extensive Browns injuries (on defensive line and secondary, plus the Browns lost their star rookie tight end, Kellen Winslow Jr.).

Usually injury-bet games lose in the NFL since most injuries are overrated. If they won any great percentage of the time, bookmakers would be out of business. However, this time the public and wise guys won as the Giants won, 27-10. The Browns' best chance was when they were down 0-10 and drove to the Giant 5 early in the third quarter. Then quarterback Jeff Garcia lost a fumble on a snap and the Giants, aided greatly by a personal foul penalty early in the drive, drove 95 yards for a touchdown. I was never in the game after that.

Packers plus 7 over Colts: Normal Play

The Colts were coming off two straight emotionally up performances in games against the Pats and Titans. Plus, they had the Jaguars—to whom they lost the last game to last year—coming up. I docked the Colts 1/2 point in my numbers, which favored them by 5. The Packers thus had value as well.

In the first half, Payton Manning was incredible. He passed for 320 yards and five touchdowns and led the Colts to a 35-17 lead. In the second half, the Colts' offense slowed down and the Packers came back to make the score just 31-38 against. With six minutes left, the Packers were driving when they lost a ball on a strip on the Colt 45. The Colts returned the fumble to the Packer 36 and then scored a touchdown. The Packers' last chance ended at the Colt 20 with an interception in the final seconds. The final was 45-31 for the Colts.

Jaguars plus 7 over Titans: Small Play

Despite the Jaguars coming off a phony win, they rated a small play in this game due to their power rating edge. My numbers favored the Titans by just two points. I needed plus 7 to bet the Jaguars since that was my number as an oddsmaker (due partly to the Titans being one game behind the Jaguars in the standings).

The Jaguars won a thriller by scoring with nine seconds left in a 15-12 win. The Jaguars are looking a little bit like last year's Panthers—a team that is winning a lot of close games.

Other Games I Looked At
Cards plus 11 over Falcons

This looked like a game the Falcons would look past. They were coming off a revenge win over the Rams last week and had a date with divisional rival Carolina next. Plus on film, the Cards looked terrible on offense. However, the Cards might not be as bad as many think. They were in both games they played (one against the defending champion Patriots) in the fourth quarter. However, since my power rating favored the Falcons by 11 1/2, I passed the game. The Cards kept things close in a poorly played game (both teams committed four turnovers) that they lost, 3-6.

Texans plus 10 over Chiefs

The Texans were the first team to be due up this season. They had the combination of due, revenge (lost to Chiefs, 42-14 last year) and number (power rating was 5 1/2 for the Chiefs) working for them. However at 0-2, the Chiefs badly needed a win and they have one of the toughest home fields in the NFL. Plus, as I noted in last week's game against the Lions, the Texans confidence was mostly shot.

One play turned this game (and maybe the Texans' season) around. Leading 14-6, late in the third quarter, the Chiefs were about to put the game away with a first and goal on the Texans 2. However an intercepted pass was returned 102 yards for a touchdown by the Texans. A two point conversion tied the score. Thus, instead of being down 21-6 (and, let's face it, being out of the game), the Texans were tied and had new life. Eventually the Texans won on a late field goal, 24-21.

Week 3 record: 1-2
Season Record: 5-5

Week Four

My slump continued as I went 0-3 this week. As usually happens in such a week, the games I pass mostly win. Easy to second guess oneself in this business!

Jaguars plus 4 1/2 over Colts: Small Play

I was uneasy about this play. The model working for the Jaguars (actually, against the Colts) was that the Colts had scored 30 plus points in two straight wins and were favored (minus 1/2 point). However, I was worried that the Colts would be very focused for this game since they were a game behind the Jaguars and had lost to them in their last meeting last season. In addition, the Jaguars were coming off two straight focused emotional efforts in wins over the Broncos and Titans (minus 1/2 point). Since I like good defensive teams playing jazzy offensive teams, I made the play on the Jaguars. With the power rating being just two for the Colts, the Jaguars had value.

For the second time this season (the Viking game against the Eagles was the first time), I was victimized by a phantom defensive holding call. The game was tied at 17 and the Colts had been stopped when there was a very late flag for this alleged penalty. Given a second chance, the Colts went down and scored a touchdown that won the game, 24-17.

Dolphins plus 5 and plus 7 over the Jets: Large Play

This was my largest bet of the season thus far. The Dolphins not only had the emotional model of losing at home as a favorite last week and now being a home underdog (plus 1/2 point); they also had tons of value in this game.

My oddsmaker line favored the Jets by 1 and my power rating was Jets by 1/2. Last week, the Dolphins were 2 1/2 point home favorites over the Steelers—a team just slightly inferior to the Jets. Now the Dolphins were getting (at the end) a touchdown. Two weeks ago, the Jets were favored by three (minus about 25 cents) over the Chargers—a team a class inferior to the Dolphins.

The Dolphins were also in a desperation situation. A loss would be their third at home for the season and would make them 0-4: a hole only one team since the merger ('92 Chargers) escaped to make the playoffs. The Dolphins were also a fresh due up with due, coverage (won last two in Miami against the Jets) and number (power rating) working for them. I expected a maximum effort both ways for the Dolphins. Thus I had everything going for me in this game.

I could not believe that the line kept going up during the week. Usually such psychotic betting behavior by the betting public results in a loss for the public and a win for the bookmakers and the smart professionals.

But four Dolphin turnovers doomed them. One was returned for a touchdown as the Dolphins lost, 17-9. The Dolphin defense held the Jets to 235 yards.In a game like this I'll win about 65 times out of 100. This was one of the 35 losing scenarios that occurred. That's why one shouldn't go overboard betting any one game.

49ers plus 4 1/2 over Rams: Normal Play

The main reason I liked the 49ers in this game was that they were a national TV home underdog that had value (my power rating was Rams by 2).

Unlike my other two losses where I probably had the right side, I was totally wrong in this game. The Rams scored on all four first half possessions to go up 24-0. They won easily, 24-14. The 49ers are probably the worst team in the NFL.

Other Games I Looked At
Chiefs plus 6 1/2 over Ravens

This was the Monday night game. The Chiefs at 0-3 badly needed a win. My power ratings favored the Ravens by just four points. The Chiefs also were a fresh due up with due, coverage (won last year in Baltimore), and number working for them. Also in terms of value, the Chiefs were 16 points behind the Ravens on the spread range.

I passed the game for three reasons: 1) In last year's win in Baltimore, the Chiefs were outplayed badly but lucked out on a punt return for a touchdown. 2) The Chiefs are a very poor defensive team. I felt that the Ravens would score too much for the Chief offense to make up. 3) Though I've done it twice this year (going 1-1) thus far, I am scared of road teams in Monday night games. The home club often plays over its head.

The Chiefs won, 27-24 and controlled the game much more than the score indicated.

Texans plus 3 over Raiders

I passed this game because there were no strong emotional edges for the Texans. I favored them a lot since I felt that last week's fairly fortunate win in Kansas City (mentioned in the week three summary) would wake them up. One thing working against the Texans was that in their history they were 1-8 (0-9 outright) on the game after a win. However the Texans were well aware of this streak. Their quarterback, David Carr (along with his father) said he wouldn't cut his hair until the Texans won two straight. With my power rating on the game being Pick, I needed plus 4 to bet the Texans. The line went nowhere near that. The Texans won, 30-17. Carr got his haircut.

Bills plus 6 over Patriots

The line on this game just seemed too high. My oddsmaker line and power rating made the game 3 1/2 for the Pats. The Bills wanted to avenge a 31-0 loss to the Pats in their last 2003 game. However, the Bills were not especially good at revenge and I had no major emotional models favoring them. Thus I passed. The Pats won and covered 31-17, though the game was much closer than the final score. The Bills trailed by seven late, but were inside the Patriot 20. Then their quarterback, Drew Bledsoe, fumbled on a sack and the Pats returned the fumble for the game and spread-clinching touchdown.

Week 4 Record: 0-3
Season Record: 5-8

Week Five

Had my best week of the season going 3-0-1. I would have done even better had I bet three other games that I was considering playing. Still, I should be happy about the week!

Dolphins plus 14 over Patriots: Small Play

I did not even post this game with the service since 14 was never close to being around for normal bettors. However, a bookmaker I advise let me have this number since at the time he was flooded with Patriots money.

The Dolphins were the first team this season to be star due up. The Dolphins had star due, revenge (the Pats had beaten them twice last season), coverage (they hadn't lost by over 12 at New England in a long time), and number (the power rating was 12) working for them.

The Dolphins were also coming off a phony loss (1/2 point). With my power rating at 12, the Dolphins had value taking 14 in the game.

The Pats really didn't show up emotionally in this game and still won by 14 (24-10), giving me a push on my bet on the Dolphins. The Dolphins outgained the Pats, 295-204 but were stopped on downs at the Patriot 21, 11, and 7 (had a first and goal on the one in that series). The Dolphins' field goal kicker, Olinda Mare, was injured in warm-ups and they had to use Wes Walker to kick. He did make a 29 yard field goal, but the Dolphins were still hurt by Mare's loss (they would have kicked a field goal from the 21 (38 yards) if Mare was in the game. Two Dolphins turnovers led to 14 Patriot points.

Lions plus 7 1/2 over Falcons: Normal Play

Two major factors favored the Lions. First, the Falcons were coming off a very emotional win over the Panthers (docked them one point for that). In addition, the Falcons were a fresh due down with the Lions having due, fatigue (the Lions had a bye last week), and number (power rating was four) working for them. With the power rating being four for the Falcons, the Lions had a lot of value.

The Lions overcame an early 0-7 deficit and won outright, 17-10. The Falcons had four turnovers and played a very uninspired game. I didn't change the letter power rating of either team after this game. The Falcons (who are a C team) are still clearly better than the Lions (a D+ team) and would probably normally win better than two of three games between the teams. However, I correctly read that the Falcons would be emotionally down in this game.

Bills plus 7 1/2 over Jets: Normal Play

Despite the Jets being 3-0 and the Bills being 0-3, I saw this as a game between two basically even teams. Before the game I rated both clubs as C teams. The Jets had beaten three below average teams (Bengals, Chargers, and Dolphins) in fairly close games while the Bills could easily have won any or all of their games against stronger teams (Jaguars, Raiders, and Patriots). My power rating on the game favored the Jets by 2 1/2, which gave the Bills tremendous value. The Jets were also coming from a phony win (minus 1/2 point) over the Dolphins.

Though I won with the Bills in a 14-16 spread covering loss, I am not at all sure I had the right side. The Jets controlled the game at all the critical times. The Jets missed an early 29-yard field goal and later lost a fumble inside the Bills 20. The Jets, despite those miscues, led 13-0 in the fourth quarter when their quarterback, Chad Pennington, threw an interception deep in Bills territory. The Bills then quickly scored two touchdowns to go up, 14-13. The Jets then drove 60 yards for the game-winning field goal. I lowered the Bills to C- after this game. I was somewhat lucky in this game.

Ravens plus 1 over Redskins: Normal Play

The Ravens lost last week to the Chiefs in a game where their defense played very poorly. I felt that they would bounce back this week. The Ravens have gone 13-1-1 to the number after their last 15 outright losses, which gave them a point in my power ratings. The Redskins, especially on offense, still look disorganized this year. With my power ratings favoring the Ravens by 1 1/2 points, I felt I had value taking 1.

The offenses did little in this game. The Ravens twice let the Redskins get the ball deep in their territory in the first half off of interceptions. The Redskins got a 10-0 lead off of these mistakes. I felt I was dead at that point since the Raven offense was doing little. However, in the third quarter, the Ravens returned a fumble and a punt for touchdowns to take a 14-10 lead. After this, the Raven defense totally shut down the Redskins. The Ravens showed some life on offense and added a field goal to win, 17-10. The Raven offense also ran out the last four minutes of the clock at the end.

Other Games I Looked At
Bucs plus 4 over Saints

I was considering betting the Bucs in this game since they were coming off a phony loss and I felt that their offense would do well with Chris Simms replacing Brad Johnson at quarterback. My power rating on the game was 3 for the Saints. However, the Saints were a fresh due up and they had also covered seven of their last nine after a loss. The Saints' loss last week was a terrible one in Arizona. They would be focused in this game. The Bucs won, 20-17, even though Simms was knocked out of the game. Brian Griese replaced him and did very well.

A FULL SEASON OF NFL BETS

Giants plus 4 1/2 over Cowboys

The Giants wanted to avenge last year's two losses to the Cowboys. Their win at Green Bay—a team better than the Cowboys, I felt—showed that the Giants were capable of getting revenge in this game. With my power rating being 2 1/2, the Giants had the value in this game. However, the Giants were a fresh may due down with the Cowboys having may due, fatigue (Cowboys were off last week), and coverage (Cowboys won two of last three at home over the Giants by over four points) going for them. The Giants were also off a phony win last week.

The Giants scored the last 23 points of the game to win, 26-10. The Giants have exceeded my expectations more than any other team in the league. Their offensive line and front seven on defense have done much, much better than I felt they would. After starting the year with a letter power rating of D, the Giants are now up to C+ and have realistic playoff hopes.

Titans plus 4 over Packers

This was virtually a must-win for the Titans. A loss would put them three games behind the Colts in their division. The Titans, who lost by 21 last week, had gone 3-1 to the number after rout losses since '99.

However, this was also a key game for the home Packers. A loss would put them three games down in the loss column to the Lions and Vikings in their division. The Packers were also a fresh due up. They figured to be as focused as the Titans.

The Titans blew out the Packers 48-27 in a game not that close. The Titans got off to a 17-0 lead in the first nine minutes and never had a worry after that. Once again, it was shown that must-win underdogs are much better bets than must-win favorites.

Week 5 Record: 3-0-1
Season Record: 8-8-1

Week Six

Because two games fell right on numbers and I get better numbers than the public, I did much better than my clients this week. I am now ahead for the season while my clients are behind. Hopefully in the coming weeks, I can stay ahead and also get my clients into the black. I went 4-2-1 for the week.

Dolphins plus 7 over Bills: Small Play

Both teams were winless going into this game. They were the last winless teams in the NFL. The Dolphins were coming off a phony loss (worth 1/2 point). With my power rating being just 3 1/2 for the Bills, the Dolphins had value. My oddsmaker line was just five, also giving the Dolphins value. With both teams being good defensive teams (the Dolphins had given up fewer yards per play than any team in the NFL going into this game) and with Miami's offense showing a little life last week, I felt that points would be at a premium.

The Dolphins lost 20-13. My clients were only able to get plus 6 1/2 on the game, which meant that I tied my bet, but it was a loss for the service.

Packers plus 3 1/2 over Lions: Large Play

I really liked the Packers in this one. At 1-4 and 2 1/2 games behind the Lions and Vikings in the division, this was a must-win game for them. That was worth a half point. Many bettors bet the Lions since the Lions had covered seven straight over the Packers in Detroit. However, all but one of those covers were as an underdog. The Packers had actually won two of the last three games in Detroit. Thus, I also felt that the Packers' well-known tendency toward struggling on turf and indoors was being overrated in the price.

Other reasons to love the Packers in this spot:

1) They were coming off a Monday night blowout loss (1/2 point).
2) They wanted to avenge a loss to Detroit in their second game last year (since they had earlier won at Carolina—a team better than the Lions—this showed that the Packers could cope and was worth 1/2 point).
3) The Lions were coming from a phony win (1/2 point versus).
4) The Lions were 2-7-1 to the number after their last seven wins (1/2 point versus).

With my power rating being 2 1/2 for the Packers, they had obscene value in this spot. My oddsmaker line was Pick, also giving the Packers great value. As a C team playing at a D+ Lions team, the Packers had super value taking 3 1/2.

With the Packers having every emotional edge plus great, great value in the price, I had to make a large bet on the game. This game was what betting the NFL is all about.

The Packers blew out the Lions, 38-10. Their maligned defense held the Lions to five first downs (none in the second half) and 125 total yards. As one old-time bettor said, a big bet should win easily. However, I'd be lying if I said I felt before the game that the Packers would win by four touchdowns.

Texans plus 7 1/2 over Titans: Normal Play

For the service this was a small play since the best widely available line was 6 1/2, even though there were sevens around for the public in spots.

I went against the Titans largely because they were coming off the blowout Monday night win (1/2 point versus). The Texans had also covered six of their last eight revenge games (1/2 point). Going into this game, the Texans had never beaten the ex-tenants of Houston, the Titans. The Texans were also 14-8 after a loss in their history (1/2 point).

The Texans were even more up for the game than I thought they'd be. They won outright, 20-10, and after the game expressed great happiness in winning this game over the team that had deserted Houston after the 1996 season.

Jaguars plus 3 and 3 1/2 over Chiefs: Small Play

When I first handicapped this game, I was actually planning to bet the Chiefs. The Jaguars had a big revenge game next up at Indianapolis and the Chiefs were a (non-fresh) may due up, plus the Chiefs were coming off a bye. However, as an oddsmaker, I had made the Jaguars a three point favorite and made them a 1 1/2 point favorite in my power ratings. I was most surprised that I was able to take three points (and later 3 1/2) with the Jaguars. With this huge edge in my power ratings, this was strictly a value bet on the Jaguars.

I nearly lost this game. The Jaguars led 14-3 and the Chiefs came back with two second half touchdowns. They missed the second extra point, which left the score at 16-14 for the Chiefs, with the Jaguars still covering. The Jaguars then turned the ball over on downs in their territory. The Chiefs missed a 42-yard field goal. After that, the Jaguars marched down the field for the winning touchdown and won, 22-16 (the Jaguars completed a two point conversion after the touchdown).

Raiders plus 3 over Broncos: Small Play

Since the line never went to three for the public except in a couple of Vegas casinos, this was a non-play for the service.

The Raiders wanted revenge for two losses to the Broncos in 2003. The Raiders had covered ten of their last 13 revenge games (1/2 point). The Broncos thus far in 2004 were 0-2-1 to the number after a win (1/2 point versus). With my power rating being Pick, I felt that the Raiders had value.

The Raiders had won their two previous home games including one where they scored 30 points on a good Bucs' defense.

The Broncos totally dominated the game, winning 31-3. The Raiders got just nine first downs in the game and gained under 150 yards. The Broncos gained 254 yards rushing. They'd had a big rushing game last week against a decent Panther rush defense. I should have attached more significance to that. This—along with my bet on the 49ers against the Rams two weeks ago—was one of my worst bets for the season.

Saints plus 4 and 4 1/2 over Vikings: Normal Play

The Saints were a Sunday night home underdog with value (power rating just 2 1/2 for the Vikings). They also had lost last week as home favorites and were now home underdogs (1/2 point).

The Vikings never had to punt in a game that they won, 38-31.

Bucs plus 7 1/2 over Rams: Normal Play

This was another game where the service and I had different results. The game fell seven for the Rams and the service price was 6 1/2. Thus I won and the clients lost.

I would still bet and select the Bucs in this game for my clients if I had to do it again.

Reasons I liked the Bucs: 1) The Rams were coming off a 1 1/2 emotional effort in their huge comeback win over the Seahawks (1 points versus), 2) The Rams were coming off a sloppy win (1/2 point versus), 3) At 1-4, the Bucs badly needed a win to stay on the fringes of playoff contention (plus 1/2 point), 4) The Bucs' physical defense had given the Rams problems in the past and they had usually beaten the Rams or at least stayed very close.

My power rating on the game favored the Rams by just four points, which gave the Bucs value.

The Rams turned two Bucs' turnovers into touchdowns in a game where they won, 28-21. On one of the takeaways, the Rams recovered a fumble on their own seven and ran it back 93 yards for a touchdown. That was a 14 point swing and cost my clients the game. Very late in the game, the Bucs lost two chances to tie the game on turnovers.

Other Games I Looked At
Seahawks plus 5 over Patriots.

The Patriots were coming off a phony win (1/2 point versus). With my power rating being 2 1/2 for the Patriots, the Seahawks had value in the price.

Two reasons I stayed off the game: 1) The Seahawks blew a 17 point lead to the Rams last week in the last 5 1/2 minutes. I wondered how they would react to that gut wrenching loss. After that loss, I noted that the Seahawk wins were all against inferior competition (Saints a D+ team, Bucs a C- team, 49ers a D- team). I rated the Patriots as a B team. 2) The Patriots had won 19 straight going into this game. It is scary to be taking just five points on the road against a team that has won 19 straight. The Pats had also covered 15 of their last 16 off a win.

The Pats won and covered, 30-20. The game had a wild ending. The Seahawks were given a last play from the Pats one-yard line because of pass interference in the endzone. With no time left and a ten-point lead, the Pats had the game locked up. Still, they gave a total defensive effort on the last play and stuffed a Seahawk run for no gain. That killed those who had bet the Seahawks. It also showed the character of the Patriots team.

Falcons minus 4 over Chargers

I almost bet my first favorite of the year in this game. The Chargers were a fresh due down and had come off two straight fairly strong emotional efforts (1/2 point versus). The Falcons were coming off a flat and phony loss to the Lions (1/2 point). I felt that the Falcons were in a position to bounce back, while the Chargers might have a letdown. With my power rating being 6 for the Falcons, they had value.

The Chargers hung in all the way and lost just 21-20. Thus, they covered. I certainly underrated the Chargers at the start of the season.

Week 6 Record: 4-2-1
Season Record: 12-10-2

Week 7

This looked like the toughest board of the year. There was only one game worthy of a bet on the parameters

I use. I didn't even much consider betting any other games.

I lost the bet I made due mostly to a factor that can't be handicapped before the game—an injury. My opinion on the other 13 games on the board was 10-2-1. Shows how strange handicapping the NFL can be.

Titans plus 7 1/2 over Vikings: Normal Play

The Titans were, I felt, a legitimate must-win underdog (add 1/2 point). They were not only 2-4 going into this game and three games behind the Colts in the loss column, but the Titans were already saddled with three divisional losses, which kill their tiebreaker chances in the division. The Vikings were coming off a sloppy win (1/2 point versus) plus had a revenge game with the Giants up next (1/2 point versus). Being a game ahead in their division meant that the Vikings could relax a little in this game. With my power rating being 3 1/2 for the Vikings and my oddsmaker line six, the Titans had value in the game.

Steve McNair, the Titan quarterback, reinjured his sternum early in the second quarter and was lost for the rest of the game. At the time of his injury, the game was tied at 3 and was anyone's game. The 7 1/2 points I was taking looked big. However, the backup quarterback, Mike Volek, gave up three interceptions, including one in the Viking endzone early in the third quarter. A penalty killed another Titan scoring chance. They ended up losing, 20-3. I lose no sleep when I lose a game due to an injury. That is one of the factors that can't be handicapped or controlled.

Week 7 Record: 0-1
Season Record: 12-11-2

Week 8

Another frustrating week for me. I went 0-3 with the service. One game that I gave out (Texans) never reached the price for the betting public that I made it a play at. Of course, the Texans won. Another game I bet (Chiefs over Colts) was never close to being available at the needed price for any length of time.

That game also won. Two games that I leaned toward but didn't give out to the service or bet for myself also won. I am now 14-14-2 on the games I've bet. I am 65-46-5 picking the whole board. I've never had a season in which I did better on the games that I've passed versus those that I bet. Might well happen this season.

Redskins plus 3 1/2 over Packers: Normal Play

The Packers were coming off two games with high emotion (minus 1/2 point) where they scored 38 and 41 points in wins (minus 1/2 point). Joe Gibbs and the Redskins had two weeks to prepare for this game since they had a bye last week (plus 1/2 point). With my power rating being one for the Redskins and my oddsmaker line making them just one point underdogs, the Redskins had value in this game.

This was the kind of game that one could fool himself into believing that he bet the right side if he took the Redskins. Trailing 20-14, the Redskins scored a touchdown with 2:35 left on the clock that was taken away on a questionable motion penalty. The Packers then intercepted the ball on the next play and scored a clinching touchdown shortly after that. Many bettors (Lem Banker would be a notable one) would whine that the bad call cost the Redskins the game.

However, it was a miracle that the Redskins even had a chance. Brett Favre, the Packer quarterback, threw two interceptions in the second half of the fourth quarter. Before these interceptions, the Packers led 20-7 and had the ball. On their two touchdown drives, the Redskins went 24 and 17 yards. They were outgained in the game, 361-272. This was a game I was wrong about.

Chiefs plus 3 over Colts: Small Play

Plus three (laying 11-10) was never close to being around for the betting public and thus this game was never close to being a play for my clients. I got this price due to my outlaw line connections.

At 2-4, the Chiefs faced a must-win situation as an underdog (plus 1/2 point). As an added bonus, the Chiefs wanted to avenge a playoff loss to the Colts from last season. With my power ratings favoring the Colts by one point, one needed plus 3 to be getting value in this game.

The Chiefs won, 45-35. Incredibly, the Chiefs blew two other scoring chances when they lost fumbles deep in Colt territory. I was certainly right on my bet in this game.

Texans Pick over Jaguars: Normal Play

Though there were Picks around in isolated spots, they weren't prevalent enough for this game to count as a selection for the service.

There were several reasons to like the Texans in this game. First, the Jaguars were coming off a supreme emotional effort in their win over the Colts last week (minus 1 point). Second, the Texans wanted revenge for a 27-0 loss to the Jaguars last year and had covered seven of their last nine revenge games (plus 1 point). The Texans, with wins at Kansas City and at Tennessee, had shown that they could cope with teams in the Jaguars' class.

With my power rating favoring the Texans by two points and my oddsmaker line favoring them by three, the Texans had value at Pick.

The Texans won the game, 20-6. They won even though they lost a touchdown when a receiver lost the ball going into the endzone (ended up being a touchback). The Texans had a 24-14 edge in first downs and a 35-25 edge in clock.

Raiders plus 7 over Chargers: Normal Play

In this game fresh dues were clashing. The Raiders were due up and the Chargers were due down. The Raiders had due, revenge, coverage (hadn't lost by over 7 at the Chargers in several years), and number (power rating was 6) working for them. The Raiders were also coming off a phony loss (plus 1/2 point). Lastly, the Raiders were in a must-win situation as an underdog (plus 1/2 point). A loss pretty much ended their season; the Raiders had expected to contend for the playoffs when the season started.

With my oddsmaker line being 4 for the Chargers, the Raiders had value. These teams had changed a lot in public perception over the season. In Week 1, the Chargers were five point underdogs in Houston. Three weeks later, the Raiders were 2 1/2 point favorites in Houston. Now, with the line as high as seven (and giving the Chargers 2 1/2 for home advantage), the Chargers were rated 4 1/2 points better than the Raiders, whereas the Texan barometer had the Raiders being 7 1/2 points better than the Chargers. The Chargers had definitely improved this season (while the Raiders had gotten worse), but I felt that this price was an overprice and an overreaction.

However, in the game, the Chargers destroyed the Raiders, 42-14. The Chargers scored on six of their first seven possessions (lost a fumble on the Raider five the time they didn't score) and won easily. I feel that this game said even more bad things about the Raiders than good things about the Chargers. My end of the week power ratings had the Raiders now the second worst team in the NFL.

Dolphins plus 7 1/2 over Jets: Normal Play

The Jets were coming off a 1 1/2 emotional effort in their loss to the Patriots last week (minus 1 point). Also, everything I read during the week seemed to indicate that the Jets were looking more back at their game against the Patriots than ahead to this game against the Dolphins.

With their season lost at 1-6, I felt that the Dolphins would try hard in this Monday night game against the Jets, a divisional rival (plus 1/2 point). The Dolphins' offense seemed to be getting untracked in efforts the last two weeks. They had outgained the Jets in their first meeting (a game I lost).

With my power rating being 3 1/2 for the Jets, the Dolphins had value.

When the Dolphins tied the game at seven with 4:30 to go in the first half, I liked my chances. Their defense had contained the Jets so far and the game seemed to be headed toward a close and low scoring finish (for one of my clients who wants predicted game scores for the Monday night game, I predicted the Jets would win, 13-10). The Jets then scored on their next six possessions and routed the Dolphins, 41-14. The Jets had 275 yards rushing in the game. They had about 50 when the game was tied at seven. This was another game that I read incorrectly.

Other Games I Looked At
Bills minus 2 1/2 over Cards

The Cards were coming off a big and emotional win over the Seahawks (minus 1 point). They were a fresh due down. The Bills had due, number (power rating was 6 1/2), and fatigue (Card emotional effort last week) working for them. The Bills were also coming off a phony loss. The Bills had value since my oddsmaker line was 5 and my power rating was 6 1/2 for the Bills.

However at 1-5, I was worried about laying points on a team with not that much incentive. I felt that the Bills might save themselves for the divisional rival Jets next week. I also had yet to bet a favorite this season and am very careful betting them.

The Bills' defense smothered the Cards and won, 38-14. However, on offense, the Bills only gained 209 yards. The Card defense continues to impress and I continue to be very worried about my under 5 1/2 win Card bet.

Titans minus 2 1/2 over Bengals

The Bengals were coming off a monster Monday night emotional home win over the Broncos (minus 1 point). Even without Steve McNair, the Titans were 4 1/2 point favorites in my power ratings and thus had value. However, I felt that the Titans must-win game was last week and that they may have considered themselves out of it with the loss to the Vikings. I don't like to lay points with teams that expected to make the playoffs but were now out of contention.

The Titans held on late to win, 27-20. The Titans forced a fumble by the Bengals on their nine-yard line to stop the final Bengal threat.

Week 8 Record: 2-3
Season Record: 14-14-2

Week Nine

I had a good week this week. I went 4-1 in my bets and 3-1 for the service. Though I am ahead in my own betting I won't really consider this season a winning one unless my clients also win.

Bills plus 3 1/2 over Jets: Normal Play

There were many reasons to like the Bills in this game: 1) The Jets were coming from a Monday night blowout win (41-14) over the Dolphins (minus 1/2 point), 2) The Jets had been emotionally up for the last two games (minus 1/2 point), 3) The Jets were a fresh due down and the Bills had due, revenge, fatigue (Jets being up the last two games), and number (power ratings favored the Bills) working for them, 4) The Jets were 0-2-1 after their last three wins (minus 1/2 point). With my power ratings favoring the Bills by 1 1/2 points, they had strong value in this game as well.

The Bills scored 12 straight points to open the second half and withstood a late Jet touchdown to win, 22-17. The Jets' quarterback, Chad Pennington, was knocked out of the game in the fourth quarter. Though the game was even at halftime, the Bills were outplayed in the first half. However, in the second half, the Bills totally outplayed the Jets—they didn't even allow them a first down until a late touchdown drive—and thus had to be considered the right side.

Bengals plus 2 over Cowboys: Small Play

Plus two never really existed for the betting public (except briefly at CRIS on Sunday night), so I didn't even give out this game to my clients.

Though I considered the Bengals one of the worst teams in the NFL (I had them in the D letter power rating class), I made a small bet on them in this game. They had won two of three at home and had beaten a strong Bronco team (though it was a Monday night win and bad teams at home sometimes play way over their heads on Monday night).

The Cowboys were coming off a sloppy win (minus 1/2 point) and had a home Monday night game with the rival Eagles next up. With my power rating being Pick on the game, the Bengals had some value taking two points.

Though the Bengals won the game, 26-3, I was not convinced I had the right side in this game. On their opening drive, the Cowboys eschewed a field goal and came up short on fourth down. The Cowboys outstated the Bengals in the first half, but were hurt by three turnovers.

Starting the second half down, 9-3, the Cowboys marched to the Bengal twenty-five, but committed a couple of dumb penalties to go out of scoring range. The Bengals then completed a third down 76-yard touchdown pass to start to break the game open. Certainly not convinced at all the Bengals are the better team!

Bucs plus 3 1/2 over Chiefs: Normal Play

At 2-5, the Bucs were a must-win underdog in this game (plus 1/2 point). The Chiefs had scored 56 and 45 points in wins the last two weeks (minus 1/2 point) but those wins were at home and this week the Chiefs were playing a tough Buc defense on the road. The Bucs, coming off a bye (plus 1/2 point), had an extra week to prepare for this game.

With my power rating being one for the Chiefs, the Bucs had value taking 3 or more.

The Bucs had some breaks in this game. On a long pass play, the Bucs forced a fumble that they recovered in their endzone. The Chiefs had two other turnovers in the game, including a pass intercepted in the Bucs' endzone. Last, Priest Holmes, the star Chiefs' running back, got injured and missed the last quarter-and-a-half. The Bucs won, 34-31. On their last touchdown, the Bucs missed the extra point, which meant that I would lose my bet if the Chiefs scored a touchdown (and made the point after). Fortunately that didn't happen—the Bucs stopped them twice, including the endzone interception.

Saints plus 7 and 7 1/2 over Chargers: Normal Play

I increased my bet slightly when I found 7 1/2 on the day of the game. I needed a lot more than that since the Saints were routed, 43-17.

The Chargers were a fresh star due down in this game and the Saints had star due, fatigue (Chargers off big win over Raiders last week), and number (power rating was 5 1/2) working for them. With the power rating being 5 1/2, the Saints had value taking 7.

I never had a chance in this game. I was more off on the Chargers in my pre-season evaluations than I was on any other team. I had them rated a D- team and projected them to win four games. Now they were 6-3, and after the game I had them at C+ in my letter power ratings. When I am that much off on a team, dues come in less often than usual.

Broncos minus 5 over Texans: Normal Play

This was the first favorite that I bet this season. The Texans were coming off a huge emotional win over the Jaguars last week (minus 1 point) and were celebrating being over .500 (4-3). In addition, the Texans had a game with the rival Colts up next (minus 1/2 point). The Broncos, meanwhile, were coming off two straight losses and were tied for the AFC West lead with the surprising Chargers. With my power rating being 7 1/2, the Broncos had value giving up to six points.

The Texans started the game with a drive to the Bronco 20. They then missed a 37-yard field goal. The Broncos scored ten straight points. The Texans then got a touchdown set up by a blocked punt. However, the Broncos scored touchdowns on their next three possessions to go up, 31-7. A late Texan touchdown made the final score 31-13 for the Broncos. On my Web site I predicted a two touchdown Bronco win in this game. I was glad to see that they won by even more than that!

Another Game I Looked At
Lions minus 2 1/2 over Redskins

The Lions had played their best ball this season off losses. They had gotten road wins in Atlanta and New York off losses. The Lions had covered after nine of their last 13 losses. With my power rating being 3 1/2, the Lions had value. However, the Redskins were 14 points behind the Lions on the spread range. That model kept me off of the game. The Redskins used a trick play and a blocked punt to win, 17-10.

Week 9 Record: 4-1
Season Record: 18-15-2

Week 10

I had my worst week of the season, going 0-4. I can't seem to keep any momentum going this season. One of my losses (Jets) was not a selection for the service since after I bet it the number needed (plus 2) was not around.

Jets plus 2 over Ravens: Small Play

The Ravens were coming off three straight fairly up emotional games (minus 1/2 point). The Ravens were also a fresh due down and the Jets had due, number (power rating was Pick), and fatigue working for them (Ravens' up efforts). The Ravens were also coming from a phony win while the Jets were coming from a phony loss (plus 1 point for the Jets). The Jets had Quincy Carter starting at quarterback for them since Chad Pennington was injured. I felt that Carter could run the Jet offense decently, though I deducted 1 1/2 points with Pennington out.

With my power rating being Pick, the Jets had value at plus 2. The Ravens' road loss to the Browns in opening week showed they could lose to a team in the Jets' class (C without Pennington).

The Jets led 14-0 and were headed for more when an option pass into the endzone was intercepted close to halftime and run back 78 yards. The Ravens then scored right before halftime. Instead of leading 17 or 21-0 at half-time, the Jets' lead was just 14-7. The Ravens then went up 17-14 late in the game. The Jets had a last ditch drive and got to the Raven 3. Bad play calling and clock management forced the Jets to settle for a field goal instead of getting the winning touchdown. In overtime the Ravens took their second possession for a field goal and won, 20-17.

Browns plus 6 over Steelers: Normal Play

The Steelers were coming off two monster wins over previously undefeated teams, the Pats and Eagles (minus 2 points). The Steelers were a fresh star due down and the Browns had star due, revenge, fatigue (Steelers' emotional efforts the last two weeks), coverage (three of last four games in Cleveland fell on three), and number (power rating was Pick). The Browns were also coming from a phony loss last week (plus 1/2 point). With my power rating being Pick, the Browns had all the value.

Three weeks before, the Browns had taken the Eagles to overtime at home before losing. This showed that the Browns could compete with a team in the Steelers class—at least at home. The Steelers had played their strong ball at home this season. The Browns also had played their best ball at home.

Before the game, a fight broke out between Steelers and Browns players. This fight served the function of getting the Steelers up for this game. They won handily,

24-10. The Steelers are probably now the best team in the NFL. They don't seem to have many weaknesses.

Redskins minus 2 1/2 over Bengals: Small Play

I don't like betting favorites, but this one seemed to stand out. I didn't feel that the Bengals were going any-place in the AFC and thought that they would save their strong efforts for divisional rivals like the Steelers, whom they played next (minus 1/2 point). At 3-5, the Redskins were still just a game out of the last playoff spot in the NFC. The Bengals were coming off a rout win against the Cowboys at home in which they were lucky, as I pointed out last week. They might letdown after that win. With my power rating favoring the Redskins by 6, they had value. My oddsmaker line was 5 1/2 for the Redskins.

The Bengals were 0-4 on the road this year. One re-cent loss was to the Titans who were without McNair at quarterback. The Redskins had beaten the Bucs at home by 6. Both of those games showed that the Redskins could cope in this game.

The Redskin offense could do nothing until the fourth quarter. Patrick Ramsey had replaced an ineffective Mark Brunell at quarterback. By then, the Bengals led, 17-0. The Redskins rallied, but fell short, 10-17.

Giants plus 1 1/2 over Cards: Normal Play

This game I bet late since money showed all week for the Cards. Giant injuries on the defensive line were the main reason for this move on the Cards.

The Giants had played well after losses, covering both times. After their last loss, the Giants won by three touch-downs in Minnesota. The Cards were 0-2 to the number after wins this season thus far (1 point for Giants). The Gi-ants last week had lost to a bad team in the Bears, which figured to make them bounce back this week (plus 1/2 point). The Cards also came from a phony win (minus 1/2 point). With my power rating favoring the Giants by four, they had value as an underdog in this game.

The Giants' wins at Minnesota, Green Bay, and Dallas showed they could beat a team in the Cards' class (D+).

The Giants' defense played well, holding the Cards to 198 total yards. But the Giants couldn't overcome ten penalties against them, most at critical times. They lost 14-17.

Another Game I Looked At
Panthers plus 2 over 49ers

In this game my power rating favored the Panthers by 3. I had over a four point edge in my power ratings—almost an automatic bet. However, going into this season, the Panthers, Super Bowl losers last year, had high hopes. They planned on reaching the Super Bowl again and winning it this time. Now, at 1-7, those hopes were gone. I wondered how they could be motivated for any games the rest of the season except maybe against divisional rivals. The 49ers, while by far the least talented team in the NFL, tried hard in every game. I thus decided to pass the Panthers. The Panthers showed heart in this game, rallying from a 0-17 deficit to win, 37-27.

Week 10 Record: 0-4
Season Record: 18-19-2

Week 11

I bounced back this week, going 3-0. One of the games I bet (Bills plus 3) wasn't given to the service since the number needed to bet this game (plus 2 1/2) was never that close to being available for normal bettors.

A FULL SEASON OF NFL BETS

Bills plus 3 over Rams: Normal Play

I needed at least plus 2 1/2 on this game since I made the Rams a 2 1/2 point favorite on my oddsmaking line, and I never go against my own line.

The Bills were coming off an embarrassing loss (6-29) at the Patriots on national TV, a Sunday night game (plus 1/2 point for the Bills). The Bills had gone 2-0-1 after their last three rout losses. The Rams were coming from a high emotional effort in their win over the divisional rival Seahawks (minus 1 point). My power rating favored the Bills by 2 1/2 points, which gave them value. The Bills' home win over the Jets, and the Rams' home loss to the Saints, as well as their road losses at Miami and at the Falcons showed that the Bills could cope in this game.

The Bills trailed early 10-0, but came back. Two long punt returns in the early third quarter—one for a touchdown and one to the Ram five that set up a touchdown—put the Bills ahead, 31-17. They won, 37-17.

Titans plus 4 over Jaguars: Normal Play

This game showed how much these teams had changed in the public's perception. In Week 3, the Titans were six point home favorites over the Jaguars (a game that I won taking seven on the Jaguars). Now, with their backup quarterback, the Jaguars were home four point favorites over the Titans, who had their quarterback, Steve McNair, returning from an injury.

The Titans still had a small chance at the playoffs at 3-6. Another loss would totally doom them. Thus they were a must-win underdog (plus 1/2 point). In addition, this was a revenge game for the Titans.

With my power rating being Pick, the Titans had value. Their win at Green Bay in Week 5 showed that the Titans could cope in this game. The Jaguars had not yet shown coping with their backup quarterback, David Garrard.

A late touchdown wiped out a 10-15 deficit and gave the Titans an 18-15 win. They stayed alive for another week in the playoff race in the AFC.

Texans plus 4 over Packers: Normal Play

This was a Sunday night nationally televised game. The home Texans would be very up for the game. The Packers were coming from a number one emotional effort in their win over the Vikings (minus 1 point). Several Texan players said that this game would define their season.

With my power rating being Pick, the Texans had value. The Texans' home win over the Jaguars (also coming from a huge emotional win the week before) and road wins at Kansas City and at the Titans showed that the Texans could cope. The Packer home losses to the Bears and Giants showed that they could well lose this game.

The Texans led 13-3 going into the fourth quarter. However, they became too conservative on offense and Brett Favre brought the Packers back. They tied the game with a touchdown and a field goal and then got the ball back with two minutes left. Favre completed six passes and led the Packers to a game winning 46-yard field goal. They thus won, 16-13. There was some plus 3 1/2 around on this game for Texan bettors. However, my service called this game a tie since most offshore books had a constant 3 on the game.

Other Games I Looked At

I actually originally bet two other games this week, but cancelled out the bets when late information made me not like my sides anymore. I would have split these games. I am not including them in my betting record, but will mention why I liked and then cancelled out these games.

A FULL SEASON OF NFL BETS

Cards plus 3 1/2 over Panthers

The Cards were now actually in playoff contention in the NFC at 4-5. A win would also get the Cards to .500, a major accomplishment for a team that had been losers for so long.

The Cards wanted to avenge a loss from last year to the Panthers (plus 1/2 point). At 2-7, the Panthers season was over and they figured to be saving their energy for divisional games against the Bucs and Saints (minus 1/2 point).

My power rating on the game was Pick, which gave the Cards value. The Cards' road win at Miami and the Panthers' home loss to the Raiders showed that the Cards could cope in this game.

The morning of the game, it was announced that the Cards quarterback, McKown, was being benched and Shaun King was starting. King had not been a decent quarterback in the league. In fact, he had been terrible. When I heard this news, I got off the game (laying 2). The Panthers won in a rout, 35-10 and King showed again that he is a poor quarterback.

Dolphins plus 10 over Seahawks

The Dolphins had a good due combination working for them in this game. They were a fresh star due up and had due, fatigue (coming off of a bye), and number working for them. The Seahawks also had done poorly after losses this year, going 0-3 to the number the next week (minus 1/2 point). My power rating on the game favored the Seahawks by 6 1/2, which gave the Dolphins value at plus 10. The Seahawks' close home win—six points—over the Panthers showed that the Dolphins could cope.

In another quarterback move, the Dolphins benched Jay Fiedler and started AJ Feely. I didn't like this move and got off the game (laying 9). The Seahawks won, 24-17, but didn't cover. Feely threw a late pass that was run back for the winning Seahawk touchdown.

Week 11 Record: 3-0
Season Record: 21-19-2

Week 12

A very frustrating week. I went 2-4. With decent luck, I probably would have gone 5-1. On the plus side, I did clinch one of the season over/under bets I made; it was the biggest one I made.

Ravens plus 7 1/2 over Patriots: Normal Play

This was strictly a value bet. With my power rating being 3 1/2 for the Pats, the Ravens had a four point edge in my power ratings at plus 7 1/2.

I felt that the Ravens' quarterback, Kyle Boller, had made significant progress in recent weeks and would avoid the big mistake. Getting 7 1/2 points with a defense as strong as the Ravens', I felt I was getting value. The Ravens' close loss at Philadelphia (by five points) showed me that they could compete in this game.

The Ravens got crushed in the game, 24-3. It was 3-3 at halftime, but the Ravens' score was a lucky one, set up on 30 yards of penalties against the Pats on a punt return near halftime. The Ravens got just 124 yards in the game, while the Pats had 314. This was the one game this weekend where I clearly had an incorrect side.

Jaguars plus 7 over Vikings: Normal Play

With Bryon Leftwich back at quarterback, the Jaguars were nearly as good as the Vikings (C+ versus B-). Leftwich had been injured the last two weeks. For the Vikings, Randy Moss returned.

A FULL SEASON OF NFL BETS

The Vikings had been emotionally up the last three weeks (minus 1/2 point) and had a game with divisional rival Chicago next (minus 1/2 point) after beating Detroit. In the weak NFC, where a .500 record might make the playoffs, the need to win wasn't as urgent for the Vikings as for the Jaguars in the AFC, where even ten wins might not make the playoffs.

With my power rating being 3 1/2 for the Vikings, the Jaguars had value. They had additional value because of all the close games they had played.

The Jaguars' win at Indianapolis and the Vikings' home loss to the Giants showed coping for the Jaguars.

The Jaguars were trailing 16-20 and were driving to the Viking twenty with just over two minutes to go. Even if they didn't score, the Jaguars had a sure cover. Then Leftwich was sacked and fumbled. The fumble was returned 77 yards for a touchdown by the Vikings. The Jaguars then drove to the Viking fifteen with a chance still to cover. However, they failed on fourth down and I had my first miracle loss of the season.

Panthers plus 3 1/2 over Bucs: Normal Play

I had thought that I might be on the Bucs in this game before I saw the line. I believed the Panthers would be favored. However, the Bucs opened as 1 1/2 point favorites at Carolina and the line went to 3. I was able to get 3 1/2. With my power rating being 1/2 a point for the Panthers, they had a four point edge in my power ratings.

The Bucs were just 2-8 after their last ten wins (minus 1/2 point). The Panthers' win at Kansas City and the Bucs' losses at Washington and Oakland showed coping ability for the Panthers.

Five field goals were missed in the game. The Panthers scored with 20 seconds left, to go up 21-14. The Bucs got to mid-field and a last ditch pass into the endzone just missed being completed. The Panthers just hung on.

Since plus 3 1/2 wasn't close to being available for the betting public, this game was not a selection for my service.

Titans plus 1 over Texans: Normal Play

Last week, the Texans were sky-high for their Sunday night home game against the Packers. Several players had said that that game would define their season. When the Texans lost a ten point fourth quarter lead and blew the game, I felt that they would be very down for this game (minus 1 point).

The Titans had lost to the Texans earlier this season and wanted revenge. Their win last week in Jacksonville told me they could get it (plus 1/2 point). The Titans had vague playoff hopes. If they could somehow run the table to finish 10-6, they had a shot. Thus, the Titans were a must-win underdog in this game (plus 1/2 point).

With my line favoring the Titans by 2 points, they had value at plus 1. The Titans' wins at Green Bay, at Jacksonville, and at Miami told me that they could win this game. Near game time, money flowed in on the Texans. I could have actually gotten 3 1/2 on the game, I found out later. I should have at least gone further on my bet.

The Titans built an early 21-3 lead. The Texans looked finished. Then they staged the biggest comeback of their brief history and won, 31-21. The Titans at 21-24, had two turnovers in Texan territory. This was at least a semi-miracle loss for me.

A FULL SEASON OF NFL BETS

Saints plus 10 over Falcons: Normal Play

In this game dues were colliding. The Saints were a fresh due up, while the Falcons were due down (non-fresh). The Saints had due, coverage (hadn't lost by over seven at Atlanta in a long time), and number (power rating was 6 1/2) working for them.

With the power rating at 6 1/2, the Saints had value. The Saints' win at St. Louis, and Falcons' home loss to the Lions and close home win over the Cards, told me that the Saints could compete.

Early on, the game didn't look good with the Saints trailing 0-14 and later 6-17 at halftime. Inspired by their coach, Jim Hasslet, going berserk at halftime, the Saints responded with two touchdowns to take a 21-17 lead. With the game in the balance, the Falcons drove easily for the winning touchdown and won, 24-21. However, the plus 10 on the Saints also won.

Rams plus 7 over Packers: Normal Play

This was another value play. With my power rating being 3 for the Packers, the Rams had a four point edge in my power ratings. I actually was able to go a little further taking 7 1/2. I felt that these teams were basically even (C+ for both).

The public by now was forgetting how the Packers had struggled at home early in the season, losing home games to the Bears, Giants, and Titans—none of whom were better than the Rams. The Rams' big win at Seattle also told me the Rams could compete in this game.

The Rams lost 45-17—a very misleading score. With two minutes left, the Packers went for it on fourth down, up 31-17. If the Rams stopped them, I could get a push on my bet with a consolation touchdown. But the Packers' running back, Davenport, broke loose for a touchdown. Then the Packers returned a fumble for a touchdown. Earlier in the game the Packers had returned another fumble for a touchdown. The Rams screwed up on three scoring chances in the game. They threw an interception in the endzone at 10-21. Earlier, they had missed a 42-yard field goal. Later the Rams botched up a fake field goal. In the game, the Rams actually outgained the Packers, 452-446 and had more first downs (25-22). Thus again, though the game was a loss, it was a misleading one.

Another Game I Looked At
Dolphins plus 2 1/2 over 49ers

This would have been another value play since my power ratings actually had the Dolphins favored by 6 1/2. The 49ers were by far the worst team in the NFL this year and one of the worst teams ever.

However, at 1-9, I felt that the Dolphins might be looking ahead to divisional rival Buffalo next week. Being totally out of contention, that seemed a legitimate worry. The Dolphins won, 24-17.

One thing on the plus side for the week was that the Titan loss to the Texans clinched my large under-10-wins season bet on the Titans.

Week 12 Record: 2-4
Season Record: 23-23-2

Week 13

I bounced back this week, going 4-1.

Ravens minus 6 over Bengals: Normal Play

I felt that the Bengals were one of the most overrated teams in the NFL. I felt that their offense would be shut down this game and the Ravens would put up decent points on a very suspect Bengal defense.

A FULL SEASON OF NFL BETS

The Ravens were coming from a rout loss at New England the week before. In recent years, the Ravens were perfect (2-0) after a rout loss. The Ravens also were an incredible 15-1-1 to the number after their last 17 losses (+ 1 1/2 points). The Bengals had been somewhat emotionally up in their last two games (loss to the Steelers and wild 58-48 win over the Browns) (minus 1/2 point). Lastly, the Bengals were coming off a sloppy win last week (minus 1/2 point).

My power rating on this game was the Ravens by 13, which gave them great value.

The Bengals' road loss at the Browns and their earlier 14 point home loss to the Ravens showed that they couldn't cope in this game. The Ravens' big home wins over the Bills and Steelers and their road win at the Bengals showed that the Ravens could cope in this spot.

The Ravens led 20-3 late in the third quarter. Their defense had stopped the Bengals virtually the whole game. The Ravens then lost a muffed punt and the game totally turned. In less than a quarter, the Bengals drove for three touchdowns against a supposedly great Raven defense and took a 24-23 lead. The Ravens then drove for a field goal (not enough for my bet) and the Bengals answered that with a game winning field goal drive. The Bengals won, 27-26. Carson Palmer, the Bengal rookie quarterback, came of age in this game.

Bucs Pick over Falcons: Normal Play

In the weak NFC, the Bucs still had wild card hopes. The Falcons were five up in the division and pretty much locked into the second seed in the NFC (the Eagles were top seed). With this incentive, and wanting revenge for an earlier loss to the Falcons, the Bucs would be the more motivated team.

289

The Bucs had covered the spread after their last three losses (plus 1/2 point).

My power rating was Bucs by three, which meant that they had value giving two points or less.

The Falcons' home loss to the Lions and the Bucs' defeat of the Chiefs at home showed that the Bucs could cope in this game and the Falcons might not be able to.

The Bucs won, 27-0, but the game was not really a rout. The Falcons twice drove to the Buc one-yard line (once when they trailed just 0-7) and threw interceptions. Another time the Falcons lost the ball on downs on the Buc twenty. Later, the Falcons lost a fumble on the Buc thirty-seven. The Falcons actually outgained the Bucs in yardage, 255-247. Thus, though it sounds strange to say, I was a little bit lucky in a game where I covered the spread by 27 points.

Panthers plus 3 over Saints: Normal Play

This was not a play for my service since the strike number (plus 2) was not around for that long, though a few clients who deal with me directly said that they were able to get it.

A few weeks ago when the Panthers were 1-7, they had looked like a totally buried team. I had certainly written off any playoff hopes they had. Now at 4-7, the Panthers were just one game out of the sixth seed. As an underdog early in the week, the Panthers were a must-win underdog (plus 1/2 point).

With my power rating being Pick, the Panthers had value at plus 2 or more. The Panthers had also covered seven of their last nine as road underdogs.

The Panther Week 2 win at Kansas City showed that they could cope in this game.

The Panthers scored 23 points before the Saints even got a first down and coasted, 32-21.

Broncos plus 3 1/2 over Chargers: Normal Play

This game was a value and standing incentive game. As an oddsmaker I made the game Pick since the Broncos were a game behind the Chargers and needed the game more. Getting 3 1/2 was getting a lot of value, I felt.

The Broncos' one point loss at the Jaguars and the Chargers' home loss to the Jets showed that the Broncos could cope in this game as field goal plus underdogs.

The Broncos lost 20-17, but I covered my bet. The Broncos would have won the game if they hadn't committed four turnovers. The last one came with under four minutes left when a pass from the Charger seven was intercepted in the endzone.

Jaguars plus 3 1/2 over Steelers: Normal Play

The Jaguars were a home underdog in a Sunday night game with a power rating edge. My power rating on the game was Steelers 1 1/2, which gave the Jaguars value at plus 3 or more.

Some of the luster had come off of Steelers' rookie quarterback Ben Roethlisberger in the last two games. The Bengal and Redskin defense put a lot of pressure on him and Roethlisberger hadn't responded that well, though the Steelers had won both games.

The Jaguars' win at Indianapolis showed that they could cope against the Steelers at home.

The Jaguars lost the game, 16-17, but I won my bet. I am not at all sure I had the right side. The Steelers drove for a touchdown the first time they had the ball. When the Jaguars tied up the game, the Steelers right away drove for another touchdown. Very late, when the Jaguars went up 16-14, the Steelers easily drove for the game-winning field goal. Thus the Steelers controlled this game at the key moments and I was lucky to cover a small spread.

Other Games I Looked At

Titans plus 13 over Colts

The Colts were a fresh star due down in this game. The Titans had revenge, number (my power rating was nine), and fatigue (the Colts fresh off several high scoring wins) working for them.

I well remembered that I was somewhat lucky to win the first matchup between these two teams (see Week 2) when the Colts won 31-17. The Titans blew all sorts of chances to blow that game open.

Reasons I favored the Titans: 1) Colts were coming off a rout win on national TV, a 41-9 Thanksgiving win over the Lions (minus 1/2 point), 2) The Titans were coming off a phony loss (plus 1/2 point), 3) The Colts were coming off wins where they had scored 31, 49, 41, and 41 points (minus 1/2 point).

With my power rating being 9, the Titans had value. The Colts' home loss to the Jaguars told me the Titans could cope.

But when Steve McNair decided his injuries would keep him from playing, I passed the game. Volek, his backup, is a huge step down.

The Colts scored the last 34 points of the game to win 51-24. Payton Manning is having perhaps the best year a quarterback has ever had in the NFL. He now has 44 touchdown passes.

The Titans tried three onside kicks in the game. It was as if they knew they couldn't compete with the Colts and needed gimmicks to stay in the game.

Dolphins plus 6 over Bills

The betting public was all over the Bills in this game, driving up the price from minus 3 during the week.

The Bills had scored 37 and 38 points in wins the last two weeks (minus 1/2 point). The Bills were a fresh may due down and the Dolphins had may due, revenge, number (power rating was 2 1/2), and fatigue (the Bills' scoring efforts the last two weeks) working for them. The Bills also were off a sloppy win (minus 1/2 point).

Until last week, the Bills hadn't won on the road in over a year. Now with that one win, the public was in love with them in Miami. The public usually loses when they think and bet like that.

The Dolphins' home win over the Rams earlier in the season told me they could win this game.

Two factors kept me off the game. First, the Dolphin quarterback, AJ Feely, had a dislocated finger on his throwing hand. It still bothered him later in the week. Second, leading Dolphin defender, Zach Thomas, was out.

The Bills came from ten points down to win, 42-32. The Dolphins had five interceptions and seven turnovers overall. The last of these interceptions was run back for a touchdown in the last two minutes that covered the spread for the Bills. Would have been a tough loss.

Week 13 Record: 4-1
Season Record: 27-24-2

Week 14

I ended up with a slight loss, going 2-2 for the weekend.

Seahawks plus 7 1/2 over Vikings: Normal Play

The Seahawks hadn't played well this season, but they were a fresh star due up and had the star due combination of revenge and number (the power rating was 6) working for them.

With my oddsmaker line being 4 and my power rating being 6, the Seahawks had value taking 7 1/2. The Viking home loss to the Giants and their close home wins over the Bears and Lions showed that the Seahawks could compete in this game.

The Seahawks overcame an early 0-10 deficit and won 27-23. A late option pass by Randy Moss into the endzone was intercepted to preserve the win for the Seahawks. I wish the Vikings had managed to win the game, though obviously I didn't want them to cover, since I was now in trouble with my over 8 1/2 win bet on them.

Bears plus 7 1/2 over Jaguars: Normal Play

The Jaguars had played almost nothing but close games this season. Their biggest win was by six points. The Jaguars also were coming off a very high emotional game against the Steelers last week (minus 1 point).

In their win last week, the Bears had good play from their new quarterback, Chad Hutchinson. I had never before been impressed by him. If he could give them decent play, the Bears would be a competitive team.

The Bears' early season win at Green Bay and their close loss to the Vikings in Minnesota showed that they could compete. With my power rating on the game being 5 1/2 for the Jaguars, the Bears had value.

Hutchinson played like he did in Dallas when he played poorly. The Jaguars won, 22-3.

Steelers minus 4 over Jets: Small Play

The Steelers wanted to avenge a loss to the Jets last season. They had covered 13 of their last 18 revenge games (plus 1/2 point). The Jets were also a fresh star due down. The Steelers had star due, revenge, and number (power rating was 8) working for them.

With my oddsmaker line being 7 and my power rating being 8, the Steelers had value. The Steeler big home wins over the Patriots and Eagles showed that they could handle the Jets and win by more than the spread.

The Steelers won, 17-6, but the game was closer than the score indicated. The yardage (295) and first downs (15) were both even. After this game I moved the Jets up in my letter power ratings to B- from C+.

Rams plus 7 1/2 over Panthers: Normal Play

Early in the week, I was hoping to get the Panthers as a home underdog. The game opened 6 for the Panthers then went up to 7. Now the Rams were the side that I liked.

The Panthers were in a divisional series sandwich. They were coming off wins over the Bucs and Saints and had the Falcons and Bucs up next (minus 1/2 point). It didn't seem to me that they should be touchdown favorites over anyone (except if they played the 49ers). The Rams had Chris Chandler starting at quarterback and were down to their third string running back, Arien Harris. However, this was more than put into the price of the game.

My oddsmaker line was Panthers by 4 and my power ratings favored them by 3 1/2. Thus the Rams had value.

The Panthers' home loss to the Raiders showed that they could lose this game.

Chandler had a terrible game, throwing six interceptions, and the Rams lost, 20-7. Despite having seven turnovers in all (versus two takeaways), the Rams still had a chance to cover late in the game. However, this didn't happen.

Another Game I Looked At
Saints plus 8 over Cowboys

This line seemed high. My oddsmaker line was 6 1/2 and my power rating on the game was 5. The Saints were a fresh due up and had due, fatigue (the Cowboys had played on Monday night), and number working for them.

The Saints' win at the Rams and the Cowboys' home loss to the Giants showed that the Saints could win this game—or at least cover. What kept me off the game were four factors:

1) The Cowboys wanted revenge for a loss to the Saints last season.
2) The Saints were in a divisional series sandwich.
3) The Saints were a terrible defensive team (the only team not to hold any opponent to 17 or less before this week) and I felt that the new Cowboy running attack spearheaded by rookie Julian Jones could have a big game on the porous defense of the Saints.
4) The Cowboys still had slight playoff hopes. I felt that their coach, Parcells, would have them win this game... possibly handily.

The Saints played better than I thought they would and won, 27-13. They overcame an early 0-10 deficit.

The Eagles' win over the Redskins made them 12-1 and made me lose the season under 11 bet I had on them.

Week 14 Record: 2-2
Season Record: 29-26-2

Week 15

Once again, I bounced back from a losing week, going 4-2. Maybe I should just bet every other week!

Panthers plus 4 1/2 over Falcons: Normal Play

At 6-7, the Panthers now had playoff hopes. Meanwhile, the Falcons had not only clinched the playoffs, but were pretty much locked into the second seed. As an underdog, the Panthers had a large motivational edge (plus 1/2 point). The Panthers also wanted revenge for an earlier loss to the Falcons. Their win at Kansas City showed that they could get it (plus 1/2 point). The Falcons also were a weak may due down. The Panthers had may due, revenge, and number (power rating was 1 1/2) working for them.

With my power rating being 1 1/2 for the Falcons, the Panthers had value. Their win at Kansas City and the Falcons' home loss to the Lions showed that the Panthers could cope.

The Panthers trailed 10-24 early in the fourth quarter, but never gave up. They scored three touchdowns to go ahead, 31-24. The Falcons tied it on a spectacular Michael Vick run on fourth down. The game went to overtime. The Falcons intercepted a pass and ran the ball back into field goal range. They then kicked the field goal to win, 34-31.

This game showed why underdogs fighting for the playoffs are good bets. The Panthers never gave up and even though they ultimately lost, they still covered the bet. As a favorite, the Panthers would have lost the money.

Lions plus 3 1/2 over Vikings: Small Play

In this game, the Vikings had the playoff incentive while the Lions were pretty close to being out of contention. However, even with a loss the Vikings could still reach the playoffs with wins in their last two games. The Vikings had been playing poorly lately and I felt that their freefall could well continue. The Lions wanted to avenge an earlier loss to the Vikings (they blew a 19-7 third quarter lead in Minnesota).

With my power rating being two for the Vikings, the Lions had value.

The Viking losses at Chicago and at home to the Giants showed that they could lose this game.

The Lions fell behind, 21-28, on a late Viking touchdown drive. I gave up at this point. However, without any timeouts, Lions quarterback Joey Harrington drove the Lions for a touchdown with eight seconds left. The Lions then flubbed the snap on the extra point and thus lost, 28-27. Taking plus 3 1/2, I had won my bet.

Bengals plus 3 and plus 3 1/2 over Bills: Normal Play

In this game, I took plus 3 early in the week. The game quickly went down to Pick. However, with Bengal quarterback Carson Palmer out for the game, the game went back up and I went a little further, taking 3 1/2.

I had been looking to go against the Bills for several weeks, but the opponent and situation were never right. I felt that now was the time. The Bills had scored 30-plus points in four straight wins (minus 1/2 point). The Bills were also a fresh star due down with the Bengals having star due, number (my power rating was Bengals by 2 1/2), revenge (the Bengals had lost to the Bills last season), and fatigue (the Bills' big scoring efforts the last few weeks) working for them. I felt that Jon Kitna, the Bengal quarterback last season who had done well, could step in and the Bengals wouldn't lose anything at quarterback. The Bengals' wanting revenge and having beaten Denver at home and the Ravens on the road would also help (plus 1/2 point).

With my power rating favoring the Bengals by 2 1/2, they had value. The Bengals' wins over the Ravens and Broncos, as well as the Bills' losses at Oakland and at Baltimore, showed that the Bengals could cope in this game.

The Bengals' defense did well, holding the Bills to 213 total yards. However, Kitna threw two interceptions (one of which was returned for a touchdown) and the Bengals also had a punt blocked and returned for a touchdown.

The Bengals had two other turnovers as well. The Bills won, 33-17. I was wrong in feeling that Kitna could adequately replace Palmer at quarterback.

Cards plus 3 1/2 over Rams: Normal Play

Last week showed that Chris Chandler could not replace Marc Bulger at quarterback for the Rams. When it was announced that Chandler would be starting again this week, I quickly bet the Cards.

The Cards were coming off a loss to the worst team in football, the 49ers (plus 1/2 point). In that game, McKown came back from his benching, did well after halftime, and nearly brought the Cards to victory from a 25-point deficit. I felt that he would be very effective this week against a soft Rams' defense.

The Cards also wanted to avenge a loss to the Rams, a game they had nearly won in St. Louis, and their home win over the Seahawks showed that they could get this revenge (plus 1/2 point). The Cards were also coming off a loss as home favorites and were now home underdogs (plus 1/2 point).

My power rating favored the Cards by four points, giving them huge value. My oddsmaker line favored the Cards by 1 1/2, also giving them value.

The Cards' home wins over the Giants and Seahawks showed that they could cope.

The Cards won in a rout, 31-7. The only Ram touchdown came on a fumble return. Chandler, who was 1 for 6 for 1 yard with an interception, was benched after the first quarter. Jamie Martin was slightly better, but could not often move the Ram offense.

No question that I had the right side in this game!

Chiefs plus 3 1/2 over Broncos: Small Play

This was mostly a value play. My power rating favored the Chiefs by one point and when the line went to three for the Broncos (from Chiefs by 1 1/2), the Chiefs had a four point edge in my power ratings.

Even though the Chiefs had been out of the playoff race for some time, they were still playing hard. The previous week in a Monday night game in Tennessee, the Chiefs overcame several deficits (including one of two touchdowns) to win. This was surprising since the Chiefs had expected to contend not only for the playoffs, but the Super Bowl. Usually teams like that are very bad bets when they fall out of contention, but the Chiefs were proving an exception to that rule.

One of my models that favored the Chiefs was that the Broncos were coming off a sloppy win (minus 1/2 point). Though the Broncos were in contention for the playoffs, they had not been playing well. Plus, the Broncos were a favorite in this game.

The Chiefs returned the opening kickoff for a touchdown and never looked back in a 45-17 rout win. And once again, the betting public and wise-guys who bet a favorite trying for the playoffs got walloped in their wallets.

Ravens plus 9 over Colts: Small Play

In this game, I went against my power ratings, which favored the Colts by 9 1/2. My oddsmaker line, however, made the Colts just a six point favorite, which gave some value to the Ravens.

I am also partial to situations in which good defensive teams like the Ravens are playing offensive powerhouses that don't have great defenses.

The Ravens had a huge incentive edge in this game. They were battling for their playoff lives while the Colts had clinched a playoff spot and would almost definitely be the three or four seed in the AFC playoffs (hosting a game on Wild Card Weekend).

The Ravens had lost a five point game in Philadelphia, while the Colts had lost a home game to the Jaguars. This showed me that the Ravens could cope as nine point underdogs.

The Ravens' defense played fairly well, holding the Colts to 20 points, their season low. However, the Ravens' offense, which had regressed in recent weeks, could only put ten points on the board. A late drive to the Colts 30 yard line ended in an interception, which ended my chances of winning the bet. The game landed very close to my power rating (9 1/2) in the Colts 20-10 win.

There were no other games that I came close to betting this week.

Week 15 Record: 4-2
Season Record: 33-28-2

Week 16

This week I split two bets. I did clinch a season over/ under win bet and leaned to the right side in three games I considered betting but passed.

Texans plus 8 over Jaguars: Normal Play

Though I lost a bet going against the Jaguars a couple of weeks ago (on the Bears, taking over a touchdown), I still felt there was value betting against the Jaguars as large favorites. Seven of their eight wins were by under a touchdown, and all had been decided in the closing moments of the game.

One model that favored the Texans was that the Jaguars were coming from a phony win (minus 1/2 point). Though the Jaguars were in the thick of playoff contention and the Texans had been mathematically eliminated when the Broncos won the day before this game, this factor was more than put into the price. In addition, the Texans would finish at .500 if they won their last games.

With my power ratings favoring the Jaguars by 5 1/2 points, the Texans had value. The Texans' outright wins at Kansas City and at Tennessee showed that they could compete in this game.

Jaguar running back Fred Taylor was a late scratch. Without him, the Jaguars really struggled on offense. They got just 126 total yards in the game. The Texans won easily, 21-0, scoring two early touchdowns to put the game out of reach.

Redskins plus 2 over Cowboys: Normal Play

This line disappeared so quickly after my bet that this game was not used as a service selection. The Redskins needed points to have value and were quickly bet to being the favorite.

The Cowboys had a huge emotional effort the week before in their close 12-7 loss in Philadelphia (minus 1 point). With the Redskins wanting revenge for an earlier loss to the Cowboys, they had the emotional edge in this game.

With my power ratings favoring the Redskins by 1 1/2 points, they had value taking points. The Redskins' win at Detroit and the Cowboys' home losses to the Giants and Saints gave the Redskins the coping edge.

Both teams missed early scoring opportunities. The Redskins scored in the middle of the fourth quarter to go up 10-6. Eventually the Cowboys had the ball on their own 25-yard line with about a minute left in the game. They went to fourth and ten. One more play stop and the Redskins would win the game. Then Vinny Testaverde completed a 15-yard pass for a first down. Four plays later he completed a 39-yard touchdown pass to win the game, 13-10. I had a very tough loss.

Other Games I Looked At
Raiders plus 10 1/2 over the Chiefs

Money came in strong on the Chiefs as they opened as seven point favorites. I made the game 5 1/2 and my power rating was six. Several models favored the Raiders. The Chiefs had scored 30 or more points in wins three straight weeks (minus 1/2 point). The Chiefs were coming from a very emotional win over the Broncos (minus 1 point). The Raiders had won a game in Denver and did have value in the price.

However, the Raiders' defense was totally crippled by injuries and I felt it would give up over 40 points to the Chiefs. I wondered if the Raider offense could keep up in hostile Kansas City. They did in a close 31-30 loss.

Steelers minus 4 over Ravens

The Steelers wanted to get revenge on the one team that had defeated them this year—the Ravens had won, 30-13, in Week 2. My power rating favored the Steelers by 9, giving them great value, and my oddsmaker line was 6 1/2. The Steelers had beaten the Patriots, Eagles, Jets, and Bengals by more than this four point spread at home. The Ravens had lost at the Colts and Browns by more than this spread on the road.

Two factors kept me away. First, the Ravens were a must-win underdog. A loss would pretty much end their playoff hopes. Second, the Ravens were 16-2-1 in their last 19 games coming off a loss (though they had lost a few weeks ago to the Bengals—by one point—and I had lost with them in that game). The Steelers won and covered, 20-7. They never had to punt in the game.

Pats plus 1 1/2 over the Jets

I hate to bet teams that are playing back-to-back on the road in a short work week. Historically, those bets have been money burners. That was the Pats' situation this week and it kept me off the game.

The Pats were coming off a loss in Miami and they had covered after their last four losses going back to late 2002. The Jets were coming off fairly strong emotional efforts in their last two games (minus 1/2 point). The Jets were a fresh due down and the Pats had due, coverage, and number working for them. The Jets were 0-2 after rout wins in 2004 (minus 1/2 point).

My power rating favored the Pats by 2, which gave them value. The Jets had lost at home to the Ravens (though Pennington didn't play that game). The Pats won easily, 23-7.

Week 16 Record: 1-1
Season Record: 34-29-2

Week 17

While I still use my power ratings in the final week of the season, I look for situations in which a team is a good bet for or a good bet against. I sometimes go further than my models on this.

I went 3-0-1 on my plays for the week, though I did lose two small season over/under win bets.

Redskins plus 6 1/2 over Vikings: Normal Play

While this bet could be considered a hedge against my Vikings over 8 1/2 win bet (they were now 8-7), the bet stood well on its own merits.

The Vikings would probably still make the playoffs even if they lost. They were playing very poorly as favorites lately and feeling the pressure of the playoff chase. They had lost to the number the last eight times they were favorites after a loss (minus 1 point). They had also lost outright in 19 of their last 21 outdoor road games.

My power ratings favored the Redskins by 1 1/2; thus there was huge value on them. Joe Gibbs' teams in the past—as I wrote last week—continued to try hard even if they were out of the playoff chase.

The Vikings' home losses to the Giants and Seahawks and road loss at Chicago showed that the Redskins could cope in this game.

The Redskins won outright, 21-18. The Vikings continued to make mistakes. A 54-yard potential touchdown pass was dropped and another possible touchdown was called back on a penalty. The Vikings, despite their loss, ended up making the playoffs when the Panthers lost.

Saints plus 8 1/2 over Panthers: Small Play

I wasn't crazy about this game. I felt that the Panthers' hot closing run was much more impressive than the Saints' three-game winning streak. The Saints won three straight when the Cowboys blew a ten-point lead, the Bucs allowed them to set up two touchdowns by returns in a four point game, and the Falcons held out several starters in a game that meant nothing to the team.

However, the price was ridiculous. My oddsmaker line on the game was five and my power rating was 3 1/2.

With the winner of this game very possibly going to the playoffs, the game figured to be played conservatively, which helped an underdog bettor taking over a touchdown.

There was a strong due combination in this game favoring the Saints. The Panthers were a fresh due down and the Saints had due, revenge (they had lost to the Panthers several weeks ago), coverage (no recent loss at Carolina by over six points), and number (power rating) working for them. The Saints had also covered seven straight times as big (seven points or plus) road underdogs.

The Saints' win at St. Louis, their close loss in Atlanta, and the Panthers' home loss to the Raiders showed that the Saints could cope.

The Saints actually won the game, 21-18. Jake Delhomme, the Panther quarterback, had a bad game. The Saints were denied a playoff berth when the Rams defeated the Jets. The Panthers would have made the playoffs had they won.

Jets plus 3 over Rams: Normal Play

I bet this one extremely early. The Jets ended up being quickly favored and the line went up to 3 1/2 on them. My oddsmaker line on the game was Pick.

Going in, both teams needed a win to make the playoffs. The Jets could get in if they lost (if the Broncos or Bills lost as well) and the Rams, too, needed help to make the playoffs. A loss would definitely eliminate them.

In a key late season game like this, I look for the better on-field team. The Jets seemed much better than the Rams. They figured to be able to run on them and the Jets' defense, I felt, could contain the Rams' offense.

My power rating on the game favored the Jets by 4 1/2, which gave them value. The Jets' win at San Diego and the Rams' home loss to the Saints showed that the Jets could easily win this game.

The Rams led 14-10 at halftime. What was most important was that the Bills trailed the Steelers at this time, 16-7. If the Bills lost, the Jets were in the playoffs. I made half a bet at halftime on the Rams in the second half at plus 3.

The Jets went ahead then fell behind, 29-26. They drove down the field for a tying field goal. Meanwhile, the Bills had lost to the Steelers—putting the Jets in the playoffs. The Rams won 32-29 on an overtime field goal. I tied my Jets bet and won my halftime bet. Since I am not recording halftime wins and losses in this book, though I did very well on them this season, I am calling this game a tie.

The Jets were lucky to get a tie on the spread for me. Two of the Jets' three touchdowns were on an interception and a kickoff return. They should have lost the game by over a touchdown.

Cards plus 3 1/2 over Bucs: Normal Play

This could also be considered a hedge bet on my Cards under 5 1/2 under win bet. However, like the Redskin bet, the bet stood out as a good bet on its own merits—the only time to make hedge bets.

Both teams were out of the playoff picture. The Bucs had expected to make the playoffs and their 5-10 record was a disgrace. Finishing 6-10 would not change the fact that this season would be a disaster for them. Traveling across the country to play this game in Arizona also didn't help the Bucs. The Cards had been trying hard all season and a win that made them 6-10 would be a good sendoff into the off-season, leaving them hopeful for next year.

My power rating on the game favored the Cards by 2 1/2 and my oddsmaker line was three, thus giving the Cards value. The Cards' home win over the Seahawks showed that they could win this one.

The Cards won, 12-7. They dominated the game. The only Buc touchdown was on a 75-yard pass play.

With the Cards' win and Vikings' loss, I lost both of those season bets, making me a disappointing 2-3 on them this season.

Other Games I Looked At
Steelers plus 10 1/2 over Bills

The Bills needed the game to possibly reach the playoffs. At 14-1, the Steelers had locked up the number one AFC seed and would be resting players.

I still favored the Steelers in this game. Under Cowher they never mailed in results. The Bills were a fresh triple star due down and had not beaten a team near the Steelers' class. My power rating on the game favored the Bills by 5 1/2 (taking incentive into account), which gave the Steelers value.

I passed the game reluctantly because it was an exhibition game for the Steelers. If they fell behind they could easily get blown out. However, the Steelers won outright, 29-24. This game showed once again that it is dangerous to bet teams with incentive (Bills) if the incentive is already put into the price.

Packers plus 4 over Bears

This game meant nothing to either team. The Packers were the number three seed in the NFC and the Bears were out of the playoffs. The Packers had lost to the Bears earlier in the season and I felt that they would want revenge. My power ratings favored the Packers by 7.

However, a few days before the game, Packer Coach Sherman announced that first stringers wouldn't play that much. Brett Favre, the Packer quarterback, wouldn't play past halftime. I also remembered that in the off-season, Bear coach, Lovie Smith, put a huge emphasis on beating the Packers. I passed the game. The Packers broke far in front early and won, 31-14. They got their revenge.

Texans minus 8 1/2 over Browns

At 7-8, the Texans would finish at .500 if they could win. I mentioned this in my bet on them last week. At 3-12, the Browns' season was a shambles and I felt that they might have salvaged a little last week in their close Sunday night loss at Miami.

However, the Texans had never been favored by this much in their history. I thus passed the game.

The Browns surprised me and won outright rather easily, 22-14. The Texans were surprisingly flat.

Week 17 Record: 3-0-1
Season Record: 37-29-3

Week 18: Wild Card Round

In the playoffs, I mostly go off of my power ratings. When there is a three-point difference between my power ratings and the line, I bet.

I did make two small futures bets on the Steelers. I bet them at plus 1.70 to win the AFC. According to my calculations, the right price was plus 1.26. I also took them at plus 3.15 to win the Super Bowl. My calculated price was plus 2.25.

With home field advantage and an undefeated record against playoff teams, I liked the Steelers' chances. With a great running game and a strong defense they play winning playoff football. But I was scared of the Patriots and their brilliant coach, Bill Bellichik. The Pats had won two of the last three Super Bowls and hadn't lost a playoff game with Tom Brady at quarterback. This is why I kept the bets small.

Jets plus 7 1/2 over Chargers: Normal Play

My power rating on this game was 3 1/2 for the Chargers. I saw this game as one between two even teams. Both could run, stop the run, and were suspect against the pass. There was Charger revenge motivation for a loss earlier to the Jets, and the Jets' short work week on a back-to-back on the road was being hugely overpriced into the line.

On my Web site, I predicted a Jets 23-20 overtime win. They won 20-17 in overtime. It would have been nice to pick an exact final score. The game was as even as

I had felt it would be. The Chargers missed a field goal in overtime that would have advanced them in the playoffs.

Vikings plus 7 over Packers: Normal Play

This was another game between even teams. Statistically, they were even in just about every category. The Packers had won two down-to-the-wire games against the Vikings this season by identical 34-31 scores.

I felt it would take some of the pressure off the Vikings because they were underdogs and not expected to win. Their offense would make fewer mistakes, I felt, and would exploit the weak Packers' defense. Of course, the Packers figured to pile up points on a suspect Vikings' defense.

I predicted a three point Packers' win and thus a Viking cover. My power rating on the game favored the Packers by 2 1/2.

The Vikings surprised me by winning 31-17. Brett Favre, the Packer quarterback, threw four interceptions. I guessed that all of the mental trauma Favre had had this season finally took its toll on him (his wife having cancer, someone killed on his Mississippi property). If Favre had had a decent game, I felt the Packers would have won... though hopefully not covered.

Week 18 Record: 2-0
Season Record: 39-29-3

Week 19: Divisional Playoff Round

This week I had just one selection. It won, continuing my late season hot run.

Patriots plus 1 1/2 over Colts: Normal Play

Almost every year in the playoffs, the public falls in love with a high scoring, poor defensive team. And virtually every time this happens, the high scoring offense gets shut down or mostly contained by a good defensive team and gets knocked out of the playoffs. You would think that the public would learn that strong defense beats good offense, but no. The public always comes back and bets the jazzy offensive team the next year and the year after that. It happened again in this game.

The Colts had scored 522 points—the fourth highest total ever—and 66 touchdowns during the regular season. Last week, the Colts destroyed the Broncos in the Wild Card round, 49-24 (leading 35-3 at half-time).

The game opened at 2 1/2 and 3 for the Patriots and the public bet the Colts until they were one point road favorites in spots, before some money finally came in on the Patriots.

I nearly made a strong play on the Patriots. However, they were without their starting cornerbacks (Ty Law and Tyrone Poole) and a key defensive lineman (Richard Seymour). And the Colts easily could've won the Week 1 game at Foxboro (a 27-24 Pat win). I bet the Pats, but kept it a normal play.

For a half, things looked scary. The Patriots led 6-3 at halftime but the Colts had moved the ball on the Patriots on the two drives before the end of the first half (one drive ended in a lost fumble and the other in a field goal). The Patriot offense was very inconsistent and was having problems running the ball.

In the second half, the Patriots had long touchdown drives on their second and third possessions to put away the game. Corey Dillon, the Patriots' running back, ended up with 144 yards. The Patriot defense totally stifled the Colts' offense. The Patriots ended up winning 20-3—even more handily than my projected 34-23 score. I'm sure that next year the betting public will make the same mistake of taking strong offense over strong defense.

Week 19 Record: 1-0
Season Record: 40-29-3

Week 20

I had bets on both games this week and ended up having a losing split (losing since, when I lost my Steeler bet, it meant that I also lost my bets on them to win the AFC and the Super Bowl).

Eagles minus 3 1/2 over Falcons: Normal Play

I was kicking myself all week since I could have given 3 on the Eagles laying 1.30, which is better than giving 3 1/2 (laying 1.10).

My numbers showed the Falcons to be barely an above average team. In the regular season, the Falcons scored and gave up the same number of touchdowns. Even without Terrell Owens, the Eagles were the class of the NFC. I felt that the Eagles' defense would contain the Falcon running game and also contain Michael Vick, who was a better runner than a passer. My power rating on the game favored the Eagles by 8 1/2.

When the score of the game was 20-10 for the Eagles, I was very worried that the game would fall 3 and that my poor decision not to lay 3 laying 1.30 would come into play. But with 3:21 left, the Eagles scored another touchdown to take me out of danger. They won, 27-10.

Steelers plus 3 1/2 over Patriots: Small Play

As I wrote earlier, I had feared the Patriots on my Steelers future bets. Last week, in a lucky win over the Jets, Steelers' quarterback Ben Roethlisberger had played like a rookie. I feared that Pats' Coach Bill Bellichek would exploit Roethlisberger's weaknesses.

Still, I go with my numbers in playoff games. My power ratings favored the Steelers by 1/2 point, which gave me more than a three-point edge for the Steelers. Because of my reservations about the Steelers and the fact that I had another full bet tied up in Steelers futures, I kept the bet a small one.

On his first pass, Roethlisberger threw an interception that the Pats converted into a field goal. The Steelers were stopped on a fourth down on their next possession at the Patriot forty. The Pats immediately got a 60-yard touchdown pass from Tom Brady to go up, 10-0. I knew then that the game was lost. Though the Steelers did get some scoring in the second half, the Patriots controlled the game at the important junctures and won rather easily, 41-27. I thus lost bets on my Steeler AFC and Super Bowl futures.

Week 20 Record: 1-1
Season Record: 41-30-3

Week 21: Super Bowl

This was a very difficult game for me to figure out. First and most important, it was unknown if Eagles' receiver Terrell Owens would play and, if he did, how effective he would be. With him effective, the Eagles were a B+ team. Without Owens—or with Owens ineffective—they were a B club. I made the assumption from my reading that if Owens did play, he would not be effective. Based on that, my power rating on the game favored the Patriots by 7, which is what the line was most of the week. I thus had no bet on the side in the Super Bowl.

In terms of how I viewed the game, I felt that with two weeks to prepare, the Patriots' defense would mostly shut down the Eagles' offense. However, I was uncertain how the improved Eagles' defense would fare against the Patriots' offense. Early in the season, the Eagles were very vulnerable to the run. That changed around the mid-point of the season when the Eagles made Jeremiah Trotter a starting linebacker.

My uncertainty over how the Patriots' offense would perform made it very difficult for me to figure out various propositions in the Super Bowl. Propositions that I had bet in the past based on field goals, whether a team would score in the last two minutes of the first half, whether a team would score in the first 6 1/2 minutes, etc. were impossible to figure out without knowing a range of points that figured to be scored in the game.

I still did bet two propositions:

1) Eagles under 21 points (laying 1.35). Normal Play. This was mostly 20 1/2 but I found 21 at Ellis Island in Las Vegas (I go to Las Vegas for Super Bowls). As I wrote above, I felt that the Patriots' defense would contain the Eagles' offense. I also was rather certain that the Pats would win. In only five of the previous thirty-eight Super Bowls had the losing team scored over 21 points.

2) Brian Westbrook under 67 1/2 and under 69 1/2 yards rushing. Normal Play. I took the under 67 1/2 at CRIS and went further when one of my clients told me that the Gold Coast had under 69 1/2. Westbrook had under 68 yards rushing in nine of the 15 games he had played. I also felt that the Patriots would take away the Eagles' running game and force Donovan McNabb to throw. Also, I felt pretty sure that the Pats would win and would be winning most of the game. Usually when that happens, the team trailing abandons the run—which would help my bet.

A FULL SEASON OF NFL BETS

The game didn't go as I forecast. The main reason for that was that not only did Terrell Owens play, but he was very effective. He caught nine passes in the game for 122 yards. No other Eagles' receiver caught more than four passes.

With the score tied at seven at halftime I made a hedge bet in the second half that the Eagles would score over 9 1/2 points in the second half. I did so since I now knew that Owens was a major factor in the game.

The Eagles ended up losing 24-21, and thus I tied my main bet (under 21) and won the halftime hedge bet. However, the Eagles probably should have scored over 21 points. McNabb twice threw interceptions when the Eagles were threatening to score.

I won the Westbrook bet fairly easily since he ended up with 44 yards rushing. I had a scary moment on this bet near the end of the first half when Westbrook ran for 22 yards (to push his rushing total to 37 yards) on the last play before halftime. I wondered angrily why the Eagles didn't try a long pass attempt instead. A run wouldn't score for them—they were on their own forty with four seconds left in the half. Fortunately, Westbrook wasn't used much as a rusher in the second half, which saved my bet.

Super Bowl Total: 1-0-1 on propositions
(1-0 on hedge)

Side Total: 0-0
Final Season Totals: 41-30-3
Season Over/Under Bets: 2-3
Playoff Futures: 0-2
Super Bowl Bets: 2-0-1

I thus ended up with a winning season, my second winning season in a row, and my seventh in the last nine years.

21

The Final Word

You have now read a book which will help you to become one of the few bettors that will have a long-term winning record against the NFL point spread. You might even join the one bettor in two hundred that is a winning bettor in his or her life.

A few final thoughts:

1) Don't be afraid to pass a game even when some of my models indicate it should be a bet. You are laying 11-10 on NFL games and need to be selective. You should feel comfortable with all of your bets.

2) The only reason to bet NFL games is to make money. Let others be the showoffs and be the ones who bet for their egos or for the thrill of being in action. In the long run, these bettors will indirectly be paying you your winnings!

3) Don't be afraid to bet against line moves. Don't be afraid even if it is so-called smart money causing these moves. If these line moves won any significant percentage of the time, bookmakers would be out of business. And never be scared of bucking a media "handicapper." Virtually no one in the media wins picking the NFL (or any other sport) for any serious length of time.

4) Make sure you are getting good prices on your bets. Getting the best of it goes a long way toward overcoming the 11-10 odds.

5) May you win more than you earn in this and future NFL seasons—the correct way of saying, "Good Luck!"

THE CHAMPIONSHIP SERIES
POWERFUL BOOKS YOU MUST HAVE

CHAMPIONSHIP OMAHA (Omaha High-Low, Pot-limit Omaha, Limit High Omaha) by Tom McEvoy & T.J. Cloutier. Clearly-written strategies and powerful advice from Cloutier and McEvoy who have won four World Series of Poker titles in Omaha tournaments. Powerful advice shows you how to win at low-limit and high-stakes games, how to play against loose and tight opponents, and the differing strategies for rebuy and freezeout tournaments. Learn the best starting hands, when slowplaying a big hand is dangerous, what danglers are and why winners don't play them, why pot-limit Omaha is the only poker game where you sometimes fold the nuts on the flop and are correct in doing so and overall, and how you can win a lot of money at Omaha! 296 pages, photos, illustrations, New Edition! $29.95!

CHAMPIONSHIP STUD (Seven-Card Stud, Stud 8/or Better and Razz) by Dr. Max Stern, Linda Johnson, and Tom McEvoy. The authors, who have earned millions of dollars in major tournaments and cash games, eight World Series of Poker bracelets and hundreds of other titles in competition against the best players in the world show you the winning strategies for medium-limit side games as well as poker tournaments and a general tournament strategy that is applicable to any form of poker. Includes give-and-take conversations between the authors to give you more than one point of view on how to play poker. 200 pages, hand pictorials, photos. $39.95.

CHAMPIONSHIP HOLD'EM by Tom McEvoy & T.J. Cloutier. Hard-hitting hold'em the way it's played today in both limit cash games and tournaments. Get killer advice on how to win more money in rammin'-jammin' games, kill-pot, jackpot, shorthanded, and other types of cash games. You'll learn the thinking process before the flop, on the flop, on the turn, and at the river with specific suggestions for what to do when good or bad things happen plus 20 illustrated hands with play-by-play analyses. Specific advice for rocks in tight games, weaklings in loose games, experts in solid games, how hand values change in jackpot games, when you should fold, check, raise, reraise, check-raise, slowplay, bluff, and tournament strategies for small buy-in, big buy-in, rebuy, incremental add-on, satellite and big-field major tournaments. Wow! Easy-to-read and conversational, if you want to become a lifelong winner at limit hold'em, you need this book! 388 Pages, Illustrated, Photos. $39.95. Now only $29.95!

CHAMPIONSHIP NO-LIMIT & POT-LIMIT HOLD'EM by T.J. Cloutier & Tom McEvoy. New Cardoza Edition! The definitive guide to winning at two of the world's most exciting poker games! Written by eight time World Champion players T.J. Cloutier (1998 and 2002 Player of the Year) and Tom McEvoy (the foremost author on tournament strategy) who have won millions of dollars each playing no-limit and pot-limit hold'em in cash games and major tournaments around the world. You'll get all the answers here—no holds barred—to your most important questions: How do you get inside your opponents' heads and learn how to beat them at their own game? How can you tell how much to bet, raise, and reraise in no-limit hold'em? When can you bluff? How do you set up your opponents in pot-limit hold'em so you can win a monster pot? What are the best strategies for winning no-limit and pot-limit tournaments, satellites, and supersatellites? You get rock-solid and inspired advice from two of the most recognizable figures in poker—advice that you can bank on. If you want to become a winning player, and a champion, you must have this book. 304 pages, paperback, illustrations, photos. $29.95

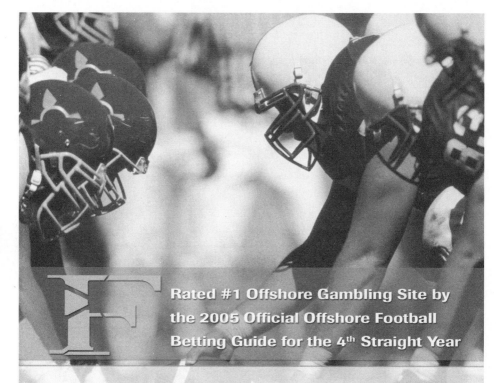